SPOTLIGHT

W9-ANE-902

NEW HAMPSHIRE HIKING

JACQUELINE TOURVILLE

How to Use This Book

ABOUT THE TRAIL PROFILES

Each hike in this book is listed in a consistent, easy-to-read format to help you choose the ideal hike. From a general overview of the setting to detailed driving directions, the profile will provide all the information you need. Here is a sample profile:

Map number and
hike number

1 SOMEWHERE USA HIKE

Round-trip mileage
(unless otherwise
noted) and the ap-
proximate amount
of time needed to
complete the hike
(actual times
can vary widely,
especially on
longer hikes)

9.0 mi/5.0 hrs

Difficulty and
quality ratings

at the mouth of the Somewhere River

General location of
the trail, named by
its proximity to the
nearest major
town or landmark

BEST

Each hike in this book begins with a brief overview of its setting. The description typically covers what kind of terrain to expect, what might be seen, and any conditions that may make the hike difficult to navigate. Side trips, such as to waterfalls or panoramic vistas, in addition to ways to combine the trail with others nearby for a longer outing, are also noted here. In many cases, mile-by-mile trail directions are included.

Symbol indicating
that the hike is
listed among the
author's top picks

User Groups: This section notes the types of users that are permitted on the trail, including hikers, mountain bikers, horseback riders, and dogs. Wheelchair access is also noted here.

Permits: This section notes whether a permit is required for hiking, or, if the hike spans more than one day, whether one is required for camping. Any fees, such as for parking, day use, or entrance, are also noted here.

Maps: This section provides information on how to obtain detailed trail maps of the hike and its environs. Whenever applicable, names of U.S. Geologic Survey (USGS) topographic maps and national forest maps are also included; contact information for these and other map sources are noted in the Resources section at the back of this book.

Directions: This section provides mile-by-mile driving directions to the trail head from the nearest major town.

Contact: This section provides an address and phone number for each hike. The contact is usually the agency maintaining the trail but may also be a trail club or other organization.

ABOUT THE ICONS

The icons in this book are designed to provide at-a-glance information on the difficulty and quality of each hike.

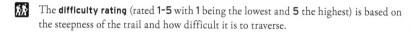

The **difficulty rating** (rated **1-5** with **1** being the lowest and **5** the highest) is based on the steepness of the trail and how difficult it is to traverse.

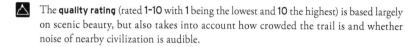

The **quality rating** (rated **1-10** with **1** being the lowest and **10** the highest) is based largely on scenic beauty, but also takes into account how crowded the trail is and whether noise of nearby civilization is audible.

ABOUT THE DIFFICULTY RATINGS

Trails rated 1 are very easy and suitable for hikers of all abilities, including young children.

Trails rated 2 are easy-to-moderate and suitable for most hikers, including families with active children 6 and older.

Trails rated 3 are moderately challenging and suitable for reasonably fit adults and older children who are very active.

Trails rated 4 are very challenging and suitable for physically fit hikers who are seeking a workout.

Trails rated 5 are extremely challenging and suitable only for experienced hikers who are in top physical condition.

MAP SYMBOLS

Symbol		Symbol		Symbol	
▭▭▭	Expressway	(80)	Interstate Freeway	✈	Airfield
▭▭▭	Primary Road	(101)	U.S. Highway	✈	Airport
▭▭▭	Secondary Road	(21)	State Highway	○	City/Town
▭ ▭ ▭	Unpaved Road	(66)	County Highway	▲	Mountain
··········	Ferry	⬤	Lake	♠	Park
▬ × ▬ ×	National Border	⬭	Dry Lake	)(	Pass
▬ ·· ▬ ··	State Border	⬭	Seasonal Lake	◉	State Capital

Hiking Tips

HIKING ESSENTIALS

It doesn't require much more than a little wilderness knowledge and a backpack's worth of key items to ensure your day hike in New England is a safe and fun adventure. Here's a list of outdoor essentials.

Water and Food

Like any physical activity, hiking increases your body's fluid needs by a factor of two or more. A good rule of thumb for an all-day hike is two liters of water per person, but even that could leave you mildly dehydrated, so carry a third liter if you can. Dehydration can lead to other—more serious—problems, like heat exhaustion, hypothermia, frostbite, and injury. If you're well hydrated, you will urinate frequently and your urine will be clear. The darker your urine, the greater your level of dehydration. If you feel thirsty, dehydration has already commenced. In short: Drink a lot.

Streams and brooks run everywhere in New England. If you're out for more than a day in the backcountry, finding water is rarely a problem (except on ridge tops and summits). But microscopic organisms *Giardia lamblia* and *Cryptosporidium* are common in backcountry water sources and can cause a litany of terrible gastrointestinal problems in humans. Assume you should always treat water from backcountry sources, whether by using a filter or iodine tablets, boiling, or another proven method to eliminate giardiasis and other harmful bacteria. Day-hikers will usually find it more convenient to simply carry enough water from home for the hike.

Similarly, your body consumes a phenomenal amount of calories walking up and down a mountain. Feed it frequently. Carbohydrate-rich foods such as bread, chocolate, dried fruit, fig bars, snack bars, fresh vegetables, and energy bars are all good sources for a quick burst of energy. Fats contain about twice the calories per pound than carbs or protein, and provide the slow-burning fuel that keeps you going all day and keeps you warm through the night if you're sleeping outside; sate your need for fats by eating cheese, chocolate, canned meats or fish, pepperoni, sausage, or nuts.

On hot days, "refrigerate" your water and perishables such as cheese and chocolate: Fill a water bottle (the collapsible kind works best) with very cold water, and ice cubes if possible. Wrap it and your perishables in a thick, insulating fleece and bury it inside your pack. Or the night before, fill a water bottle halfway and freeze it, then fill the remainder with water in the morning before you leave for the hike.

Trail Maps

A map of the park, preserve, or public land you are visiting is essential. Even if you have hiked a trail a hundred times, carry a map. Unexpected trail closures, an injury requiring a shorter route, bad weather, or an animal encounter can all result in a sudden change of plans that require map assistance. Some may believe a GPS device takes the place of a map, but this isn't always true. If you get lost, a detailed trail map showing lakes, rivers, ridge lines, trail junctions, and other landmarks is still the most reliable way to get back on trail.

Many land agencies provide free paper maps at the trailhead, though be aware that some state parks and land agencies are much more vigilant about restocking than others.

GLOBAL POSITIONING SYSTEM (GPS) DEVICES

Working with a system of orbiting satellites, GPS receivers are able to accurately pinpoint your position, elevation, and time anywhere on the face of the earth. Out on the trail, GPS devices can help you navigate from point to point, indicating bearings and the distance remaining to reach your destination. It can also help should you become lost.

Despite these advances, GPS technology is not a replacement for the old standby of a compass and paper topographical map. GPS units are not yet able to provide an adequately detailed view of the surrounding landscape, batteries typically wear out in less than a day, and some landscape conditions can interfere with signal strength. Still, when used in concert with topographical maps, GPS is an extremely useful addition to your navigational toolbox.

Every hike in this book lists GPS coordinates for the hike's trailhead. Use these for better road navigation on the drive to your destination. Inputting the trailhead GPS coordinates before leaving on your hike will also help you retrace your steps if you become lost.

Check the agency's website to see if maps can be printed out beforehand or call to request a map be sent to you. For hikers along the Appalachian Trail, numerous trail maps are available. The best—and most complete—maps are published by the Appalachian Mountain Club and the Appalachian Trail Conservancy.

BLAZES AND CAIRNS

New England's forests abound with blazes—slashes of paint on trees used to mark trails. Sometimes the color of blazes seems random and unrelated to other trails in the same area, but most major trails and trail systems are blazed consistently. The Appalachian Trail (AT) bears white blazes for its entire length, including its 734 miles through five New England states. Most side trails connecting to the AT are blue-blazed. Vermont's 270-mile Long Trail, which coincides with the AT for more than 100 miles, is also blazed in white. Connecticut's Blue Trails system of hiking paths scattered across the state is, as the name suggests, marked entirely with blue blazes.

Although not all trails are well blazed, popular and well-maintained trails usually are—you'll see a colored slash of paint at frequent intervals at about eye level on tree trunks. Double slashes are sometimes used to indicate a sharp turn in the trail. Trails are blazed in both directions, so whenever you suspect you may have lost the trail, turn around to see whether you can find a blaze facing in the opposite direction; if so, you'll know you're still on the trail.

Above tree line, trails may be marked either with blazes painted on rock or with cairns, which are piles of stones constructed at regular intervals. In the rocky terrain on the upper slopes of New England's highest peaks, care may be needed to discern artificially constructed cairns from the landscape surrounding them, but the cairns in rocky areas are usually built higher and are obviously constructed by people.

Extra Clothing

At lower elevations amid the protection of trees or on a warm day, you may elect to bring no extra clothing for an hour-long outing, or no more than a light jacket for a few hours or more. The exception to this is in the Seacoast region, where hikes are more exposed to cool wind. But higher elevations, especially above tree line, get much colder than the valleys—about three degrees Fahrenheit per thousand feet—and winds can grow much stronger. Many a White Mountains hiker has departed from a valley basking in summerlike weather and reached a summit wracked by wintry winds and lying under a carpet of fresh snow, even during the summer months.

Insulating layers, a jacket that protects against wind and precipitation, a warm hat, gloves, a rain poncho, and extra socks are always a good idea to bring along when out on a long hike, especially when scaling New England's highest peaks. Look for wool blends or the new breed of high tech synthetics, fabrics that wick moisture from your skin and keep you dry. Even on a shorter trek, stowing a jacket, hat, and extra pair of socks in your backpack is always a good idea.

Flashlight

Carrying a flashlight in your pack is a must, even when your hike is planned to end well before dusk. Emergencies happen, and being stuck on the trail after dark without a flashlight only compounds the situation. Plus, if you have ever been in New England right before a thunderstorm, you know fast moving cloud cover can turn the landscape pitch dark in seconds. Micro flashlights with alloy skins, xenon bulbs, and a battery life of eight hours on two AA batteries provide ample illumination and won't add much weight to your pack. Throw in some spare batteries and an extra light—or just pack two flashlights to always be covered. A reliable, compact, and waterproof micro flashlight can typically be purchased for under $20.

Sunscreen and Sunglasses

As you climb to higher elevations, the strength of the sun's ultraviolet rays increases. Applying sunscreen or sunblock to exposed skin and wearing a baseball cap or wide-brimmed hat can easily prevent overexposure to sun. SPF strengths vary, but applying sunscreen at least a half-hour before heading out gives the lotion or spray enough time to take effect. When deciding which sunscreen to buy, look for a fragrance-free formula; strongly scented lotions and sprays may attract mosquitoes. And don't forget your sunglasses. Squinting into the sun for hours on end is not only bad for the delicate skin around your eyes, it's almost a certain way to develop a bad case of eye strain. Look for sunglasses with lenses that provide 100 percent UVA and UVB protection.

First-Aid Kit

It's wise to carry a compact and lightweight first-aid kit for emergencies in the back-country, where an ambulance and hospital are often hours, rather than minutes, away. Prepare any first-aid kit with attention to the type of trip, the destination, and the needs of people hiking (for example, children or persons with medical conditions).

A basic first-aid kit consists of:
- aspirin or an anti-inflammatory
- 4 four-inch-by-four-inch gauze pads
- knife or scissors
- moleskin or Spenco Second Skin (for blisters)
- 1 roll of one-inch athletic tape
- 1 six-inch Ace bandage

- paper and pencil
- safety pins
- SAM splint (a versatile and lightweight splinting device available at many drug stores)
- several alcohol wipes
- several one-inch adhesive bandages
- tube of povidone iodine ointment (for wound care)
- 2 large handkerchiefs
- 2 large gauze pads

Pack everything into a thick, clear plastic resealable bag. And remember, merely carrying a first-aid kit does not make you safe; knowing how to use what's in it does.

HIKING GEAR

Much could be written about how to outfit oneself for hiking in a region like New England, with its significant range of elevations and latitudes, alpine zones, huge seasonal temperature swings, and fairly wet climate.

Don't leave your clothing, gear, and other equipment choices to chance. New England is packed with plenty of friendly, locally owned stores that offer quality, outdoor clothing and footwear options (and knowledgeable staff to help you). Or, take part in the venerable Yankee tradition of the swap meet. Many of New England's mountain clubs hold semi-annual or seasonal meets, giving hikers the irresistible chance to scoop up quality used gear at a very frugal price. Swap meets are also a fun and easy way to meet others in the hiking community.

Clothing

Clothes protect you against the elements and also help to regulate body temperature. What you wear when you go hiking should keep you dry and comfortable, no matter what the weather and season. From underwear to outerwear, pick garments that offer good "breathability." Wool blends and the new breed of synthetic microfibers do a good job at wicking moisture away from the skin. Shirts and pants made from microfiber polyesters are also extra-light and stretchy, allowing for maximum range of movement.

You will also want to dress in layers: underwear, one or more intermediate layers, and, finally, an outer layer. Wearing multiple layers of clothing offers you lots of flexibility for regulating body temperature and exposure. Test your clothing at different temperatures and levels of activity to find out what works best for you.

Rain Gear

Coastal currents smashing up against weather fronts dropping south from Canada give New England its famously fickle weather. Especially in summer, a sunny late morning start to your hike could mean a return trip in a raging rainstorm, often with very little warning time. No matter where you go or how long you expect to be out on the trail, bring along rain gear. It doesn't need to be elaborate: a vinyl foul weather poncho left in its packaging until needed is a compact addition to your pack.

If you do end up getting caught in a thunderstorm or sudden downpour, move away from high ground and tall trees immediately. Take shelter in a low spot, ravine, or thin place in the woods, cover up with your poncho, and wait for the storm to pass. Also,

HIKING GEAR CHECKLIST

Long-distance backpackers need to worry about hauling along camping and cooking equipment, but besides good boots, comfortable clothes, water, food, and a trusty map, it doesn't take much to have all the gear you need for a day hike. Here are some must-haves for your next outing.

IN CASE OF EMERGENCY

Altimeter

Compass

Extra clothes

First-aid kit

Lightweight (or mylar) blanket

Pen/pencil and paper

Swiss army-style knife

Waterproof matches

CREATURE COMFORTS

Binoculars

Bird, wildlife, and tree/flower identification guides

Bug spray/sunscreen

Camera

Face cloths

Fishing pole and fishing license

Picnic supplies

Trekking pole

And, of course, bring along your hiking guide!

look carefully at your surroundings, making sure you are not standing in a dry riverbed or wash while waiting, in case of flash floods.

Being out in rainy weather is also a concern for your feet and legs. Brushing up against wet ferns or low-lying plants can make for uncomfortably damp pant legs and soaked socks and boots. In case you do get stuck in the rain, another good piece of equipment to have on hand is a pair of gaiters, leggings made of Gore-Tex or other water-repellant materials. Gaiters are held in place under each boot with a stirrup and extend over your pants to just below the knee.

Shoes and Socks

The most important piece of gear may be well-fitting, comfortable, supportive shoes or boots. Finding the right footwear requires trying on various models and walking around in them in the store before deciding. Everyone's feet are different, and shoes or boots that feel great on your friend won't necessarily fit you well. Deciding how heavy your footwear should be depends on variables like how often you hike, whether you easily injure feet or ankles, and how much weight you'll carry. My general recommendation is to hike in the most lightweight footwear that you find comfortable and adequately supportive.

There are three basic types of hiking boots. Sneaker-like trail shoes are adequate when you are hiking in a dry climate and on well-established paths. Traditional hiking boots, sometimes called trail hikers or trail boots, are constructed with a higher cut and slightly stiffer sole to provide support on steep inclines and muddy paths. Mountaineering boots are for those who might need to attach crampons for a better grip on glaciers or hard-packed snow on mountain hikes and rock or ice climbing. Mountaineering boots are built with a very stiff sole to give your feet and ankles support and protection as you climb more challenging terrain.

The hiking boot experts at L.L.Bean, New England's premier shopping destination for outdoor gear and equipment, recommend hikers consider the various advantages of fabric-and-leather boots and all-leather boots. Fabric-and-leather boots are lighter and easier to break in, but all-leather boots offer added protection and durability in rigorous terrain, as well as being water resistant and breathable. Quality boots can be found in either style.

HIKING BOOTS

Try boots on at the end of the day when your feet are more swollen and wear the socks you plan to wear on the trail. Boots should feel snug but comfortable, so you can still wiggle your toes. Most hiking boots won't feel as instantly comfortable as sneakers, but they shouldn't pinch, cause hot spots, or constrict circulation. They should fit securely around your ankle and instep. Try walking down an incline at the store. Your feet should not slide forward, nor should your toenails scrape against the front of your boot. If your foot slides forward, the boot could be too wide. If the back of your heel moves around, your boots might not be laced up tight enough.

Once you purchase a pair of boots, break them in slowly with short hikes. Leather boots in particular take a while to break in, so take a couple of two- or three-hour hikes before your big trip or wear them around the house. If you find any sharp pressure points, use leather conditioner to soften the leather.

SOCKS

With exertion, one foot can sweat up to two pints of vapor/fluid per day. That's why wicking technology in hiking socks is so important. Without it, bacteria and fungus can become a problem. The best hiking socks are made from 100 percent wool or a wool blend of at least 50 percent wool. Unlike most synthetic fibers, which have to wait for moisture to condense into a liquid before wicking it away from your skin, wool socks absorb and transfer moisture in its vapor state, before it condenses. When it's hot, this creates a mini air-conditioning unit next to your feet, releasing heat through your socks and boots. And when it's cold, wicking keeps bone-chilling moisture at bay.

Some newer synthetics and synthetic blends are engineered to wick moisture; read the package label carefully and ask the store clerk for recommendations. The one fiber to stay away from is cotton, which absorbs water and perspiration and holds it next to your skin. If you are hiking with wet feet and the temperature drops below freezing, you risk getting frostbite. A good sock system and hiking boots reduce that possibility.

For comfort and good circulation, look for socks that won't bind your feet and avoid those made with excessive stitching or a scratchy knit that could lead to chafing. Terry woven socks are a good pick to distribute pressure and support your natural posture. And thicker isn't always better. Depending on the fit of your boots and the climate you'll be hiking in, a medium-weight wool sock that fits to mid-calf is often your best bet.

FOOTCARE

At an Appalachian Mountain Club hiking seminar, one instructor wisely noted that, besides the brain, "Your feet are the most important part of your body." Hurt any other

THE APPALACHIAN TRAIL

Perhaps the most famous hiking trail in the world, the Appalachian Trail (AT) runs 2,174 miles from Springer Mountain in Georgia to Mount Katahdin in Maine, along the spine of the Appalachian Mountains in 14 states. About 734 miles – or more than one-third – of the AT's length passes through five New England states: Connecticut (52 miles), Massachusetts (90 miles), Vermont (150 miles), New Hampshire (161 miles), and Maine (281 miles). New England boasts some of the AT's most spectacular, best-known, and rugged stretches, including the White Mountains, the southern Green Mountains, the Riga Plateau of Massachusetts and Connecticut, and Maine's Mahoosuc, Saddleback, and Bigelow ranges, 100-mile Wilderness, and Katahdin. A few hundred people hike the entire trail end to end every year, but thousands more take shorter backpacking trips and day hikes somewhere along the AT.

Maintained by hiking clubs that assume responsibility for different sections of the AT, the trail is well marked with signs and white blazes on trees and rocks above tree line. Shelters and campsites are spaced out along the AT so that backpackers have choices of where to spend each night. But those shelters can fill up during the busy season of summer and early fall, especially on weekends. The prime hiking season for the AT in New England depends on elevation and latitude, but generally, that season runs May-October in southern New England and mid-June-early October at higher elevations in northern New England.

body part and we might conceivably still make it home under our own power. Hurt our feet, and we're in trouble.

Take care of your feet. Wear clean socks that wick moisture from your skin while staying dry. Make sure your shoes or boots fit properly, are laced properly, and are broken in if they require it. Wear the appropriate footwear for the type of hiking you plan to do. If you anticipate your socks getting wet from perspiration or water, bring extra socks; on a multiday trip, have dry socks for each day, or at least change socks every other day. On hot days, roll your socks down over your boot tops to create what shoe manufacturers call "the chimney effect," cooling your feet by forcing air into your boots as you walk.

On longer treks, whenever you stop for a short rest on the trail—even if only for 5 or 10 minutes—sit down, pull off your boots and socks, and let them and your feet dry out. When backpacking, wash your feet at the end of the day. If you feel any hot spots developing, intervene before they progress into blisters. A slightly red or tender hot spot can be protected from developing into a blister with an adhesive bandage, tape, or a square of moleskin.

If a blister has formed, clean the area around it thoroughly to avoid infection. Sterilize a needle or knife in a flame, then pop and drain the blister to promote faster healing. Put an antiseptic ointment on the blister. Cut a piece of moleskin or Second Skin (both of which have a soft side and a sticky side with a peel-off backing) large enough to overlap the blistered area. Cut a hole as large as the blister out of the center of the moleskin, then place the moleskin over the blister so that the blister is visible through the hole. If done properly, you should be able to walk without aggravating the blister.

Backpack

When just out for the day, a roomy backpack will do to hold your belongings; toting an over-sized metal frame pack is not necessary unless you plan on camping overnight and need to bring along camp stove, bed roll, tent, and other extra gear. Shoulder straps should be foam padded for comfort. Look for backpacks made of water-resistant nylon. And just like clothes or shoes, try the pack on to make sure it has the fit you want.

Trekking Poles

For hikers who need a little extra physical support, trekking poles or walking sticks relieve feet and legs of tens of thousands of pounds of pressure over the course of an all-day hike. They are particularly useful in helping prevent knee and back pain from rigorous hiking. If you find a good walking stick along your journey, before heading back to your car, leave the stick in an obvious spot for another weary hiker to stumble upon. It warmed the bottom of my heart one day to find at least a dozen walking sticks leaning against a trailhead signpost in Massachusetts, free for anyone to use.

CLIMATE

With New England's biggest peaks in the northern states and its smaller hills and flatlands in the southern states, as well as an ocean moderating the Seacoast climate, this region's fair-weather hikers can find a trail to explore virtually year-round. But the wildly varied character of hiking opportunities here also demands some basic knowledge of and preparation for hitting the trails.

The ocean generally keeps coastal areas a little warmer in winter and cooler in summer than inland areas. Otherwise, any time of year, average temperatures typically grow cooler as you gain elevation or move northward.

New England's prime hiking season stretches for several months from spring through fall, with the season's length depending on the region. In general, summer high temperatures range 60°F–90°F with lows from 50°F to around freezing at higher elevations. Days are often humid in the forests and lower elevations and windy on the mountaintops. July and August see occasional thunderstorms, but July through September is the driest period. August is usually the best month for finding ripe wild blueberries along many trails, especially in northern New England.

September is often the best month for hiking, with dry, comfortable days, cool nights, and few bugs. Fall foliage colors peak anywhere from mid-September or early October in northern New England to early or mid-October in the south; by choosing your destinations well and moving north to south, you can hike through vibrant foliage for three or four successive weekends. The period from mid-October into November offers cool days, cold nights, no bugs, few people, and often little snow.

In the higher peaks of Vermont's Green Mountains, New Hampshire's White Mountains, Maine's northern Appalachians, and along the Appalachian Trail in parts of western Massachusetts and Connecticut, high-elevation snow disappears and alpine wildflowers bloom in late spring; by late October, wintry winds start blowing and snow starts flying (though it can snow above 4,000 feet in any month of the year). Spring trails are muddy at low elevations—some are closed to hiking during the April/May "mud season"—and buried under deep, slushy snow up high, requiring snowshoes. Winter conditions set in by mid-November and can become very severe, even life threatening.

CROSS-COUNTRY SKIING AND SNOWSHOEING

Many hikes in this book are great for cross-country skiing or snowshoeing in winter. But added precaution is needed. Days are short and the temperature may start to plummet by mid-afternoon, so carry the right clothing and don't overestimate how far you can travel in winter. Depending on snow conditions and your own fitness level and experience with either snowshoes or skis, a winter outing can take much longer than anticipated – and certainly much longer than a trip of similar distance on groomed trails at a cross-country ski resort. Breaking your own trail through fresh snow can also be very exhausting – take turns leading and conserve energy by following the leader's tracks, which also serve as a good return trail.

The proper clothing becomes essential in winter, especially the farther you wander from roads. Wear a base layer that wicks moisture from your skin and dries quickly, middle layers that insulate and do not retain moisture, and a windproof shell that breathes well and is waterproof or water-resistant (the latter type of garment usually breathes much better than something that's completely waterproof). Size boots to fit over a thin, synthetic liner sock and a thicker, heavyweight synthetic-blend sock. For your hands, often the most versatile system consists of gloves and/or mittens that also can be layered, with an outer layer that's waterproof and windproof and preferably also breathable.

Most importantly, don't overdress: Remove layers if you're getting too hot. Avoid becoming wet with perspiration, which can lead to too much cooling. Drink plenty of fluids and eat snacks frequently to maintain your energy level; feeling tired or cold on a winter outing may be an indication of dehydration or hunger.

As long as you're safe, cautious, and aware, winter is a great time to explore New England's trails. Have fun out there.

Going above the tree line in winter is considered a mountaineering experience by many (though these mountains lack glacier travel and high altitude), so be prepared for harsh cold and strong winds.

The second strongest wind gust ever recorded on Earth was measured on April 12, 1934, at the weather observatory on the summit of New Hampshire's Mount Washington. The gust was clocked at 231 mph. The summit of Mount Washington remains in clouds 60 percent of the time. Its average temperature year-round is 26.5°F; winds average 35 mph and exceed hurricane force (75 mph) on average 104 days a year. Be aware that in the higher peaks of the Whites as well as alpine peaks in Vermont and Maine, weather conditions change rapidly. It is not uncommon to set off from the trailhead in hot, sunny weather only to hit driving rain and hail on the summit.

In the smaller hills and flatlands of central and southern New England, the snow-free hiking season often begins by early spring and lasts into late autumn. Some of these trails are even occasionally free of snow during the winter, or offer opportunities for snowshoeing or cross-country skiing in woods protected from strong winds, with warmer temperatures than you'll find on the bigger peaks up north. Many Seacoast trails, even in Maine, rarely stay snow-covered all winter, though they can get occasional heavy snowfall and be very icy in cold weather. For more information about weather-related trail conditions, refer to the individual hike listings.

SAFETY AND FIRST AID

Few of us would consider hiking a high-risk activity. But like any physical activity, it does pose certain risks, and it's up to us to minimize them. For starters, make sure your physical condition is adequate for your objective—the quickest route to injury is over-extending either your skills or your physical abilities. You wouldn't presume that you could rock climb a 1,000-foot cliff if you've never climbed before; don't assume you're ready for one of New England's hardest hikes if you've never—or not very recently—done anything nearly as difficult.

Build up your fitness level by gradually increasing your workouts and the length of your hikes. Beyond strengthening muscles, you must strengthen the soft connective tissue in joints like knees and ankles that are too easily strained and take weeks or months to heal from injury. Staying active in a variety of activities—hiking, running, bicycling, Nordic skiing—helps develop good overall fitness and decreases the likelihood of an overuse injury. Most importantly, stretch muscles before and after a workout to reduce the chance of injury.

New England's most rugged trails—and even parts of its more moderate paths—can be very rocky and steep. Uneven terrain is often a major contributor to falls resulting in serious, acute injury. Most of us have a fairly reliable self-preservation instinct—and you should trust it. If something strikes you as dangerous or beyond your abilities, don't try it, or simply wait until you think you're ready for it.

An injury far from a road also means it may be hours before the victim reaches a hospital. Basic training in wilderness first aid is beneficial to anyone who frequents the mountains, even recreational hikers. New England happens to have two highly respected sources for such training, and the basic course requires just one weekend. Contact SOLO (Conway, NH, 603/447-6711, www.soloschools.com) or Wilderness Medical Associates (Scarborough, ME, 207/730-7331, www.wildmed.com) for information.

Plants

From fern-choked forest floors to fields filled with wild blueberries, plant life in New England is varied and diverse. And luckily, there are only a few poisonous plant species to be wary of: poison ivy, poison oak, and poison sumac. The three plants contain urushiol, an oil that causes an allergic reaction and rash in humans. According to the American Academy of Dermatology, humans typically come in contact with urushiol by brushing up against or touching the plants, touching an object or animal that has come in contact with the oil, or breathing in urushiol particles if a poison plant is burned in a campfire.

Urushiol penetrates the skin in minutes, but the rash usually takes anywhere from 12 to 72 hours to appear, followed quickly by severe itching, redness, swelling, and even blisters. When the rash develops, streaks or lines often reveal where the plant brushed against the skin. A rash triggered by urushiol does not spread and is not contagious.

RECOGNIZING POISONOUS PLANTS

Hikers best protection against the itchy rash caused by urushiol is learning how to identify the plants that contain the oil.

Poison Ivy: Leaves of three, let them be… Poison ivy grows as vines or low shrubs almost everywhere in New England and true to that famous phrase from summer camp, the plant consists of three pointed leaflets; the middle leaflet has a much longer stalk than the two side ones. Leaflets are reddish when they bud in spring, turn green during the summer, and then become various shades of yellow, orange, or red in the autumn. Small greenish flowers grow in bunches attached to the main stem close to where each leaf joins it. Later in the season, clusters of poisonous berries form. They are whitish, with a waxy look.

Poison Oak: There are two main species of poison oak, but the species commonly found in New England is the Atlantic Poison Oak a vine plant or bush. Poison oak leaves grow in clusters of three leaves; the lobbed appearance of each leaf resembles the white oak. Plants put out berries in spring that are white or yellowish-green in color and leaflets change color with the seasons. Poison oak tends to grow in sandy soils.

Poison Sumac: Though it is one of New England's native tree species, poison sumac is the rarest of the urushiol-containing plants. Sumac can be identified by its row of paired

Avoiding Poison Oak: Remember the old Boy Scout saying: "Leaves of three, let them be."

leaflets that contains an additional leaflet at the end. Often the leaves have spots that resemble blotches of black enamel paint. These spots are actually urushiol, which when exposed to air turn brownish-black. Poison sumac tends to grow near wet areas and bogs.

TREATING POISON IVY, POISON OAK, AND POISON SUMAC

When an allergic reaction develops, the skin should be washed well with lukewarm water and soap. All clothing should be laundered, and everything else that may be contaminated with urushiol should be washed thoroughly. Urushiol can remain active for a long time. For mild cases, cool showers and an over-the-counter product that eases itching can be effective. Oatmeal baths and baking-soda mixtures also can soothe the discomfort. When a severe reaction develops contact a dermatologist immediately, or go to an emergency room. Prescription medication may be needed to reduce the swelling and itch.

Insects

Black flies, or mayflies, emerge by late April or early May and pester hikers until late June or early July, while mosquitoes come out in late spring and dissipate (but do not disappear) by midsummer. No-see-ums (tiny biting flies that live up to their name) plague some wooded areas in summer. Of particular concern in recent years has been the small, but growing number of cases of eastern equine encephalitis (EEE) in humans, spread by EEE-infected mosquitoes. It's still very rare, but cases of EEE tend to emerge each year at the end of summer and early fall. Mosquitoes acquire EEE through contact with diseased birds.

LYME DISEASE

Deer ticks are often carriers of the bacteria that causes Lyme disease. Hundreds of cases of the disease – most mild and treatable with antibiotics – are diagnosed in New England each year. The easiest way to avoid tick bites is to wear socks, long pants, and a long-sleeve shirt whenever you hike, and especially when you hike in areas with tall grass and/or large deer populations. Tucking your pant legs into your socks prevents the best protection against the tiny ticks, but never fail to check your skin thoroughly at the end of a hike. Most tick bites cause a sharp sting, but some may go unnoticed.

If you do find a tick, don't panic. Take a pair of tweezers and place them around the tick as close to your skin as possible. Gently pull the tick straight out to avoid parts of it breaking off still attached to the skin. The majority of tick bites are no more of a nuisance than a mosquito or black fly bite. If you do notice a rash spreading out from around the bite within a week of finding the tick, it may be an early sign of Lyme disease. Other symptoms are similar to the flu – headache, fever, muscle soreness, neck stiffness, or nausea – and may appear anywhere from a few days to a week or so after being bitten. If you do notice any symptoms, seek medical help immediately. When caught in its early stages, Lyme disease is easily treated with antibiotics; left untreated, the disease can be debilitating.

You will want to have some kind of bug repellant with you no matter where your hike takes you. (Even the windswept coast isn't free of insects; New England's swarms of black flies first appear on the coast and then move inland.) There is much debate about the health effects of wearing sprays containing the chemical DEET; some may prefer ointments made with essential oils and herbs believed to deter bugs. Or skip the sprays and salves and wear a lightweight jacket made of head-to-waist (or head-to-toe) mosquito netting. These unusual creations are made by Bug Baffler, a New Hampshire-based company, and sold on the web (www.bugbaffler.com).

Wildlife

The remarkable recovery of New England's mountains and forests during the past century from the abuses of the logging industry has spawned a boom in the populations of many wild animals, from increased numbers of black bears and moose to the triumphant return of the bald eagle and peregrine falcon. For the most part, you don't have to worry about your safety in the backcountry when it comes to wildlife encounters. It's typical for hikers to see lots of scat and a traffic jam of prints on the trail without ever actually spotting the animals that left this evidence behind.

Still, a few sensible precautions are in order. If you're camping in the backcountry, know how to hang or store your food properly to keep it from bears and smaller animals like mice, which are more likely to be a problem. You certainly should never approach the region's two largest mammals: moose, which you may see in northern New England, or bear, which you may never see. These creatures are wild and unpredictable, and a moose can weigh several hundred pounds and put the hurt on a much smaller human. The greatest danger posed by moose is that of hitting one while driving on dark back roads at night; hundreds of collisions occur in Maine and New Hampshire every year, often wrecking vehicles and injuring people. At night, drive more slowly than you would during daylight. As one forest ranger warns, "the most dangerous part of hiking in the mountains is the drive to the trailhead."

First Aid

HYPOTHERMIA

In humans and other warm-blooded animals, core body temperature is maintained near a constant level through internal temperature regulation. When the body is over-exposed to cold, however, internal mechanisms may be unable to replenish excessive heat loss. Hypothermia is defined as any body temperature below 95°F (35 °C). Despite its association with winter, hypothermia can occur even when the air temperature is in the 50s. Often the victim has gotten wet or over-exerted himself or herself on the trail. Hypothermia is a leading cause of death in the outdoors.

Symptoms of hypothermia include uncontrollable shivering, weakness, loss of coordination, confusion, cold skin, drowsiness, frost bite, and slowed breathing or heart rate. If a member of your hiking party demonstrates one or more of these symptoms, send a call out for help and take action immediately. Get out of the wind and cold and seek shelter in a warm, dry environment. Help the victim change into windproof, waterproof clothes and wrap up in a blanket, if one is available; start a fire to add extra warmth. Encourage the victim to eat candy, energy bars, and other high-sugar foods to boost energy. Do not offer alcohol, it only makes heat loss worse.

Victims of mild to moderate hypothermia may be suffering from impaired judgment and not be making rational decisions. They might try to resist help; be persistent.

HEAT STROKE

Our bodies produce a tremendous amount of internal heat. Under normal conditions, we cool ourselves by sweating and radiating heat through the skin. However, in certain circumstances, such as extreme heat, high humidity, or vigorous activity in the hot sun, this cooling system may begin to fail, allowing heat to build up to dangerous levels.

If a person becomes dehydrated and cannot sweat enough to cool their body, their internal temperature may rise to dangerously high levels, causing heat stroke. Symptoms include headache, mental confusion, and cramps throughout the entire body. If you have these symptoms, or notice them in a member of your hiking party, take immediate action to lower the body's core temperature. Get out of the sun and move to a shadier location. Pour water over the victim and fan the skin to stimulate sweating; sit in a nearby stream, if possible. Encourage the victim to drink liquids and rest. If symptoms are severe or don't improve within a few minutes of starting first aid, do not hesitate to call for help.

Probably the most effective way to cut risk for heat stroke is to stay adequately hydrated. When the temperatures soar on a New England summer day, stop frequently on the trail for water and rest breaks.

SPRAINS AND BREAKS

For any sprain or strain, remember RICE: rest, ice, compression, elevation. First, have the patient rest by lying down on the ground or nearest flat surface. Next, reduce swelling by gently placing a plastic freezer bag filled with cold water on the injury. To compress the ankle, snugly wrap the injury in an ACE bandage. (First-aid tape will also work.)

The wrap should cover the entire foot except for the heel and end several inches above the ankle. Most compression wraps are self-fastening or come with clip fasteners—or use tape to secure the end. If toes become purplish or blue, cool to the touch, or feel numb or tingly according to the patient, the wrap is too tight and should be loosened.

Keep the leg elevated until swelling is visibly reduced. When you or someone you are with suffers a sprained ankle or other minor injury on the trail, keep an open mind about finishing the hike. Because it's always more enjoyable when everyone can fully participate, it might be best to cut your losses and come back another time.

Navigational Tools

At some point, almost every hiker becomes lost. Torn down trail signs, trail detours, faded blazes, and snow, fog, and other conditions can make staying the course very rough going. First, take every step to prevent becoming lost. Before you hike, study a map of the area to become familiar with the trails, nearby roads, streams, mountains and other features. Leave a trip plan with family or friends and sign in at the trailhead register or nearby ranger cabin, if a hiker registry is available.

Always hike with a map and compass. And as you ramble along the trail, observe the topography around you (ridges, recognizable summits, rivers, etc.). They serve as good reference points, particularly when you are above the tree line. Some hikers leave small piles of rocks spaced at regular intervals to help them navigate treeless, alpine areas. Should you become disoriented, stop, pull out your map and look at the countryside for familiar landmarks.

Few people remain truly lost after consulting a map and calmly studying the terrain for five minutes. If you still need help orienting yourself, you may want to head to a ridge or high ground so you can identify hills or streams that are marked on your topographical map. Lay your map on the ground and put your compass on top to orient north. Another helpful gadget is an altimeter, which can tell you your approximate elevation; you can then pinpoint this elevation on a topographic map. Until you have your bearings, don't wander too far from your original route. If you told family members or fellow hikers where you plan to hike, that area is where rescuers will start searching for you.

Should you continue to be lost, S.T.O.P. (stop, think, observe, and plan). And don't panic. Not only does it cloud your judgment, you will be using up energy that you may need later on. Stay put and, if you carry a whistle, blow it at timed intervals to signal rescuers or other hikers (yelling also works).

HIKING ETHICS

Trail Etiquette

One of the great things about hiking is the quality of the people you meet on the trail. Hikers generally do not need an explanation of the value of courtesy, and one hopes this will always ring true. Still, with the popularity of hiking on the increase, and thousands of new hikers taking to the trails of New England every year, it's a good idea to brush up on some etiquette basics.

As a general rule and a friendly favor to other hikers, yield the trail to others whether you're going uphill or down. All trail users should yield to horses by stepping aside for the safety of everyone present. Likewise, horseback riders should, whenever possible, avoid situations where their animals are forced to push past hikers on very narrow trails.

Mountain bikers should yield to hikers, announce their approach, and pass nonbikers slowly. During hunting season, nonhunters should wear blaze orange, or an equally bright, conspicuous color. The hunters you may come across on the trail are usually responsible and friendly and deserve like treatment.

Many of us enjoy the woods and mountains for the quiet, and we should keep that in mind on the trail, at summits, or backcountry campsites. Many of us share the belief that things like cell phones, radios, and CD players do not belong in the mountains. High tech devices may also pose serious safety risks when used on the trail. Texting while hiking? Not a good idea when you should be watching out for exposed tree roots and rocky footing. Likewise, listening to a MP3 player could prevent you from hearing another hiker alerting you to dangers ahead.

New England has seen some conflict between hikers and mountain bikers, but it's important to remember that solutions to those issues are never reached through hostility and rudeness. Much more is accomplished when we begin from a foundation of mutual respect and courtesy. After all, we're all interested in preserving and enjoying our trails.

Large groups have a disproportionate impact on backcountry campsites and on the experience of other people. Be aware of and respect any restrictions on group size. Even where no regulation exists, keep your group size to no more than 10 people.

TIPS FOR AVOIDING CROWDS

Even on New England's most popular peaks, it is still possible to beat the crowds and have the trail all—or mostly—to yourself. Timing is everything. For hikes of less than six or seven miles round-trip, try to arrive at the trailhead early in the morning. Depending on the elevation gain, a seven-mile round-tripper will take the average hiker somewhere around three hours to complete—the perfect length for a late morning or early afternoon trek. Start your hike by 7 A.M. on a sunny Saturday morning and you will probably be returning to your car just as the weekend crush is arriving. For very short hikes, waiting until late afternoon or early evening before hitting the trail almost always ensures low boot traffic. But keep these late day hikes short and to destinations with easy footing just in case you're still out on the trail when night falls.

For very long hikes of nine miles round-trip or more, this early-bird strategy will not work, since early morning is the normal start time for most longer hikes. To still salvage a little solitude on your journey, you might want to consider breaking high mileage hikes into a two-day trek with an overnight stay at a shelter or backcountry campground. Start out on the trail later in the day and aim to camp at least halfway to the summit (within a mile of the summit is ideal). As early as you can the next day, finish the climb and enjoy the peaceful stillness.

Another way to avoid the crowds is to hike during the work week, when even the busiest of New England's trailheads are almost empty. If it felt as though you were part of a conga line climbing to the top of Mount Washington on a warm, sunny Sunday afternoon, come back on Wednesday and find almost no one around. Similarly, time your hikes according to the seasons. With the exception of a few places in northern New England that tend to stay muddy and even icy well into late spring, June is often the best month for encountering light boot traffic. Birds chirp, the air is fresh, wildflowers bloom in the meadows, and the throngs of summer tourists—and swarms of mosquitoes—have yet to arrive. Similarly, the week after Labor Day weekend is often quiet on the trail, with family vacationers gone back to school and the fall foliage season not yet underway.

Hiking with Children

Exploring the great outdoors with kids is one of life's great rewards. Starting from a very young age, a baby can be placed in a front carrier and taken out on almost any trail where the walking is flat and the environment serene; the rhythmic pace of hiking tends to lull even the fussiest of infants right to sleep. Backpack carriers are a good way to tote toddlers on-trail and, depending on the model, can accommodate a child of up to 35 pounds. When hiking with a child-carrier pack, keep a small mirror in your pocket so you can frequently check on your passenger without having to stop and remove the pack.

Around age three, kids are ready to hit the trail along with the rest of the family. But, little legs don't travel very far. Make your family outings kid-centric by picking short hikes that lead to such exciting features as waterfalls, duck-filled ponds, giant glacial erratics, huge gnarled tree trunks, beaver dams, and small hills with big views. Even if the hike is under a half mile in total length, plan extra time for rest stops and lots of unfettered exploration. Most children love the grown-up feel of having their own lightweight backpack; fill the pack with a water bottle and snack treats.

When a child reaches school age, physical ability rises dramatically. And so does his or her responsibility as a hiker. Teach your children how to read maps, how to use a compass, and what to do if lost. Show by example how to be courteous to the other hikers you encounter on the trail. Your efforts will be appreciated.

Hiking with Pets

Dogs are great trail companions and generally love the adventure of hiking every bit as much as their owners do. But dogs can create unnecessary friction in the backcountry. Dog owners should respect any regulations and not presume that strangers are eager to meet their pet. Keep your pet under physical control whenever other people are approaching. And for your dog's protection, always bring a leash along, even if regulations don't call for one.

Due to its large wildlife population, Baxter State Park in Maine is one notable destination that does not permit pets of any kind inside its borders. If you do have your dog along, check in with the campsites lining the access roads to Baxter. Many offer day boarding for dogs. Several bird refuges and Audubon sanctuaries also prohibit dogs. Call ahead to these and other destinations to find out trail regulations for pets.

Leave No Trace

Many of New England's trails receive heavy use, making it imperative that we all understand how to minimize our physical impact on the land. The nonprofit organization Leave No Trace (LNT) advocates a set of principles for low-impact backcountry use that are summarized in these basic guidelines:

- Be considerate of other visitors.
- Dispose of waste properly.
- Leave what you find.
- Minimize campfire impact.
- Plan ahead and prepare.

• Respect wildlife.

• Travel and camp on durable surfaces.

LNT offers more in-depth guidelines for low-impact camping and hiking on its website: www.lnt.org. You can also contact them by mail or phone: Leave No Trace Inc., P.O. Box 997, Boulder, CO 80306; 303/442-8222 or 800/332-4100.

Camping

The following are more recommendations that apply to many backcountry areas in New England:

• Avoid building campfires; cook with a backpacking stove. If you do build a campfire, use only wood found locally as a way to prevent the spread of destructive forest pests introduced from areas outside New England. In all six states, campers are encouraged not to move firewood more than 50 miles from its original source. Store-bought, packaged firewood is usually okay, as long as it is labeled "kiln dried" or "USDA Certified." Wood that is kiln dried is generally free of pests, although if the wood is not heated to a certain temperature, insects can survive.

• Avoid trails that are very muddy in spring; that's when they are most susceptible to erosion.

• Bury human waste beneath six inches of soil at least 200 feet from any water source.

• Burn and bury, or carry out, used toilet paper.

• Carry out everything you carry in.

• Choose a campsite at least 200 feet from trails and water sources, unless you're using a designated site. Make sure your site bears no evidence of your stay when you leave.

• Do not leave any food behind, even buried, as animals will dig it up. Learn how to hang food appropriately to keep it from bears. Black bears have spread their range over much of New England in recent years, and problems have arisen in isolated backcountry areas where human use is heavy.

• Even biodegradable soap is harmful to the environment, so simply wash your cooking gear with water away from any streams or ponds.

• Last but not least, know and follow any regulations for the area you will be visiting.

THE WHITE MOUNTAINS

© VINCENT VANNICOLA

BEST HIKES

Poet, naturalist, and avid hiker Henry David Thoreau once observed, "thousands annually seek the White Mountains to be refreshed by their wild and primitive beauty." Change that figure to millions and the famous New Englander's words are as true now as they were when he wrote them over 150 years ago. Comprised of an 800,000-acre national forest, countless state parks, seven soaring summits of over 5,000 feet, and more than 1,200 miles of trails, this great alpine outcropping of the Appalachian chain is, for many, simply the most spectacular range east of the Rockies.

Besides the classic and popular summits of the Presidentials — including Mount Washington and Mount Adams — hiking "the Whites" takes you from the dizzying heights of Franconia Ridge and Mount Chocorua to the scenic lowlands of Zealand and Crawford Notches and to the largest federal wilderness in the Northeast (the Pemigewasset). Walks to waterfalls, gorges, rock-strewn rivers, and quiet mountain ponds also await — as well as the chance to glimpse moose, fox, deer, bear, and other northern wildlife roaming freely across the landscape of mixed evergreen and deciduous forest.

Many hikes in the White Mountains (Mounts Lincoln and Lafayette, Mount Chocorua, Mount Moosilauke) are among the most popular in New England. You are likely to find trails crowded with boots on nice weekends in summer and fall — and even in winter. Some of the lower peaks (Welch and Dickey, North Moat, Mount Willard) offer the best views per ounce of sweat that you'll find anywhere, while still other summit climbs (Flume and Tripyramid) rank among the region's most rugged and difficult. For isolation, the hikes along the newly constructed Cohos Trail, a winding 162-mile footpath leading from the northern edge of the Presidentials all the way to the Canadian border, is remote, backcountry summiting at its New England best.

Hikes to the bigger peaks of the Whites often entail more than 3,000 or even 4,000 feet of elevation gain, at least several miles round-trip, very rugged terrain, and the possibility of severe weather. Some of the worst weather conditions in North America have been recorded at the Mount Washington weather observatory and hikers must always be prepared for unpredictable changes in the weather at any time and in any season. The Pinkham Notch AMC visitors center offers updated weather conditions for Mount Washington and other major peaks.

In the White Mountain National Forest, fires are prohibited above timberline and camping is prohibited within a quarter mile of any hut or shelter except at authorized tent sites. Camping is permitted above timberline only where there exists a base of at least two feet of snow. Timberline is defined as that elevation at which trees are less than eight feet tall and is often indicated by trailside signs. Stay on the trail in the alpine zone (the area above timberline) to avoid damaging fragile alpine vegetation.

Along the Appalachian Trail as it passes through the White Mountains, dogs must be kept under control, and horses, bikes, hunting, and firearms are prohibited. Cross-country skiing and snowshoeing are allowed, though the trail is often too rugged for skiing. In areas where the Appalachian Trail crosses through New Hampshire state park land, dogs must be leashed.

Keep group sizes to no more than 10 people in any federal wilderness area in the White Mountain National Forest (a good guideline to follow in non-wilderness areas as well, because large groups disproportionately affect the land and the experience of other hikers). Contact the White Mountain National Forest for information on permits for larger groups.

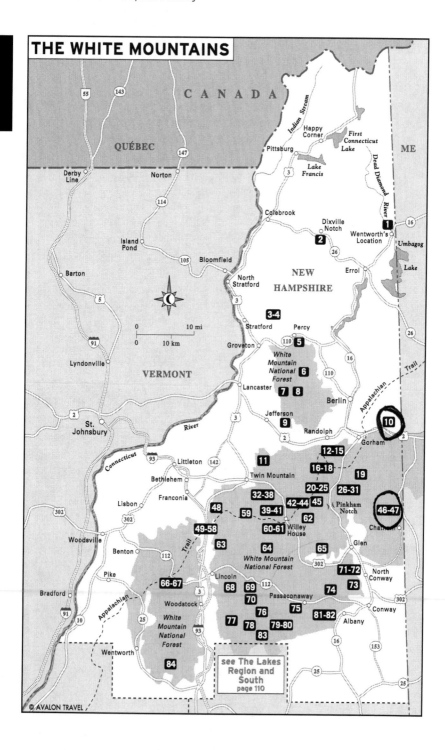

THE WHITE MOUNTAINS

1 DIAMOND PEAKS
6.6 mi/3.5 hr

in the Second College Grant near Wentworth's Location

Tucked away in the vast wilds of the North Country, this moderate trek to two of Diamond Mountain's three peaks (West Peak, 2,010 ft. and East Peak, 2,050 ft.) takes you to a scenic ridge rising high between the Dead Diamond and Magalloway Rivers. The land is part of the Second College Grant, a tract of land given by the state to Dartmouth College in 1807. Hikers not affiliated with the college are welcome on the trails, but will need to park outside the grant and walk or bike the 2.2 miles of flat road to the trailhead (making for a total hiking distance of 6.6 miles round-trip). The hike up Diamond Peaks climbs about 600 feet.

Across from the Dartmouth Forest Management Center, the yellow-blazed Diamond Peaks Trail begins at a sign on the right (east) side of the road. Bikes are prohibited on the trail, but can be left near the trailhead. The trail rises gently through the woods at first before beginning a short but steep ascent up the rocky hillside. At 0.3 mile, a spur trail on the left leads to Alice Ledge, a lookout with good views of the Dead Diamond River Valley. Turning sharply right, the main trail pushes almost due west, passing Linda Ledge (at 0.5 mile), before reaching West Peak at approximately one mile from the trailhead. Just below the peak's wooded summit is an open ledge overlooking precipitous cliffs. Continuing its ascent along the top of the cliffs, the trail offers several good views of the valley below and the surrounding wooded hills. In this fine spot for bird-watching, ravens and red-tailed hawks are frequently seen around the Diamond Peaks. The trail then ends in another 0.1 mile atop the tall cliffs of East Peak. Follow the same route back.

User Groups: Hikers and dogs. Bikes are prohibited past the trailhead. No horses or wheelchair facilities.

Permits: The hike is on private land within the Second College Grant, a township of nearly 27,000 acres owned by Dartmouth College in Hanover. The college uses gates to control access. A permit from the Outdoor Programs Office at Dartmouth College is required to park within the grant and is available only to persons affiliated with the college or its Outing Club. However, day use by the public is allowed, provided you park outside the grant.

Maps: The Outdoor Programs Office at Dartmouth College sells a waterproof contour trail map of the Second College Grant for $2. For a topographic area map, request Wilsons Mills from the USGS.

Directions: From the junction of Routes 16 and 26 in Errol, follow Route 16 north for 8.7 miles into Wentworth's Location. About 0.2 mile past the Mount Dustan Store in the Wentworth's Location village center, turn left at a small cemetery onto Dead Diamond Road, a gravel logging road; find the parking turnout in another 0.2 mile, just before the gate. Remember how far north you are—this road could be snow covered from mid-autumn well into spring and may be a mud bog until July. Follow it for 2.2 miles to the Forest Management Center.

GPS Coordinates: 44.8860 N, 71.0740 W

Contact: Dartmouth College Outdoor Programs Office, 119 Robinson Hall, Dartmouth College, Hanover, NH 03755, 603/646-2834, www.dartmouth.edu/~doc.

2 TABLE ROCK, DIXVILLE NOTCH
0.7 mi/1.5 hr

in Dixville Notch State Park

Not for the faint of heart—or those afraid of heights, this hike takes you to the soaring precipice of spectacular Table Rock (2,510 ft.), a narrow promontory jutting out an incredible

100 feet from the north shoulder of Mount Gloriette, one of the mountains flanking narrow, winding Dixville Notch. Only four feet at its tip with sheer drops of up to 800 feet off either side, Table Rock is a lookout perch unlike any other in New England.

From the roadside trailhead, the trail climbs very steeply over difficult, rocky ground for 0.3 mile as it rises 600 feet to the cliff top. Once on the ledge, turn right with the trail, climbing uphill another 40 feet to walk the long gangplank of Table Rock. The giant buttress of shattered rock thrusting far out from the main cliff face rises hundreds of feet above the floor, with sheer drops off either side of the narrow walkway. Edging along Table Rock is an unnerving adventure for even the most experienced hikers. But if you stay put along the wider base of the ledge, you might be able to put anxiety aside as you take in panoramic views of the surrounding mountains and the Balsams, a grand resort hotel and Dixville Notch landmark. The Balsams maintains a crisscrossing network of trails in this area, leading to and from the hotel, but this hike descends the way you came—arguably more difficult and dangerous than the ascent because of the steepness and frequently wet rock.

User Groups: Hikers only. This trail is not suitable for bikes, dogs, or horses; no wheelchair facilities.

Permits: Parking and access are free.

Maps: A guidebook with map for the Cohos Trail, including information about Table Rock, is available from the Cohos Trail Association ($21.95). For a topographic area map, request Dixville Notch from the USGS.

Directions: From the main entrance to the Balsams Resort on Route 2, head east for 0.1 mile. Park in the ample turnout where a sign marks the Dixville Notch Heritage Trail start (behind the state park sign).

GPS Coordinates: 44.8651 N, 71.3010 W

Contact: The Cohos Trail Association, 266 Danforth Rd., Pittsburg, NH 03592, 603/363-8902, www.cohostrail.org. Dixville Notch

State Park, Route 26, Dixville, NH 03576, 603/538-6707, www.nhstateparks.org.

❸ SUGARLOAF MOUNTAIN
3.5 mi/2.5 hr

in Nash Stream State Forest

The North Country's 39,601-acre Nash Stream State Forest offers some of the most remote and lonely hiking in the Granite State—and on some sizable hills, no less. Sugarloaf fronts a large range of peaks that are virtually unknown to many hikers and that nearly rival in size the Pilot Range of the northern White Mountain National Forest to the south. Were the 3,701-foot bare rock summit of Sugarloaf just a few hundred feet taller, peak-baggers would flock here. As it is, the state forest sees few visitors. Even during prime hiking season don't be surprised if you find moose, deer, and other northern wildlife your only companions as you enjoy a vista of peaks stretching all the way north into Quebec. This 3.5-mile hike offers a net elevation gain of about 2,100 feet.

From the parking area, pick up the westbound Sugarloaf Trail, an old jeep road (look for the sign marker). Starting off as a gradual climb, at 0.2 mile, the trail comes to a fork. Here, bear right (the yellow-blazed trail bearing to the left is the Cohos Trail). Soon listing to the northwest, the trail begins to ascend steeply and without pause—a real calf-burner. At 1.2 miles, a sharp change of course faces you almost due north as the trail eases out somewhat and begins to skirt the summit. Changing direction again a short distance further, the trail turns left and heads south to reach the craggy summit ledges, a little more than 1.7 miles from the trailhead. Hike back the same way.

User Groups: Hikers and leashed dogs. This trail is not suitable for bikes or horses; no wheelchair facilities.

Permits: Parking and access are free.

Maps: A guidebook with map for the Cohos

Trail, including information about Sugarloaf Mountain, is available from the Cohos Trail Association ($21.95). For topographic area maps, request Tinkerville, Blue Mountain, Stratford, and Percy Peaks from the USGS.

Directions: From the junction of Route 110 and U.S. 3 in Groteton, follow Route 110 east for 2.6 miles to Emerson Road. Turn left and drive 2.2 miles to a left hand turn onto the dirt Nash Stream Road. Continue a half mile to an open area with an oversized locator map posted on a sign. From the sign, follow Nash Stream Road another 4.6 miles, bear left, and continue 3.2 miles. Drive over a bridge and another 100 feet to a parking area on the left. Nash Stream Road is typically open Memorial Day–early November, depending on weather conditions.

GPS Coordinates: 44.7371 N, 71.4392 W

Contact: New Hampshire Division of Forests and Lands, P.O. Box 1856, Concord, NH 03302-1856, 603/271-3456, www.nhdfl.org. Cohos Trail Association, 266 Danforth Rd., Pittsburg, NH 03592, 603/363-8902, www.cohostrail.org.

🄸 NORTH PERCY PEAK
4 mi/3 hr   👫4 ⛰9

in Nash Stream State Forest

 BEST (

Though located in the remote Nash Stream State Forest, direct road access makes the 3,418-foot North Percy Peak a bit more accessible than other trailheads in the Nash Stream region. A challenging climb over rock slabs that are dangerously slippery when wet, this hidden gem of a hike rewards you with long views in every direction from the mountain's scrub-covered summit. Hiking to the top of North Percy Peak offers a net elevation of about 2,200 feet.

From the parking area on Nash Stream Road, follow the orange-blazed Percy Peaks Trail as it begins a moderate ascent through hardwood forest, crossing a stream at 0.3 mile,

and then reaching a large boulder at the one-mile mark. Here, the trail turns left and quickly grows steep and rough as it reaches exposed slabs. At 1.2 miles, the trail comes to a junction with the former Slide Trail. Now officially closed due to unsafe conditions, the Slide Trail forges straight up the exposed slabs. This hike stays on Percy Peaks Trail as it angles southeast away from the slabs and rounds the peak to a col between North Percy and South Percy. At 1.7 miles, the trail passes a junction with the Cohos Trail and then takes a sharp left, emerging above the tree line and running at a steep angle up vast southern slabs another 0.5 mile to the summit. Remember where the trail reenters the woods at the tree line: Sporadic blazes and cairns and the landscape of scrub brush on the mountain's flat summit make it easy to lose the way back to the trail. Return the way you came.

User Groups: Hikers and leashed dogs. This trail is not suitable for bikes or horses; no wheelchair facilities.

Permits: Parking and access are free.

Maps: A guidebook with map for the Cohos Trail, including information about the Percy Peaks Trail, is available from the Cohos Trail Association ($21.95). For topographic area maps, request Tinkerville, Blue Mountain, Stratford, and Percy Peaks from the USGS.

Directions: From the junction of Route 110 and U.S. 3 in Groteton, follow Route 110 east for 2.6 miles to Emerson Road. Turn left and drive 2.2 miles to a left hand turn onto the dirt Nash Stream Road. Continue a half mile to an open area with an oversized locator map posted on a sign. From the sign, follow the Nash Stream Road another 2.2 miles to a turnout on the right. Nash Stream Road is typically open Memorial Day–early November, depending on weather conditions.

Contact: New Hampshire Division of Forests and Lands, P.O. Box 1856, Concord, NH 03302-1856, 603/271-3456. The Cohos Trail Association, 266 Danforth Rd., Pittsburg, NH 03592, 603/363-8902, www.cohostrail.org.

5 DEVIL'S HOPYARD

2.4 mi/1.5 hr   👣1 ⛰8

in the northern White Mountain National
Forest east of Lancaster and west of Berlin

A short detour off the Kilkenny Ridge Trail leads to the wild and otherworldly Devil's Hopyard, a small gorge almost completely overgrown with moss, ferns, and trees. In the middle of all this lush green, water cascades and then rushes out of sight beneath massive boulders—a sight that can make you think you've stepped into some kind of emerald fairyland. This short hike nets an easy elevation gain of 250 feet.

From the South Pond parking area, head south on the Kilkenny Ridge Trail/Devil's Hopyard Trail. (The two trails coincide for the first 0.6 mile, but on many maps, only the Kilkenny Ridge Trail is listed.) In 60 yards after crossing the Devil's Hopyard stream, the Devil's Hopyard Trail turns right (west) at a signed trail junction and leaves the Kilkenny. As the Devil's Hopyard Trail continues, the path narrows and becomes somewhat rocky. At 0.8 mile, the trail crosses the stream again and soon enters the Hopyard gorge. Crossing over moss-covered rocks (which can be very slippery even when not very wet), the trail turns steep as it rises to the ledges above the cascades (at 1.2 miles). Return the way you came.

User Groups: Hikers and dogs. No bikes, horses, or wheelchair facilities.

Permits: A permit is required for day use or overnight parking at any White Mountain National Forest trailhead. Permits are available at several area stores and from the national forest at a cost of $5 for seven consecutive days or $20 per year. A $3 one-day permit can be purchased at self-service stations at national forest trailheads, but the permit is good only for the trailhead at which it's purchased.

Maps: A waterproof area trail map is available from the Appalachian Mountain Club (Carter Range–Evans Notch/North Country–Mahoosuc, $9.95). For a topographic map, request West Milan from the USGS.

Directions: From the intersection of U.S. 3 and Route 110 in Groveton, drive east on Route 100 for approximately 10 miles to reach a right hand turn for South Pond Road. Follow South Pond Road 0.7 mile to the White Mountain National Forest South Pond Recreation Area; continue 0.2 mile to the parking area and trailhead.

GPS Coordinates: 44.5971 N, 71.3675 W

Contact: White Mountain National Forest Headquarters, 71 White Mountain Dr., Campton, NH 03246, 603/536-6100, TDD for hearing impaired 603/536-3665, www.fs.fed.us/r9/white.

6 ROGERS LEDGE

10 mi/6 hr   👣3 ⛰7

in the northern White Mountain National
Forest east of Lancaster and west of Berlin

This long, though fairly easy, hike is a pleasant walk in the woods as it passes through a relatively quiet area of the White Mountain National Forest on the way to Rogers Ledge (2,945 ft.) and its beautiful mountain views. With a net elevation gain of about 1,500 feet spread out over five miles, the rugged terrain that dominates so much of the rest of this region is relatively absent here, allowing you more time to spot moose and bear tracks, watch spotted salamanders and tree frogs scamper from the trail, and catch sight of such birds as the American redstart, black-throated blue warbler, and red-eyed vireo—some of the over 72 varieties of neotropical migrant birds who summer in these parts of the Whites.

From the parking area, follow the Mill Brook Trail a relatively flat 3.8 miles to the Kilkenny Ridge Trail. Turn right (north) and walk this easy stretch of the Kilkenny 0.6 mile to Rogers Ledge. At 2,945 feet, this high ledge overlooks the Presidentials to the south, the

Pilot Range to the southwest, and Berlin and the Mahoosuc Range to the east. After enjoying the view, return the way you came. For those who wish to camp overnight before the return trip back, the Rogers Ledge Tentsite is located at the junction of the Kilkenny Ridge and Mill Brook trails.

User Groups: Hikers and dogs. No bikes, horses, or wheelchair facilities.

Permits: No backcountry permit is needed, but a permit is required for day use or overnight parking at any White Mountain National Forest trailhead. Permits are available at several area stores and from the national forest at a cost of $5 for seven consecutive days or $20 per year. A $3 one-day permit can be purchased at self-service stations at national forest trailheads, but the permit is good only for the trailhead at which it's purchased.

Maps: A waterproof area trail map is available from the Appalachian Mountain Club (Carter Range–Evans Notch/North Country–Mahoosuc, $9.95). For topographic area maps, request West Milan, Milan, Pliny Range, and Berlin from the USGS.

Directions: From the junction of Routes 16 and 110 in Berlin, drive north on Route 110 for approximately seven miles. At a sign for the U.S. Fish Hatchery, turn left onto York Pond Road. Follow the paved road to the hatchery and then follow the Mill Brook Trail signs to a small parking area at the end of a short dirt road behind the hatchery office. The entrance gate to the U.S. Fish Hatchery on York Pond Road is closed 4 P.M.–8 A.M., but not locked; close and pin the gate again after passing through if it is closed when you arrive.

GPS Coordinates: 44.4986 N, 71.3390 W

Contact: White Mountain National Forest Headquarters, 71 White Mountain Dr., Campton, NH 03246, 603/536-6100, TDD for hearing impaired 603/536-3665, www.fs.fed.us/r9/white.

⑦ KILKENNY LOOP
18.5 mi/2 days

In the northern White Mountain National Forest east of Lancaster and west of Berlin

BEST (

This backpacking loop is good proof that even in a national forest as heavily used as the White Mountains, trails strewn with pine-needle duff and moss so untrod upon that it actually gives softly like a cushion underfoot, still exist—and exist in abundance. This two-day traverse of the Pilot Range, much of it on the Kilkenny Ridge Trail, takes place along the national forest's northernmost reaches. Far removed from population centers, the Pilot Range boasts no giant peaks to attract hikers, but it does offer the chance to revel in the solitude and quiet of the forest. This hike includes side trips to Rogers Ledge and the Horn, perhaps the two best views in the range, and offers a net elevation gain of about 4,000 feet.

From the small parking area behind the fish hatchery office, follow the gently rising Mill Brook Trail 3.8 miles to the Kilkenny Ridge Trail, passing through an extensive area of birch forest. Drop your packs and turn right (north) for the 1.2-mile side trip to Rogers Ledge, an open ledge atop cliffs with sweeping views south to the Presidentials, southwest to the unfolding Pilot Range, and southeast to Berlin's smokestacks and the Mahoosuc Range beyond. Double back to your packs and hike southwest on the Kilkenny Ridge Trail for 2.1 miles, much of it an easy walk, with a moderate hill climb just before you reach Unknown Pond and the intersection with the Unknown Pond Trail. The Unknown Pond Tentsite is on the left, a good place to camp for the night.

On the hike's second day, head back to the trail junction to rejoin the southbound Kilkenny Ridge Trail. Climbing steeply, the trail gains several hundred feet in elevation. At 1.7 miles from Unknown Pond, a side trail leads left (east) 0.3 mile to the craggy, 3,905-foot summit of the Horn, with expansive views in every direction. Reaching the very summit of the Horn requires a little hand and foot scrambling, but it's not too difficult.

Back on the Kilkenny Ridge Trail, continue southwest over the wooded summit of the Bulge (3,920 ft.) and on to the highest point on the ridge, 4,170-foot wooded summit of Mount Cabot, 2.8 miles from Unknown Pond. From Cabot's summit, the Kilkenny Ridge Trail coincides with the Mount Cabot Trail for 1.4 miles, with great views from an open ledge along the way. Where the two trails split, bear left (east) with the Kilkenny Ridge Trail and follow it for another 0.3 mile to the Bunnell Notch Trail. They coincide for 0.1 mile; where they split, stay left (east) on the Bunnell Notch Trail for another 2.6 miles. Turn left on the York Pond Trail and follow it 0.2 mile back to York Pond Road. From here, bear right and follow the road for two miles back to the fish hatchery parking area.

There are two backcountry campsites on the Kilkenny Ridge Trail: 0.1 mile north of the Mill Brook Trail junction and at Unknown Pond. There's also a cabin with bunks on the Kilkenny Ridge Trail 0.4 mile south of the Mount Cabot summit.

User Groups: Hikers and dogs. Trail is not suitable for bikes or horses. No wheelchair facilities.

Permits: No backcountry permit is needed, but a permit is required for day use or overnight parking at any White Mountain National Forest trailhead. Permits are available at several area stores and from the national forest at a cost of $5 for seven consecutive days or $20 per year. A $3 one-day permit can be purchased at self-service stations at national forest trailheads, but the permit is good only for the trailhead at which it's purchased.

Maps: A waterproof area trail map is available from the Appalachian Mountain Club (Carter Range–Evans Notch/North Country–Mahoosuc, $9.95). For topographic area maps, request West Milan, Milan, Pliny Range, and Berlin from the USGS.

Directions: You can either shuttle vehicles to either end of this hike or use one vehicle and hike two miles of road at the end of the trip. From the junction of Routes 16 and 110 in Berlin, drive north on Route 110 for about seven miles. At the U.S. Fish Hatchery sign, turn left onto York Pond Road. Follow the paved road to the hatchery and then follow signs for the Mill Brook Trail to a small parking area at the end of a short dirt road behind the hatchery office. The hike begins there and ends at the York Pond Trail, which begins two miles farther down York Pond Road.

The U.S. Fish Hatchery entrance gate on York Pond Road is closed 4 P.M.–8 A.M., but not locked; close and pin the gate again after passing through if it is closed when you arrive.

GPS Coordinates: 44.4986 N, 71.3390 W

Contact: White Mountain National Forest Headquarters, 71 White Mountain Dr., Campton, NH 03246, 603/536-6100, TDD for hearing impaired 603/536-3665, www.fs.fed.us/r9/white.

8 MOUNT CABOT
11.5 mi/7 hr   🏃4 ⛰8

in the northern White Mountain National Forest east of Lancaster and west of Berlin

Although Mount Cabot (4,170 ft.) has a wooded summit with no views, it attracts hikers for its status as the tallest peak in New Hampshire's North Country, the wild, hilly land of forests and lakes that stretches from the northern White Mountain all the way to the Canadian border. Bunnell Rock, an open ledge along this hike, and the Horn (3,905 ft.), one of Cabot's subsidiary peaks, offer broad views of this corner of the Pilot Range and add greatly to the hike's scenic quality. There is a net elevation gain of nearly 3,000 feet over the course of the hike.

From the parking area on York Pond Road, follow the York Pond Trail for 0.2 mile before bearing right onto the Bunnell Notch Trail.

For the next 2.9 miles, the gently descending Bunnell Notch Trail generally tracks along the north side of a stream and then ends at the junction with the Kilkenny Ridge Trail. Here, turn right, and follow the Kilkenny Ridge/ Mount Cabot Trail uphill for 1.4 miles to the wooded summit of Mount Cabot, passing the great view from Bunnell Rock along the way. The Kilkenny Ridge Trail continues northward past Cabot's summit, bouncing up and down along a wooded ridge. It passes over the 3,920-foot summit of the Bulge, and, 1.1 miles from Cabot's summit, reaches a side path that leads 0.3 mile to the craggy, 3,905-foot summit of the Horn, which is reached by an easy scramble and offers great views of the Whites. Backtrack to the Kilkenny Ridge Trail, turn right (north), and descend, steeply at times, for 1.7 miles to Unknown Pond. Turn right (southeast), following the pond's shoreline briefly; where the Kilkenny Ridge Trail swings left (northeast), continue straight ahead on the Unknown Pond Trail, descending 3.3 miles to York Pond Road. Turn right and walk a short distance back to the York Pond Trail parking area.

User Groups: Hikers and dogs. No bikes, horses, or wheelchair facilities.

Permits: No backcountry permit is needed, but a permit is required for day use or overnight parking at any White Mountain National Forest trailhead. Permits are available at several area stores and from the national forest at a cost of $5 for seven consecutive days or $20 per year. A $3 one-day permit can be purchased at self-service stations at national forest trailheads, but the permit is good only for the trailhead at which it's purchased.

Maps: A waterproof area trail map is available from the Appalachian Mountain Club (Carter Range–Evans Notch/North Country–Mahoosuc, $9.95). For topographic area maps, request Pliny Range and Stark from the USGS.

Directions: From the junction of Routes 16 and 110 in Berlin, drive north on Route 110 for about seven miles and turn left onto York Pond Road at the U.S. Fish Hatchery sign. Follow the paved road to the hatchery and then continue about two miles farther to a small parking area on the right, just before the end of York Pond Road. The York Pond Trail begins at the end of the road. The U.S. Fish Hatchery entrance gate on York Pond Road is closed 4 P.M.–8 A.M., but not locked; close and pin the gate again after passing through if it is closed when you arrive. The York Pond Road has been plowed all the way to its end in recent winters, but check first with the White Mountain National Forest.

GPS Coordinates: 44.4963 N, 71.3593 W

Contact: White Mountain National Forest Headquarters, 71 White Mountain Dr., Campton, NH 03246, 603/536-6100, TDD for hearing impaired 603/536-3665, www.fs.fed.us/r9/white.

9 MOUNTS STARR KING AND WAUMBEK
7.2 mi/3.5 hr   🏃3 7

in the White Mountain National Forest near Jefferson

This trek along the Cohos Trail leads to two peaks in the Pliny Range: Mount Starr King (3,914 ft.), named for Thomas Starr King, a Boston pastor who wrote an early book on the White Mountains, and Mount Waumbek (4,006 ft.), one of the White Mountain's lesser known 4,000-footers and sometimes labeled on older maps as Pliny Major, the mountain's former name. This not-so-steep climb gains approximately 2,400 feet in elevation as it reaches the scenic top of Starr King; continuing to Waumbek adds another 200 feet of ascent.

From the access road parking area, look for the Starr King/Cohos Trail sign marker. The yellow-blazed trail ascends at a steady, but moderate grade for almost the entire length of its 2.6-mile push northeast to the Starr King summit. From a cleared area at the top, the site of a long gone summit shelter, sweeping views of the Whites, from the Presidential Range (southeast) to the Pemigewasset Wilderness peaks (south) and Franconia Ridge (southwest) are still stunning, even as they are being rapidly encroached upon by returning forest growth (scramble atop a boulder for the better views). The trail continues off the summit and onward for another mile on easy terrain to Mount Waumbek. The sporadically marked trail is almost completely in the woods and low trees obstruct any kind of view from the Waumbek summit. Still, for peak baggers, Waumbek is worth the boot mileage. From Waumbek's summit, the Kilkenny Ridge Trail/Cohos Trail leads east and north into the Pilot Range, toward Mount Cabot, Unknown Pond, and Rogers Ledge. This hike descends the same way you came.

User Groups: Hikers and dogs. No bikes, horses, or wheelchair facilities.

Permits: No backcountry permit is needed, but a permit is required for day use or overnight parking at any White Mountain National Forest trailhead. Permits are available at several area stores and from the national forest at a cost of $5 for seven consecutive days or $20 per year. A $3 one-day permit can be purchased at self-service stations at national forest trailheads, but the permit is good only for the trailhead at which it's purchased.

Maps: A waterproof area trail map is available from the Appalachian Mountain Club (Carter Range–Evans Notch/North Country–Mahoosuc, $9.95). For a topographic area map, request Pliny Range from the USGS.

Directions: From the junction of Route 115A and U.S. 2 in Jefferson, follow U.S. 2 east for 0.2 mile. Turn left up a narrow road at a sign for the Starr King Trail. The road ends in about 0.1 mile at a small parking area at the trailhead.

GPS Coordinates: 44.4194 N, 71.4654 W

Contact: White Mountain National Forest Headquarters, 71 White Mountain Dr., Campton, NH 03246, 603/536-6100, TDD for hearing impaired 603/536-3665, www.fs.fed.us/r9/white.

10 MAHOOSUC RANGE: GENTIAN POND

6 mi/3.5 hr   🏃2 ⛰8

in Shelburne

BEST (

Gentian Pond is a picturesque and quite large puddle of water tucked away in the evergreen woods of the rugged Mahoosucs. Go in June to see hundreds of rare white and pink lady's slippers in bloom along the trail and, if you have time, load up a backpack for two or three days and stay in the shelter at Gentian Pond—the dusk view southward to the Androscoggin Valley and the Carter-Moriah Range is fantastic. The shelter is also a good base for exploring the surrounding Mahoosuc Range. This out-and-back hike to the pond climbs about 800 feet uphill.

From the trailhead on North Road, pick up the northbound Austin Brook Trail, an old logging road. After a level two miles, the road narrows to a hiking trail as it begins to skirt the edge of a swampy area. At 2.5 miles, the trail turns sharply right, continuing its modest ascent before growing quite steep in its final 0.5 mile push to the pond and shelter. Just before the Gentian Pond shelter, the Austin Brook Trail meets the Appalachian Trail (also known along this stretch as the Mahoosuc Trail). Return the way you came.

Camping is only allowed at shelters and designated camping areas.

User Groups: Hikers and dogs. This trail is not suitable for bikes or horses; no wheelchair facilities.

Permits: Parking and access are free.

Maps: A waterproof area trail map is available from the Appalachian Mountain Club (Carter Range–Evans Notch/North Country–Mahoosuc, $9.95). For a topographic area map, request Shelburne from the USGS.

Directions: From the intersection of U.S. 2

and Route 16 in Gorham, head southeast on Main Street/Route 16 for 6.9 miles. Turn left at Meadow Road, crossing the Androscoggin River. In 0.9 mile, turn left on North Road and continue for another 0.5 mile. The trailhead is on the right (north) side of the road; park along the road. The Mahoosuc Range is on private property, not within the White Mountain National Forest.

GPS Coordinates: 44.4125 N, 71.0680 W

Contact: Appalachian Mountain Club Pinkham Notch Visitor Center, P.O. Box 298, Gorham, NH 03581, 603/466-2721, www.outdoors.org.

🔟 CHERRY MOUNTAIN: OWL'S HEAD TRAIL

3.8 mi/2.5 hr

In the White Mountain National Forest south of Jefferson

Almost due west of the Presidential Range, the broad, open ledges of the Owl's Head (3,258 ft.) offer dramatic views of the Presidentials' soaring peaks. A climb with a net elevation gain of just under 2,000 feet, this hike takes place on a completed portion of the new Cohos Trail, a 162-mile footpath that will eventually run the entire length of Coos County, from the Presidentials (of which Cherry Mountain is technically a western outpost) to the Canadian border.

From the parking area on Route 115, the yellow-blazed Owl's Head Trail/Cohos Trail heads south, briefly entering a thin strip of woods before crossing a small brook and emerging into a cleared area. Head straight across the clearing to a post marker that reads "Path." The trail has been relocated a bit in this area in recent years due to heavy logging operations, so keep an eye out for signs of recent trail work and brush clearing. The hiking is fairly easy at first, crossing some logged areas—watch for cairns and trail markers. At 0.7 mile, the trail swings left (south)

towards the mountain and begins climbing at a moderate grade. About 1.8 miles from the road, the trail crests the Cherry Mountain ridge; walk a relatively flat 0.1 mile to the Owl's Head ledges. To the south, the trail continues on to Mount Martha (3,573 ft.), 0.8 mile farther, where there is a good view. This hike turns back from the Owl's Head ledges and returns to the trailhead along the same route.

User Groups: Hikers and dogs. Trail is not suitable for bikes or horses; no wheelchair facilities.

Permits: No backcountry permit is needed, but a permit is required for day use or overnight parking at any White Mountain National Forest trailhead. Permits are available at several area stores and from the national forest at a cost of $5 for seven consecutive days or $20 per year. A $3 one-day permit can be purchased at self-service stations at national forest trailheads, but the permit is good only for the trailhead at which it's purchased.

Maps: A waterproof area trail map is available from the Appalachian Mountain Club (Franconia–Pemigewasset Range, $9.95). For a guidebook and maps to the Cohos Trail, contact the Cohos Trail Association. For topographic maps, request Bethlehem and Mount Washington from the USGS.

Directions: From the junction of Route 115 and U.S. 3 in Carroll, follow Route 115 north 5.8 miles to the parking area on the right (with Stanley Slide historical marker).

GPS Coordinates: 44.3590 N, 71.4901 W

Contact: White Mountain National Forest Headquarters, 71 White Mountain Dr., Campton, NH 03246, 603/536-6100, TDD for hearing impaired 603/536-3665, www.fs.fed.us/r9/white. The Cohos Trail Association, 266 Danforth Road, Pittsburg, NH 03592, 603/363-8902, www.cohostrail.org.

12 MOUNTS ADAMS AND MADISON: THE AIR LINE
9.9 mi/8 hr   🥾5 ⛰10

in the White Mountain National Forest south of Randolph

This is the most direct route to the second-highest peak summit in New England—5,799-foot Mount Adams—though not necessarily the fastest. It follows the mountain's spectacular Durand Ridge, giving hikers extended views down into King Ravine, southwest across the prominent ridges on the northern flanks of Mounts Adams and Jefferson, and north across the Randolph Valley to the Pilot Range peaks. Some scrambling is necessary, and you need to be comfortable with exposure—there's an interesting little foot ledge traverse that can get your heart pumping. In good weather, this route allows a fit hiker the option of hitting both Adams and Madison in a day. The vertical ascent to Adams is nearly 4,500 feet, and Madison adds about another 500 feet.

From the parking lot at Appalachia, the Air Line heads almost due south as it makes a beeline to Adams's summit, passing straight through several trail junctions and coinciding briefly with the Randolph Path at 0.9 mile. Emerging above the tree line at three miles, the trail makes a sharp ascent up Durand Ridge, the rocky, bare crest of King Ravine (the ravine plunges to the right; this part of the trail is also called the Knife-edge). Still ascending steeply and without cover, the trail veers right and coincides with the Appalachian Trail/Gulfside Trail at 3.7 miles. A mere 70 yards later, the Air Line bears left for the final 0.6 mile push to the Mount Adams summit. Descend via the Air Line—or go for Madison's summit (5,366 ft.). To reach Madison from Adams's summit, backtrack 0.6 mile back to where the Air Line and AT/Gulfside Trail coincide. This time, stay on the AT heading northwest and in 0.2 mile reach the Madison AMC hut. From the hut, follow the AT (it now coincides with the Osgood Trail) another 0.5 mile to Madison's summit. To descend, retrace your steps to the Madison AMC hut and then head north on the Valley Way all the way back to the parking area, a return trip of 4.3 miles. While on the

alpine scrub growth

© PETER DAME

Valley Way, be sure to take the side paths that parallel it past scenic Tama Fall and Gordon Fall, which are marked by signs not far from the trailhead and do not add any appreciable distance to this hike.

Note: Weather conditions, especially above the tree line, may change rapidly. In the event of bad weather, even the most expert of hikers should turn back. The Valley Way re-enters the woods more quickly than other trails and is the best escape route.

User Groups: Hikers and dogs. No wheelchair facilities. This trail should not be attempted in winter except by hikers experienced in mountaineering and prepared for severe winter weather, and is not suitable for bikes, horses, or skis.

Permits: Parking and access are free.

Maps: A waterproof area trail map is available from the Appalachian Mountain Club (Presidential Range, $9.95). For a topographic area map, request Mount Washington from the USGS.

Directions: From the junction of U.S. 2 and Route 16 in Gorham, follow U.S. 2 west for 2.1 miles. The Appalachia parking area is on the left (south), marked by a sign.

GPS Coordinates: 44.3709 N, 71.2893 W

Contact: White Mountain National Forest Headquarters, 71 White Mountain Drive, Campton, NH 03246, 603/536-6100, TDD for hearing impaired 603/536-3665, www.fs.fed.us/r9/white. The Appalachian Mountain Club Pinkham Notch Visitor Center has up-to-date weather and trail information about the Whites; call 603/466-2725.

13 MOUNT ADAMS: KING RAVINE

9.2 mi/8 hr 👣5 ⛰️10

In the White Mountain National Forest south of Randolph

BEST (

This route through King Ravine is one of the most difficult and spectacular hikes in the White Mountains and an adventurous way up the second-highest peak in New England: 5,799-foot Mount Adams. Besides involving hard scrambling over boulders and up the talus of a very steep ravine headwall, you will gain nearly 4,400 feet in elevation from the trailhead to Adams's summit.

From the Appalachia parking lot, pick up the Air Line Trail and follow it for 0.8 mile, ascending steadily but at an easy grade through mixed deciduous forest; at the trail junction with the Short Line, bear right. The Short Line parallels the cascading Cold Brook, drawing near the brook in spots—though much of the trail is separated from the brook by forest too dense to bushwhack through. Follow the Short Line for 1.9 miles—it coincides for nearly a half mile with the Randolph Path—until it joins the King Ravine Trail. Immediately after you turn onto the King Ravine Trail, a sign marks Mossy Fall on the right, a five-foot-tall waterfall that drops into a shallow pool. The forest here is dense but low, and you start getting views of the ravine walls towering high overhead. Beyond Mossy Fall, the trail grows much steeper, weaving amid massive boulders that have tumbled off the ravine cliffs over the eons. Scrambling atop one of these boulders offers an unforgettable view of King Ravine; the cabin visible on the western wall is Crag Camp, managed by the Randolph Mountain Club.

Just past the junction with the Chemin des Dames at 2.9 miles—a trail that scales the steep ravine wall to the left (east) to join the Air Line—the King Ravine Trail divides. To the right, the Subway will have you crawling through boulder caves, at times removing your pack to squeeze through narrow passages. To the left is an easier route known as the Elevated, which skirts most of the boulders and offers more ravine views. The two trails rejoin within about 200 yards. Soon afterward, the King Ravine Trail passes a trail junction with the Great Gully Trail and offers another choice of options: to the left, the main trail; to the right, a side loop through the Ice Caves, where ice tends to linger year-round. Again, these two paths rejoin within a short distance. The trail emerges completely from the trees and reaches the base of the King Ravine headwall at 3.4 miles. The King Ravine Trail grows its steepest up the headwall, basically following a talus slope. In just over 0.5 mile, the trail gains 1,100 feet in elevation, and footing is tricky on the sometimes-loose rocks.

Atop the headwall, the trail passes between rocky crags at a spot called the Gateway. On the other side, turn right on the Air Line and follow it for 0.6 mile over treeless alpine terrain to the Adams summit (4.6 miles from the Appalachia parking area), with stunning views in every direction. On the way down, you have the option of bagging the Mount Madison summit as well. (See the *Mounts Adams and Madison: the Air Line* listing in this chapter.) Descend via the Air Line; it's 4.3 miles back to the trailhead.

User Groups: Hikers and dogs. No bikes, horses, or wheelchair facilities. This trail should not be attempted in winter except by hikers experienced in mountaineering and prepared for severe winter weather.

Permits: Parking and access are free.

Maps: A waterproof area trail map is available from the Appalachian Mountain Club (Presidential Range, $9.95). For a topographic area map, request Mount Washington from the USGS.

Directions: From the junction of U.S. 2 and Route 16 in Gorham, follow U.S. 2 west for 2.1 miles. The Appalachia parking area is on the left (south), marked by a sign.
GPS Coordinates: 44.3709 N, 71.2893 W

Contact: White Mountain National Forest Headquarters, 71 White Mountain Drive, Campton, NH 03246, 603/536-6100, TDD for hearing impaired 603/536-3665, www.fs.fed.us/r9/white. Randolph Mountain Club, P.O. Box 279, Randolph, NH 03581, www.randolphmountainclub.org.

14 MOUNT ADAMS: LOWE'S PATH

9.6 mi/6 hr

In the White Mountain National Forest south of Randolph

This is the easiest route to the Mount Adams summit, which at 5,799 feet is the second-highest peak in New England and one of the most interesting. The trail has moderate grades and is well protected until timberline, but the last 1.5 miles are above the trees. It's also the oldest trail coming out of the Randolph Valley, cut in 1875–1876.

Lowe's Path ascends gently at first, making several crossings of brooks through an area often wet and muddy. After 2.5 miles you reach the Log Cabin, a Randolph Mountain Club shelter. Another 0.6 mile brings you to both the timberline and a spur trail branching left which leads 0.1 mile to the RMC's Gray Knob cabin. This trail junction also offers the hike's first sweeping views, with the Mount Jefferson Castellated Ridge thrusting its craggy teeth skyward and much of the White Mountains visible on a clear day. From here, Lowe's Path cuts through some krummholz (the dense stands of stunted and twisted conifers that grow at timberline) and then ascends barren talus, where it can be tricky to find the cairns. At 4.1 miles, the trail forces a scramble over a rock mound known as Adams 4 and then begins the final 0.7-mile uphill stretch to the 5,799-foot summit. From Adams's aery heights, hikers are rewarded with some of the best views in these mountains. To the south are Mounts Jefferson, Clay, and Washington and the vast Great Gulf Wilderness; to the north lies neighboring Mount Madison.

User Groups: Hikers and dogs. No bikes, horses, or wheelchair facilities. This trail should not be attempted in winter except by hikers experienced in mountaineering and prepared for severe winter weather.

Permits: Access is free. There is a parking

fee of $2 per day per vehicle at Lowe's Store parking lot.

Maps: A waterproof area trail map is available from the Appalachian Mountain Club (Presidential Range, $9.95). For a topographic area map, request Mount Washington from the USGS.

Directions: From the junction of U.S. 2 and Route 16 in Gorham, follow U.S. 2 west for 8.4 miles to Lowe's Store (on the right). Park at the store and cross U.S. 2. To the right (west) is a dirt driveway that leads about 50 yards to Lowe's Path (on the right).

GPS Coordinates: 44.3637 N, 71.3306 W

Contact: White Mountain National Forest Headquarters, 71 White Mountain Drive, Campton, NH 03246, 603/536-6100, TDD for hearing impaired 603/536-3665, www.fs.fed.us/r9/white. The Appalachian Mountain Club Pinkham Notch Visitor Center has up-to-date weather and trail information about the Whites; call 603/466-2725. Randolph Mountain Club, P.O. Box 279, Randolph, NH 03581, www.randolphmountainclub.org.

15 MOUNT MADISON: MADISON GULF AND WEBSTER TRAILS
11.5 mi/10 hr   🏃5 ⛰10

in the White Mountain National Forest south of Randolph

BEST (

The Madison headwall ascent on the Madison Gulf Trail is without question one of the most difficult hikes in New England. With its intimidating 11.5 miles round-trip and 4,000 feet of elevation gain, this hike also rates as one of the wildest hikes in these mountains—and you may well see no other hikers on the trail. Still, the rugged physical challenge and scenic reward from the top of Madison make this a butt kicker not to miss. Portions of the route coincide with the Appalachian Trail (AT).

From the parking area, follow the Great Gulf Link Trail a flat mile to the Great Gulf Trail. Turn right and continue about three easy miles (passing the Osgood Trail junction in less than two miles); soon after a jog left in the trail, turn right (north) onto the Madison Gulf Trail. You are in the Great Gulf, the enormous glacial cirque nearly enclosed by the high peaks of the northern Presidentials, which loom around you. The Madison Gulf Trail grows increasingly steep, following the boulder-filled Parapet Brook through a dense forest for about two miles to the base of the formidable headwall. Crossing a lush, boggy area along a shelf at the headwall's base, you then attack the main headwall, a scramble over steep, exposed rock ledges that can be hazardous in wet weather.

After a strenuous mile, the trail reaches the flat saddle between Mounts Madison and Adams, where you find the AMC's Madison hut and Star Lake, a beautiful little tarn and one of the few true alpine ponds in the Whites. From the hut, turn right (east) on the Appalachian Trail/Osgood Trail leading to Madison's ridge-like summit (5,366 ft.). Continue over the summit and down the open AT/Osgood Trail for a half mile. The Daniel Webster Trail branches left (northeast) at Osgood Junction, heading diagonally down a vast talus slope to the woods, leading another 3.5 miles to the campground road in Dolly Copp. Turn right and walk 0.2 mile down the road to your car.

User Groups: Hikers and dogs. No bikes, horses, or wheelchair facilities. This trail should not be attempted in winter except by hikers experienced in mountaineering and prepared for severe winter weather.

Permits: No backcountry permit is needed, but a permit is required for day use or overnight parking at any White Mountain National Forest trailhead, as indicated by signs posted at most trailheads. Permits are available at several area stores and from the national forest at a cost of $5 for seven consecutive days or $20 per year. A $3 one-day permit can be purchased at self-service stations at national forest trailheads, but the permit is good only for the trailhead at which it's purchased.

Maps: A waterproof area trail map is available from the Appalachian Mountain Club (Presidential Range, $9.95). For a topographic area map, request Mount Washington from the USGS.

Directions: From the Pinkham Notch Visitor Center, drive north on Route 16 approximately two miles to the entrance of the Dolly Copp Campground (on your left). Drive to the end of the campground road and park in the dirt lot at the start of the Great Gulf Link Trail. About a quarter mile before the parking lot, you pass the start of the Daniel Webster (scout) Trail, which is where you will end this hike. GPS Coordinates: 44.3236 N, 71.2187 W

Contact: White Mountain National Forest Headquarters, 71 White Mountain Drive, Campton, NH 03246, 603/536-6100, TDD for hearing impaired 603/536-3665, www.fs.fed.us/r9/white. The Appalachian Mountain Club Pinkham Notch Visitor Center has up-to-date weather and trail information about the Whites; call 603/466-2725.

Mount Jefferson's summit and Castellated Ridge (visible to the right of the summit)

© PETER DAME

16 MOUNT JEFFERSON: THE CASTELLATED RIDGE

10 mi/9 hr   🏃5 ⛰10

in the White Mountain National Forest south of Bowman

BEST (

The stretch of the Castle Trail above timberline ranks among the most spectacular ridge walks in New England—but you must work hard to get there, climbing some 4,200 feet on this 10-mile round-tripper. The Castellated Ridge narrows to a rocky spine jutting above the krummholz (the dense stands of stunted and twisted conifers that grow at timberline), with long, sharp drops off either side. The ridge acquired its name from the three castles, or towers, of barren rock you scramble over and around. This can be a dangerous place in nasty weather. But on a clear day, from Jefferson's summit (5,716 ft.), you can see almost all of the Whites and all the way to

Vermont's Green Mountains, and even beyond to New York's Adirondacks. You also walk briefly on the Appalachian Trail where it coincides with the Gulfside Trail north of Jefferson's summit.

From the parking area, follow the dirt driveway to the right for about 150 yards until you reach a somewhat hidden marker on the right where the Castle Trail enters the woods. The hiking is fairly easy at first, but in the first half mile there's a bridgeless crossing of the Israel River, which can be difficult at high water. Approximately one mile beyond the stream crossing, the trail passes the junction with the Israel Ridge Path on the left, on which you will return. The trail then ascends the ridge, growing steep and passing through an interesting subalpine forest before passing a junction with the Link at 3.5 miles out.

The Castle Trail requires scrambling from this point, reaching the first castle a quarter mile past the Link junction. Continue up the ridge to the vast talus field covering the upper flanks of Mount Jefferson, watching carefully for cairns. The trail follows a direct line to the summit, where twin rock mounds are separated by a short distance; the first you encounter, farther west, is the true summit, five miles from the trailhead.

Descend to the trail junction between the two summits, walk north on the Jefferson Loop Trail toward Mount Adams for 0.4 mile, and then continue on the Gulfside Trail for another 0.2 mile into Edmands Col. Bear left onto the Randolph Path, which then leads to the right (northeast) around the Castle Ravine headwall. At 0.7 mile from Edmands Col, the trail coincides briefly with the Israel Ridge Path. Where they split, stay to the left on the Israel Ridge Path, continuing approximately 0.5 mile to a junction with the Emerald Trail. If you have time, take a left on the Emerald Trail and make the worthwhile 20-minute detour to Emerald Bluff, which offers a stunning view of Castle Ravine. The Israel Ridge Path continues down into the woods, eventually rejoining the Castle Trail 2.5 miles below the Emerald Trail. Turn right and continue to the trailhead parking area, 1.3 miles ahead.

User Groups: Hikers and dogs. No bikes, horses, or wheelchair facilities. This trail should not be attempted in winter except by hikers experienced in mountaineering and prepared for severe winter weather.

Permits: No backcountry permit is needed, but a permit is required for day use or overnight parking at any White Mountain National Forest trailhead. Permits are available at several area stores and from the national forest at a cost of $5 for seven consecutive days or $20 per year. A $3 one-day permit can be purchased at self-service stations at national forest trailheads, but the permit is good only for the trailhead at which it's purchased.

Maps: A waterproof area trail map is available from the Appalachian Mountain Club (Presidential Range, $9.95). For a topographic area map, request Mount Washington from the USGS.

Directions: From the junction of U.S. 2 and Route 115 in Randolph, follow U.S. 2 east for 4.1 miles to the parking area on the right (south) side of the road.

GPS Coordinates: 44.3564 N, 71.3468 W

Contact: White Mountain National Forest Headquarters, 71 White Mountain Drive, Campton, NH 03246, 603/536-6100, TDD for hearing impaired 603/536-3665, www.fs.fed.us/r9/white. The Appalachian Mountain Club Pinkham Notch Visitor Center has up-to-date reports on weather in the Presidential Range; call 603/466-2721.

17 MOUNT JEFFERSON: RIDGE OF THE CAPS

6.6 mi/5 hr 🏃4 ⛰10

in the White Mountain National Forest south of Jefferson

Beginning at an elevation of 3,008 feet, the highest trailhead accessed by a public road in the White Mountains, the Caps Ridge Trail provides the shortest route from a trailhead to a 5,000-foot summit in these mountains: five miles round-trip if you go up and down the Caps Ridge Trail. This hike extends the distance to 6.6 miles to make a loop and incorporate the spectacular Castellated Ridge. Despite the relatively short distance compared to other Presidential Range hikes, rugged trails and a net climb of 2,700 feet still make this alpine loop fairly strenuous.

Follow the Caps Ridge Trail, which rises steadily through conifer forest; at mile one, an open ledge offers sweeping views to the Ridge of the Caps above, the Castellated Ridge to the north, and the southern Presidentials to the south. You may also see the black smoke from the cog railway chugging up Mount Washington. Continue up the Caps Ridge Trail, immediately passing the junction with the Link trail, on which this route returns. The Caps Ridge Trail soon emerges from the woods and zigzags up the craggy ridge, with excellent views of most of the Whites. At 2.1

miles, the trail passes through a junction with the Cornice Trail. Continue on for another 0.4 mile; when the ridge becomes less distinct in a sprawling talus slope, you are near Jefferson's summit, a pile of rocks rising to 5,716 feet above sea level.

For a five-mile total hike, descend the way you came. To continue on this hike, descend the other side of Jefferson's summit cone, follow the summit loop trail northward just a few steps, and then turn left (northwest) onto the Castle Trail (marked). Follow its cairns, descending at a moderate angle over the vast boulder fields of Jefferson, to the prominent Castellated Ridge. The trail follows close to the ridge crest, passing the three distinct stone castles along it. At 1.5 miles below the summit, turn left (south) on the Link, which wends a rugged—and in spots heavily eroded—path through dense forest for 1.6 miles back to the Caps Ridge Trail. Turn right (west) and descend a mile back to the trailhead.

User Groups: Hikers and dogs. No bikes, horses, or wheelchair facilities. This trail is not accessible in winter.

Permits: No backcountry permit is needed, but a permit is required for day use or overnight parking at any White Mountain National Forest trailhead. Permits are available at several area stores and from the national forest at a cost of $5 for seven consecutive days or $20 per year. A $3 one-day permit can be purchased at self-service stations at national forest trailheads, but the permit is good only for the trailhead at which it's purchased.

Maps: A waterproof area trail map is available from the Appalachian Mountain Club (Presidential Range, $9.95). For a topographic area map, request Mount Washington from the USGS.

Directions: From the junction of U.S. 2 and route 115 in Jefferson, follow U.S. 2 east a short distance to Valley Road. Turn right and follow the road more than a mile. Then turn left onto the gravel Jefferson Notch Road and continue on it for about four miles to the trailhead. From U.S. 302 in Bretton Woods, turn onto the Base Road at a sign for the Mount Washington Cog Railway and drive 5.6 miles. Then turn left on Jefferson Notch Road and follow it to Jefferson Notch. Or from U.S. 302 in Crawford Notch, 0.2 mile north of the visitor information center, turn onto Mount Clinton Road. Follow it 3.7 miles, cross Base Road, and continue straight ahead onto Jefferson Notch Road.

GPS Coordinates: 44.2961 N, 71.3536 W

Contact: White Mountain National Forest Headquarters, 71 White Mountain Drive, Campton, NH 03246, 603/536-6100, TDD for hearing impaired 603/536-3665, www.fs.fed.us/r9/white. The Appalachian Mountain Club Pinkham Notch Visitor Center has up-to-date reports on weather in the Presidential Range; call 603/466-2721.

18 PRESIDENTIAL RANGE TRAVERSE

20 mi one-way/2.5 days 🏃5 ⛰10

in the White Mountain National Forest between Gorham and Crawford Notch

BEST (

This is the premier backpacking traverse in New England—in fact, nowhere else east of the Rockies can you hike a 15-mile ridge entirely above timberline. The route hits nine summits, seven of them higher than 5,000 feet—including New England's highest, 6,288-foot Mount Washington—and each with its own unique character. The route covers some very rugged terrain and is quite strenuous, with a cumulative vertical ascent of well over 8,000 feet. The task is complicated by the fact that the odds of having three straight days of good weather in these peaks may be only slightly better than those of winning the lottery. Finding appropriate campsites can be difficult, too, because of the White Mountain National Forest regulations that prohibit against camping above timberline. Skipping the side paths to summits and staying on the Gulfside Trail, Westside Trail, and

Crawford Path will reduce the distance slightly and the elevation gain significantly. Masochistic types have been known to attempt this traverse in a single day, a feat known in some circles as the Death March. From the junction of the Osgood and Daniel Webster Trails to the junction of the Crawford Path and the Webster Cliffs Trail, this hike coincides with the Appalachian Trail (AT).

From the parking area near the entrance to the Dolly Copp Campground, take the Daniel Webster-Scout Trail (marked), ascending moderately through the woods. Starting around the 2.0-mile mark, the trail grows rockier and increasingly steep until, at 2.9 miles, it begins a rough climb almost directly up a steep talus slope; scrambling will be necessary in parts. At 3.5 miles, the trail ascends open Osgood Ridge, with stunning views of the Great Gulf Wilderness and the peaks of the northern Presidentials. Approaching the ridge crest, the trail reaches Osgood Junction. Here, bear right on the Appalachian Trail/Osgood Trail and follow another 0.6 mile to the top of Mount Madison (a narrow ridge of boulders marks the summit). Continue over the summit on the AT/Osgood Trail a half mile down to the Madison AMC hut and turn left for the Star Lake Trail, a less-traveled footpath that passes the beautiful Star Lake tarn and winds a mile up the steep east side of 5,799-foot Mount Adams, the second-highest peak in New England. Adams has five distinct summits, several ridges and ravines, and excellent views. Descend via Lowe's Path nearly a half mile over an expansive talus field to the giant cairn at Thunderstorm Junction, where several trails meet.

From here, you can descend the Spur Trail a mile to the Randolph Mountain Club's Crag Camp cabin, or follow Lowe's Path for 1.3 miles to the Gray Knob cabin—both are good places to spend the night. To continue on, turn left (southwest) onto the Gulfside Trail. At 0.6 mile south of Thunderstorm Junction, you pass the Israel Ridge Path branching to the right toward the RMC's Perch camping

area. From Edmands Col (the saddle 1.3 miles south of Thunderstorm Junction), hike 0.2 mile southwest and bear right onto the Jefferson Loop Trail, climbing 0.4 mile to Mount Jefferson's top. Of its two summits, the westernmost (to your right from this direction) is the highest at 5,716 feet. The other summit is 11 feet lower.

Continue between the two summits on the loop trail and rejoin the Gulfside Trail. About 0.5 mile farther, after dipping down through Sphinx Col, bear left onto the Mount Clay Loop Trail. On a day when you see two dozen hikers on Jefferson, you may have Clay to yourself. This is probably because Clay is considered a shoulder of Mount Washington rather than a distinct peak. Yet, on Clay's broad 5,533-foot summit, you can observe abundant alpine wildflowers (particularly in the second half of June) and peer down the sheer headwall of the Great Gulf. The Clay Loop rejoins the Gulfside in 1.2 miles, and then it's another mile to the roof of New England, Washington's 6,288-foot summit, finishing via the Crawford Path. The summit has a visitors center with a cafeteria and bathrooms—seen by weary hikers as either a welcome respite or a blemish on this otherwise wild trek.

From the summit, turn southwest onto the Crawford Path and follow it 1.4 miles down to Lakes of the Clouds, the location of another AMC hut. Just south of the hut, bear right off the Crawford onto the Mount Monroe Loop Trail for the steep half-mile climb to its 5,372-foot summit (a great place to catch the sunset if you're staying at the Lakes hut). The Monroe Loop rejoins the Crawford Path southbound 0.3 mile past the summit. The Crawford then traverses the bump on the ridge known as Mount Franklin (5,001 ft.), also not considered a distinct summit. About two miles south of the Lakes hut, bear right for the loop over 4,760-foot Mount Eisenhower. A mile south of Eisenhower, follow the Webster Cliffs Trail 0.1 mile to the 4,312-foot summit of Mount Pierce, then double back and turn left on the Crawford Path, descending nearly three miles. Just before reaching U.S. 302 in Crawford Notch, turn right onto the Crawford Connector path leading 0.2 mile to the parking area on the Mount Clinton Road.

The Appalachian Mountain Club operates the Madison and Lakes of the Clouds huts, where a crew prepares meals and guests share bunkrooms and bathrooms. The Randolph Mountain Club operates two cabins on Mount Adams: Crag Camp (capacity 20) and the winterized Gray Knob (capacity 15), both of which cost $12 per person per night and are run on a first-come, first-served basis. The RMC also operates two open-sided shelters on Adams, the Perch (capacity 8, plus four tent platforms) and the Log Cabin (capacity 10), both of which cost $7 per night, with the fee collected by a caretaker. All shelters are open year-round.

User Groups: Hikers and dogs. No bikes, horses, or wheelchair facilities. This hike should not be attempted in winter except by hikers experienced in mountaineering and prepared for severe winter weather.

Permits: No backcountry permit is needed, but a permit is required for day use or overnight parking at any White Mountain National Forest trailhead, as indicated by signs posted at most trailheads. Permits are available at several area stores and from the national forest at a cost of $5 for seven consecutive days or $20 per year. A $3 one-day permit can be purchased at self-service stations at national forest trailheads, but the permit is good only for the trailhead at which it's purchased.

Maps: A waterproof area trail map is available from the Appalachian Mountain Club (Presidential Range, $9.95). For a topographic area map, request Mount Washington from the USGS.

Directions: From Gorham, drive 4.4 miles south on Route 16 to the U.S. Forest Service's Dolly Copp Campground (entrance on right), which is operated on a first-come, first-served basis. Drive to the end of the campground road to a dirt parking lot at the Great Gulf

Link trailhead. About a quarter mile before the parking lot is the start of the Daniel Webster-Scout Trail, which is where you begin this hike. Leave a second vehicle at the other end of this traverse, just off U.S. 302 in Crawford Notch State Park. The Crawford Path Trailhead parking area is on Mount Clinton Road, opposite the Crawford House site and just north of Saco Lake. The AMC-run hiker shuttle bus also provides service in this area to many popular trailheads and may be able to provide transportation for the return trip. GPS Coordinates: 44.3236 N, 71.2187 W

Contact: White Mountain National Forest Headquarters, 71 White Mountain Drive, Campton, NH 03246, 603/536-6100, TDD for hearing impaired 603/536-3665, www.fs.fed.us/r9/white. The Appalachian Mountain Club Pinkham Notch Visitor Center has up-to-date weather and trail information about the Whites; call 603/466-2725. For route information and to make reservations for the AMC-run hiker shuttle bus, call 603/466-2727.

🔢 THE CARTER-MORIAH RANGE

20 mi one-way/3 days   🏃5   ⛰9

in the White Mountain National Forest between Pinkham Notch and Shelburne

BEST (

This section of the Appalachian Trail (AT) just might have you cursing one moment, uttering expressions of awe the next. This is a great three-day ridge walk on the AT, with excellent views of the Presidential Range to the west and the Wild River Valley to the east. The cumulative elevation gained on this 20-mile hike is more than 6,700 feet.

From the Appalachian Mountain Club Visitor Center, follow the Lost Pond Trail to the Wildcat Ridge Trail; turn left (east), and you will soon begin the steep climb to the ridge, passing over open ledges with commanding views of Mount Washington—a good destination for a short day hike. The first of Wildcat's five summits that you'll encounter—Peak E, 4,041 feet high—is a 3.8-mile round-trip hike of about three hours. The trail traverses the roller coaster Wildcat Ridge, up and down five humped summits with few views. Just beyond the final peak is a short spur trail to a view atop cliffs overlooking Carter Notch and the Carter Range that will make you eat all your nasty comments about this trail. Descend north a steep mile—including a traverse of about 25 feet across a loose, very steep rockslide area—turning right (east) onto the Nineteen-Mile Brook Trail for the final 0.2 mile into the notch and to the larger of two ponds there. Tent sites can be found near the junction of the Wildcat Ridge and Nineteen-Mile Brook Trails, or ask a caretaker at the AMC hut in Carter Notch about nearby sites.

Leaving from the notch, head north on the steep Carter-Moriah Trail, passing one ledge with a view of the entire notch from high above it. A bit more than a mile from the notch, the trail passes over the highest point on this ridge, Carter Dome, at 4,832 feet. Unfortunately, trees block any views. The trail continues nearly a mile to the rocky summit of Mount Hight (4,675 ft.)—the nicest summit in the range, with 360-degree views of the Presidentials and far into Maine to the east. From Hight, the Carter-Moriah Trail turns sharply left (west) a short distance, drops north down a steep slope into the forest for a half mile to Zeta Pass, then continues north over the wooded summits of South Carter and Middle Carter (2.7 miles from Mount Hight). As the ridge ascends gradually again toward North Carter, you break into the alpine zone and some of the best views on this hike, particularly west to Mount Washington. From the viewless summit of North Carter, the trail drops several hundred feet over rock ledges that require scrambling, passes over the hump known as Imp Mountain, and reaches the spur trail to the Imp campsite in two miles. Check out the view at sunset from the ledge just below the shelter.

Continuing north on the Carter-Moriah Trail, you cross over some open ledges on Imp Mountain before the trail ascends steadily onto the open southern ledges of Mount Moriah two miles from the shelter. A short distance farther, the Carter-Moriah Trail peels off left toward the town of Gorham. This hike continues on the AT, which at this point coincides with the Kenduskeag Trail—but drop your pack and make the short detour on the Carter-Moriah for the rocky scramble up the spur trail to Moriah's summit. Backtrack to the Kenduskeag (an Abenaki word meaning "a pleasant walk") and follow its often wet path 1.5 miles to the Rattle River Trail, where you'll turn left (north). The trail descends steeply at first, through a dense, damp forest, then levels out before reaching the Rattle River shelter in 2.5 miles. From there, it's less than two miles to a parking lot on U.S. 2 in Shelburne, the terminus of this traverse.

Backcountry campsites along this route are scarce, and camping is prohibited along much of the high ridge; bring adequate equipment for off-trail camping, which is permitted 200 feet away from any trails or water sources. Carry cash for camping overnight at the Appalachian Mountain Club hut in Carter Notch ($25 per person per night) or the AMC's Imp campsite ($8 per person per night). **User Groups:** Hikers and dogs. No bikes, horses, or wheelchair facilities. This trail should not be attempted in winter except by hikers experienced in mountaineering and prepared for severe winter weather, and is not suitable for skis.

Permits: No backcountry permit is needed, but a permit is required for day use or overnight parking at any White Mountain National Forest trailhead. Permits are available at several area stores and from the national forest at a cost of $5 for seven consecutive days or $20 per year. A $3 one-day permit can be purchased at self-service stations at national forest trailheads, but the permit is good only for the trailhead at which it's purchased.

Maps: A waterproof area trail map is available

from the Appalachian Mountain Club (Carter Range–Evans Notch/North Country–Mahoosuc, $9.95). For a topographic area map, request Carter Dome from the USGS.

Directions: To shuttle two vehicles for this traverse, leave one at the hike's terminus, a parking area where the Appalachian Trail crosses U.S. 2, 3.6 miles east of the southern junction of U.S. 2 and Route 16 in Shelburne. The hike begins at the Appalachian Mountain Club Visitor Center on Route 16 in Pinkham Notch at the base of Mount Washington, 12 miles south of the junction with U.S. 2 in Gorham and about 8 miles north of Jackson. An AMC-run hiker shuttle bus also provides service in this area to select trailheads.

GPS Coordinates: 44.2564 N, 71.2525 W

Contact: White Mountain National Forest Headquarters, 71 White Mountain Drive, Campton, NH 03246, 603/536-6100, TDD for hearing impaired 603/536-3665, www.fs.fed.us/r9/white. The Appalachian Mountain Club Pinkham Notch Visitor Center has up-to-date weather and trail information about the Whites; call 603/466-2725. For information and reservations for the AMC-run hiker shuttle bus, call 603/466-2727.

⓴ MOUNT WASHINGTON: HUNTINGTON RAVINE AND THE ALPINE GARDEN

8 mi/8 hr   🏃5 ⛰10

In the White Mountain National Forest in Pinkham Notch

Discard all your preconceived notions of difficult trails. Huntington Ravine has earned a reputation as the most difficult regular hiking trail in the White Mountains—and for good reason. The trail ascends the ravine headwall, involving very exposed scrambling up steep slabs of rock with significant fall potential. Inexperienced scramblers should shy away from this route and persons carrying a heavy pack may want to consider another way up

the mountain. The ravine is strictly a summer and early fall hike, and even in those seasons snow can fall, treacherous ice can form, or the steep rock slabs may be slick with water. The headwall, the Alpine Garden, and the top of the Lion Head all lie above the tree line and are exposed to the weather. This eight-mile loop, with a net elevation gain of 3,400 feet, will lead you through mountain terrain found on few other peaks east of the Rockies.

From the Appalachian Mountain Club Visitor Center, follow the wide Tuckerman Ravine Trail. Less than 1.5 miles up, the Huntington Ravine Trail diverges right (north); watch closely for it, because the sign may be partly hidden by trees, and the path is narrow and easily overlooked. This trail climbs steeply in spots and you get fleeting glimpses of the ravine headwall above. Within 1.5 miles from the Tuckerman Ravine Trail, you reach a flat, open area on the Huntington Ravine floor—and your first sweeping view of the massive headwall, riven by several ominous gullies separating tall cliffs. Novice hikers can reach this point without any trouble and the view of the ravine is worth it. Nearby is a first-aid cache bearing a plaque memorializing Albert Dow, a climber and mountain rescue volunteer killed by an avalanche in Huntington Ravine during a 1982 search for a pair of missing ice climbers.

The trail leads through a maze of giant boulders to the headwall base and then heads diagonally up the talus. On the headwall proper, the well-blazed trail ascends rock slabs, which may be wet, and sections of blocky boulders. Two miles from the Tuckerman Ravine Trail, you reach the top of the ravine and the broad tableland known as the Alpine Garden, where colorful wildflowers bloom mid-June–August.

By following the Huntington Ravine Trail a quarter mile farther, you can pick up the Nelson Crag Trail for the final mile to Washington's summit and then descend the Tuckerman Ravine and Lion Head Trails to rejoin this loop at the other side of the Alpine Garden—adding two miles and about 800 feet of ascent to this hike. But this hike takes a finer route—free from the tourists who flock to the summit via the auto road or cog railway—crossing the Alpine Garden to the Lion Head. Turn left (south) onto the Alpine Garden Trail, which traverses the mile-wide, tundra-like plain. In a short distance, you see to your left the top of a prominent cliff known as the Pinnacle, which is part of the Huntington Ravine headwall. The view from atop the Pinnacle merits the short detour, but take care to walk on rocks and not the fragile alpine vegetation—some plants found here are the only known of their kind. The sprawling boulder pile of the mountain's upper cone rises up on your right.

Once you're across the Alpine Garden, turn left (east) onto the Lion Head Trail. The flat trail follows the crest of a prominent buttress, above the cliffs that form the northern or right-hand wall of Tuckerman Ravine. There are numerous good views down into the ravine before the trail drops back into the woods again, descending steeply and eventually rejoining the Tuckerman Ravine Trail about two miles from the AMC Visitor Center. Turn left (east) and head down.

User Groups: Hikers only. No bikes, horses, or wheelchair facilities. This hike should not be attempted in winter except by hikers experienced in mountaineering and prepared for severe winter weather.

Permits: No backcountry permit is needed, but a permit is required for day use or overnight parking at any White Mountain National Forest trailhead. Permits are available at several area stores and from the national forest at a cost of $5 for seven consecutive days or $20 per year. A $3 one-day permit can be purchased at self-service stations at national forest trailheads, but the permit is good only for the trailhead at which it's purchased.

Maps: A waterproof area trail map is available from the Appalachian Mountain Club (Presidential Range, $9.95). For a topographic area map, request Mount Washington from the USGS.

Directions: The hike begins from the Appalachian Mountain Club Visitor Center on Route 16 in Pinkham Notch at the base of Mount Washington, 12 miles south of the junction of Route 16 and U.S. 2 in Gorham and about 8 miles north of Jackson. The trailhead is behind the visitors center.

GPS Coordinates: 44.2575 N, 71.2533 W

Contact: White Mountain National Forest Headquarters, 71 White Mountain Drive, Campton, NH 03246, 603/536-6100, TDD for hearing impaired 603/536-3665, www.fs.fed.us/r9/white. The Appalachian Mountain Club Pinkham Notch Visitor Center has up-to-date reports on weather in the Presidential Range; call 603/466-2721.

21 MOUNT WASHINGTON: THE LION HEAD
8.6 mi/7 hr   🏃5 ⛰10

in the White Mountain National Forest in Pinkham Notch

The Lion Head Trail, a less-traveled route up New England's highest peak than the Tuckerman Ravine Trail in summer, is the standard route for a challenging winter ascent. The actual winter Lion Head Trail follows a different route than the summer trail to avoid avalanche hazard. Trail signs are posted in the appropriate places when each trail is opened or closed for the season. To check on the status of the changeover, call the AMC's Pinkham Notch Visitor Center.

From Pinkham Notch, pick up the wide Tuckerman Ravine Trail, follow it for 2.3 miles, and then turn right onto the Lion Head Trail. It soon begins steep switchbacks up the face of the Lion Head ridge, breaking out of the forest within a half mile of the Tuckerman Ravine Trail junction for excellent views of Pinkham Notch and the Carter Range across the notch. Shortly after leaving the forest, the trail crests the Lion Head for much flatter walking across the Alpine Garden, a tundra-like

looking up at Tuckerman Ravine, Mount Washington

plateau that's one of the best places in these mountains to view alpine wildflowers from late spring well into summer, depending on how long the snow lingers. To your left, the ridge drops away abruptly into Tuckerman Ravine; straight ahead lies Washington's summit, still more than 1,200 feet higher.

At 1.1 miles from the Tuckerman Ravine Trail, the Lion Head Trail crosses the Alpine Garden Trail and soon afterward begins climbing Mount Washington's summit cone. A half mile farther, turn right onto the Tuckerman Ravine Trail and follow it another 0.4 mile to Washington's summit. Descend the way you came.

User Groups: Hikers only. Trail is not suitable for bikes, dogs, or horses; no wheelchair facilities. This hike should not be attempted in winter except by hikers experienced in mountaineering and prepared for severe winter weather.

Permits: No backcountry permit is needed, but a permit is required for day use or overnight parking at any White Mountain National Forest trailhead. Permits are available at several area stores and from the national forest at a cost of $5 for seven consecutive days or $20 per year. A $3 one-day permit can be purchased at self-service stations at national forest trailheads, but the permit is good only for the trailhead at which it's purchased.

Maps: A waterproof area trail map is available from the Appalachian Mountain Club (Presidential Range, $9.95). For a topographic area map, request Mount Washington from the USGS.

Directions: The hike begins from the Appalachian Mountain Club Visitor Center on Route 16 in Pinkham Notch at the base of Mount Washington, 12 miles south of the junction of Route 16 and U.S. 2 in Gorham and about 8 miles north of Jackson. The trailhead is behind the visitors center.

GPS Coordinates: 44.2575 N, 71.2533 W

Contact: White Mountain National Forest Headquarters, 71 White Mountain Drive, Campton, NH 03246, 603/536-6100, TDD for hearing impaired 603/536-3665, www.fs.fed.us/r9/white. The AMC's Pinkham Notch Visitor Center has up-to-date reports on weather in the Presidential Range; call 603/466-2721.

22 MOUNT WASHINGTON: TUCKERMAN RAVINE

8.4 mi/7 hr   🥾5 ⛰️10

in the White Mountain National Forest in Pinkham Notch

BEST (

This trail is the standard route and most direct way up the 6,288-foot Mount Washington, the Northeast's highest peak, so it typically sees hundreds of hikers on nice weekends in summer and early autumn. It's also a busy place in spring, when skiers make the hike up into Tuckerman Ravine to ski its formidable headwall. Although the crowds can diminish the mountain experience, the ravine is stunningly scenic, an ascent of the headwall is a serious challenge, and reaching Washington's summit is an accomplishment sought by many. This is the common route for first-time hikers of Washington. The trail on the ravine headwall is sometimes closed due to ice; check on weather and conditions at the visitors center. While hiking the headwall, watch out for rocks kicked loose by hikers above you and be careful not to dislodge any rocks yourself. When you pass over the Mount Washington summit, you'll be walking on the Appalachian Trail. The elevation gained on this hike to the rooftop of New England is about 4,300 feet.

From behind the visitors center, the wide Tuckerman Ravine Trail ascends at a moderate grade, passing the short side path to Crystal Cascade within a half mile. As you continue up the Tuckerman Ravine Trail, you'll pass intersections with several trails. At 2.5 miles the trail reaches the floor of the ravine, a worthwhile destination in itself; to the right is the Lion Head and to the left the cliffs of Boott Spur. (From the Hermit Lake shelter, which is along the Tuckerman Ravine Trail, walk to the right less than a quarter mile for a striking reflection of Boott Spur in Hermit Lake.) The trail then climbs the headwall, reaching its lip a mile from Hermit Lake, and follows rock cairns nearly another mile to the summit. Although many hikers descend Tuckerman's headwall, an easier way down is via the Lion Head Trail, which diverges left from the Tuckerman Ravine Trail just below the summit and then rejoins it 0.1 mile below Hermit Lake.

User Groups: Hikers only. Trail is not suitable for bikes, dogs, or horses; no wheelchair facilities. This hike should not be attempted in winter except by hikers experienced in mountaineering and prepared for severe winter weather.

Permits: No backcountry permit is needed, but a permit is required for day use or overnight parking at any White Mountain National Forest trailhead. Permits are available at several area stores and from the national forest at a cost of $5 for seven consecutive days or $20 per year. A $3 one-day permit can be purchased at self-service stations at national forest trailheads, but the permit is good only for the trailhead at which it's purchased.

Maps: A waterproof area trail map is available from the Appalachian Mountain Club (Presidential Range, $9.95). For a topographic area map, request Mount Washington from the USGS.

Directions: The hike begins from the Appalachian Mountain Club Visitor Center on Route 16 in Pinkham Notch, at the base of Mount Washington, 12 miles south of the junction of Route 16 and U.S. 2 in Gorham and about 8 miles north of Jackson. The trailhead is behind the visitors center.

GPS Coordinates: 44.2575 N, 71.2533 W

Contact: White Mountain National Forest Headquarters, 71 White Mountain Drive, Campton, NH 03246, 603/536-6100, TDD for hearing impaired 603/536-3665, www.fs.fed.us/r9/white. The Appalachian Mountain Club Pinkham Notch Visitor Center has up-to-date reports on weather in the Presidential Range; call 603/466-2721.

23 MOUNT WASHINGTON: AMMONOOSUC RAVINE/ JEWELL TRAIL

9.8 mi/7.5 hr 🏃5 ⛰10

in the White Mountain National Forest north of Crawford Notch

Like every other route to the 6,288-foot summit of Mount Washington, this loop hike offers great views, rough terrain, and the chance to run into some really nasty weather. A northeasterly approach to the mountain that uses the Appalachian Trail (AT) for part of its ascent, this climb traverses exposed ground from just below the Lakes of the Clouds hut until descending more than a half mile down the Jewell Trail; always bring warm, weatherproof clothes along for what can be very rapidly shifting conditions. And even on the sunniest of days, hikers should also watch out for tricky—and often wet—stretches on the Ammonoosuc Ravine's steep upper headwall as well as several brook crossings, some of which are impossible to ford in times of high water. This hike climbs about 3,800 feet in elevation.

From the parking lot, follow the moderately ascending Ammonoosuc Ravine Trail, passing picturesque Gem Pool about two miles out. For the next half mile, the trail makes a steep ascent of the headwall, passing several cascades and pools and good views back into Ammonoosuc Ravine. At three miles, you leave the last scrub vegetation behind and enter the alpine zone; take care to walk on rocks and not the fragile plant life. From the Lakes of the Clouds AMC hut (reached at 3.1 miles), the detour south to the 5,372-foot summit of Monroe adds a relatively easy one-mile round-trip and 360 feet of climbing to this hike.

To continue the hike, turn left (north) from the Lakes of the Clouds hut onto the Appalachian Trail/Crawford Path, which passes by the two tiny tarns that give the hut its name. It's 1.4 more miles and more than 1,000 vertical feet to the top of Washington, where there is a visitors center and amazing views. Descend the AT/Crawford Path from the summit for 0.2 mile and bear right with the AT, now coinciding with the Gulfside Trail heading north. Follow it 1.4 miles, walking the crest of the exposed ridge, passing the loop trail up Mount Clay, and finally reaching a junction with the Jewell Trail. Turn left and descend the Jewell for 3.7 miles, descending steep ground through several switchbacks at first, and then proceeding at a more moderate grade back to the parking area.

The Appalachian Mountain Club operates the Lakes of the Clouds hut, where a crew prepares meals and guests share bunkrooms and bathrooms.

User Groups: Hikers and dogs. No bikes, horses, or wheelchair facilities. This trail should not be attempted in winter except by hikers experienced in mountaineering and prepared for severe winter weather.

Permits: No backcountry permit is needed,

but a permit is required for day use or overnight parking at any White Mountain National Forest trailhead. Permits are available at several area stores and from the national forest at a cost of $5 for seven consecutive days or $20 per year. A $3 one-day permit can be purchased at self-service stations at national forest trailheads, but the pass is good only for the trailhead at which it's purchased.

Maps: A waterproof area trail map is available from the Appalachian Mountain Club (Presidential Range, $9.95). For a topographic area map, request Mount Washington from the USGS.

Directions: From the junction of U.S. 302 and U.S. 3 in Twin Mountain, drive east on U.S. 302 for 4.6 miles and turn left at signs for the Mount Washington Cog Railway. Continue 6.7 miles to a large parking lot on the right. Or from U.S. 302 in Crawford Notch, 0.2 mile north of the visitor information center, turn onto Mount Clinton Road (not maintained in winter). Follow it 3.7 miles and turn right. Continue 1.1 miles and turn right into the parking lot.

GPS Coordinates: 44.2699 N, 71.3498 W

Contact: White Mountain National Forest Headquarters, 71 White Mountain Drive, Campton, NH 03246, 603/536-6100, TDD for hearing impaired 603/536-3665, www.fs.fed.us/r9/white. The Appalachian Mountain Club Pinkham Notch Visitor Center has up-to-date reports on weather in the Presidential Range; call 603/466-2721. The Appalachian Mountain Club, 603/466-2727 for reservation and rate information.

24 MOUNTS WASHINGTON AND MONROE: CRAWFORD PATH

16.4 mi/11 hr   👤4 ⛰10

in the White Mountain National Forest and Crawford Notch State Park

This is a hike typically covered in two days, with a stay at the AMC's Lakes of the Clouds

© VINCENT VANNICOLA

the AMC's Lakes of the Clouds hut in the saddle between Mounts Washington and Monroe

hut, but the gentle nature of the Crawford Path allows very fit hikers to do this in a day. The southern ridge of the Presidentials is far less rugged than the northern ridge, yet the views surpass those of most hikes in New England. Another draw: the Lakes of the Clouds, among the few true alpine tarns in the White Mountains. The 5,372-foot Mount Monroe rolls like a wave south from the 6,288-foot Mount Washington. If you do spend a night at the hut, make the short walk up onto Monroe to watch the sunset. Remember that weather changes quickly on these peaks and may even be radically different atop Washington than on the other summits. Even on a sunny September day in the valley, it's not unusual to encounter a snowstorm atop Washington.

From the parking area, follow the Crawford Connector 0.2 mile to the Crawford Path, considered the oldest continuously maintained footpath in the country. (Nearby, a side path leads left for 0.4 mile over rough ground to Crawford Cliff, with a good view of Crawford Notch.) From the connector trail junction, the Crawford Path ascends steadily, passing a short side path in 0.4 mile that leads to Gibbs Falls. Less than three miles from U.S. 302, the trail emerges from the forest and meets the Appalachian Trail/Webster Cliff Trail (turning right and walking about 150 yards south on that trail brings you to the 4,312-foot summit of Mount Pierce). From this point to Washington's summit, the Appalachian Trail and Crawford Path coincide; turn left on the now white-blazed trail or enjoy more level ground with views in all directions. A bit more than a mile from the Webster Cliffs Trail junction, the Mount Eisenhower loop trail diverges for the 0.4-mile climb to Eisenhower's 4,760-foot summit, then descends, steeply in spots, another 0.4 mile to rejoin the Crawford Path. Although bagging Eisenhower entails 300 feet of climbing and 0.2 mile more hiking than taking the Crawford Path around the summit, the view from its summit is worth the small effort. The AT/Crawford Path continues to ascend at a very gentle grade until, six miles from U.S. 302, the Mount Monroe Loop branches left for its two summits (from this direction, the second, or northernmost, summit is the highest).

It's the same distance, 0.7 mile, via either the Crawford Path or the Monroe Loop to where the two trails meet again north of Monroe, but the Monroe Loop involves another 350 feet of elevation gain and is much more exposed. From the northern junction of the trails, the Crawford Path leads a flat 0.1 mile to the Lakes of the Clouds hut. From there, it's a steady climb for 1.4 miles over very rocky terrain up the barren summit cone of Washington to the roof of New England. Return via the same route.

The Appalachian Mountain Club operates the Lakes of the Clouds hut in the saddle between the summits of Washington and Monroe, where a crew prepares meals and guests share bunkrooms and bathrooms.

User Groups: Hikers and dogs. No bikes, horses, or wheelchair facilities. This trail should not be attempted in winter except by hikers experienced in mountaineering and prepared for severe winter weather, and is not suitable for skis.

Permits: No backcountry permit is needed, but a permit is required for day use or overnight parking at any White Mountain National Forest trailhead. Permits are available at several area stores and from the national forest at a cost of $5 for seven consecutive days or $20 per year. A $3 one-day permit can be purchased at self-service stations at national forest trailheads, but the pass is good only for the trailhead at which it's purchased.

Maps: A waterproof area trail map is available from the Appalachian Mountain Club (Presidential Range, $9.95). For a topographic area map, request Mount Washington from the USGS.

Directions: From the Appalachian Mountain Club Highland Center on U.S. 302 in Crawford Notch, turn left onto U.S. 302 and drive north for less than 0.1 mile to a right turn for Mount Clinton Road. Follow the road only a short distance to the trailhead parking area. GPS Coordinates: 44.2200 N, 71.4100 W

Contact: White Mountain National Forest Headquarters, 71 White Mountain Drive, Campton, NH 03246, 603/536-6100, TDD for hearing impaired 603/536-3665, www.fs.fed.us/r9/white. The Appalachian Mountain Club Pinkham Notch Visitor Center has up-to-date reports on weather in the Presidential Range; call 603/466-2721. The Appalachian Mountain Club, 603/466-2727 for reservation and rate information, www.outdoors.org

25 MOUNT WASHINGTON: BOOTT SPUR/GULF OF SLIDES

6.9 mi/5 hr

in the White Mountain National Forest in Pinkham Notch

The summit of 6,288-foot Mount Washington, with its commercial development

and access by road and cog railway, may be a turn-off for some alpine purists. This climb—onto a high shoulder of Washington with views down into two of its ravines—skips the summit, but doesn't skimp on breathtaking scenery or natural beauty. The ascent to the high point named Boott Spur (5,500 ft.) is about 3,500 feet.

From the Appalachian Mountain Club Visitor Center, follow the Tuckerman Ravine Trail for nearly a half mile. Shortly after passing the side path to Crystal Cascade, turn left at a junction with the Boott Spur Trail. In another 1.7 miles, a side path leads a short distance right to Ravine Outlook, a worthy detour that takes you high above Tuckerman Ravine (but adds no appreciable mileage). Return to the Boott Spur Trail, which emerges from the woods nearly two miles from where it left the Tuckerman Ravine Trail. In another 0.2 mile, the trail passes between the halves of Split Rock and begins the 0.7-mile push to the open ridge known as Boott Spur, with excellent views down into Tuckerman Ravine. Although the grade is moderate, a few false summits along the step-like ridge deceive many hikers. Once atop the shoulder, approximately three miles from the Boott Spur Trailhead, turn left (south) onto the Davis Path and follow it for a half mile. Then turn left again (southeast) onto the Glen Boulder Trail, which circles around the rim of the Gulf of Slides, another of Washington's scenic ravines. Much of the Glen Boulder Trail is above the tree line, with long views to the south and good views east toward Wildcat Mountain and the Carter Range. At 1.5 miles from the Davis Path, you'll pass the Glen Boulder, an enormous glacial erratic set precariously on the mountainside. A bit more than a mile past the boulder, back down in the woods, turn left onto the Direttissima, the trail heading the last mile back to the visitors center parking lot.

User Groups: Hikers only. No bikes, dogs, horses, or wheelchair facilities. This trail should not be attempted in winter except by hikers experienced in mountaineering and prepared for severe winter weather.

Permits: No backcountry permit is needed, but a permit is required for day use or overnight parking at any White Mountain National Forest trailhead. Permits are available at several area stores and from the national forest at a cost of $5 for seven consecutive days or $20 per year. A $3 one-day permit can be purchased at self-service stations at national forest trailheads, but the pass is good only for the trailhead at which it's purchased.

Maps: A waterproof area trail map is available from the Appalachian Mountain Club (Presidential Range, $9.95). For a topographic area map, request Mount Washington from the USGS.

Directions: The hike begins from the Appalachian Mountain Club Visitor Center on Route 16 in Pinkham Notch, at the base of Mount Washington, 12 miles south of the junction of Route 16 and U.S. 2 in Gorham and about 8 miles north of Jackson. The trailhead is behind the visitors center. GPS Coordinates: 44.2575 N, 71.2533 W

Contact: White Mountain National Forest Headquarters, 71 White Mountain Drive, Campton, NH 03246, 603/536-6100, TDD for hearing impaired 603/536-3665, www.fs.fed.us/r9/white. The Appalachian Mountain Club Pinkham Notch Visitor Center has up-to-date reports on weather in the Presidential Range; call 603/466-2721.

26 SQUARE LEDGE

1.2 mi/0.75 hr

in the White Mountain National Forest in Pinkham Notch

Square Ledge is the aptly named cliff that's obvious when you're standing in the parking lot at the Appalachian Mountain Club Visitor Center on Route 16 and looking due east across the road. The view from atop this cliff is one of the best you can get of Pinkham Notch and the deep ravines on the east side of New England's highest peak, 6,288-foot Mount Washington. A good taste of White Mountains adventure for first time hikers, this route offers a bit of easy scrambling up the last six or eight feet of rock to get onto Square Ledge, with a total net climb of 400 feet.

From the Appalachian Mountain Club Visitor Center, cross Route 16 and walk south about 100 feet to where the Lost Pond Trail, a part of the white-blazed Appalachian Trail, crosses a bog on a boardwalk and enters the woods. About 50 feet into the woods, turn left on the blue-blazed Square Ledge Trail. The trail almost immediately crosses a ski trail and then ascends gradually through a mixed forest with lots of white birch trees. Watch for the sporadic blazes marking the trail, especially in winter, when the pathway may be less obvious. At 0.1 mile from the road, turn left and follow a side path 100 feet to Ladies Lookout, where you'll get a decent view toward Washington. Back on the Square Ledge Trail, continue through the woods, skirting around Hangover Rock—easy to recognize—then turn right and climb more steeply uphill. At 0.6 mile, scramble up the gully to the right of the cliffs and at the top of the gully, scramble up the rocks to the top of the ledge with excellent views towards Washington and Pinkham Notch. Return the way you came.

User Groups: Hikers and dogs. Dogs must be under control at all times. Trail is not suitable for bikes, horses, or wheelchairs.

Permits: No backcountry permit is needed, but a permit is required for day use or overnight parking at any White Mountain National Forest trailhead. Permits are available at several area stores and from the national forest at a cost of $5 for seven consecutive days or $20 per year. A $3 one-day permit can be purchased at self-service stations at national forest trailheads, but the permit is good only for the trailhead at which it's purchased.

Maps: A waterproof area trail map is available from the Appalachian Mountain Club (Presidential Range, $9.95). For a topographic area map, request Mount Washington from the USGS.

Directions: The hike begins from the Appalachian Mountain Club Visitor Center on Route 16 in Pinkham Notch, at the base of Mount Washington, 12 miles south of the junction of Route 16 and U.S. 2 in Gorham and about 8 miles north of Jackson. The trailhead is across the highway from the visitors center.

GPS Coordinates: 44.2565 N, 71.2523 W

Contact: White Mountain National Forest Headquarters, 71 White Mountain Drive, Campton, NH 03246, 603/536-6100, TDD for hearing impaired 603/536-3665, www.fs.fed.us/r9/white. The Appalachian Mountain Club Pinkham Notch Visitor Center has up-to-date reports on weather in the Presidential Range; call 603/466-2721.

27 MOUNT HIGHT/CARTER DOME/CARTER NOTCH

10 mi/7.5 hr   🏃5 ⛰10

in the White Mountain National Forest north of Pinkham Notch

This scenic 10-mile loop through the Carter Range, a series of rugged hills extending south of Gorham on the eastern side of Route 16, takes you over the summit of craggy Mount Hight (4,675 ft.); onto the ninth-highest peak in the Granite State, the 4,832-foot Carter Dome; and into a boulder-strewn mountain notch where towering cliffs flank a pair of tiny ponds. The hike climbs approximately 3,500 feet and coincides in portions with the Appalachian Trail.

From the parking turnout on the east side of Route 16, pick up the Nineteen-Mile Brook Trail at the trail marker and follow it southeast for an easy stretch. Just before two miles out, the trail reaches a junction. Turn left (east) onto the Carter Dome Trail. In about two miles, at Zeta Pass, head south (right), picking up the Carter-Moriah Trail, which coincides with the white-blazed Appalachian Trail (AT).

The trail climbs steeply, requiring some scrambling over rocks, to the bare summit of Mount Hight. There you have a 360-degree panorama of the Presidential Range dominating the skyline to the west, the Carters running north, and the lower hills of eastern New Hampshire and western Maine to the south and east. Continue south on the AT/Carter-Moriah Trail, over the viewless summit of Carter Dome, and descend into Carter Notch. There's a great view of the notch from open ledges before you start the knee-pounding drop. At the larger of the two Carter Lakes in the notch, two miles past Mount Hight, leave the AT and turn right (northwest) onto the Nineteen-Mile Brook Trail for the nearly four-mile walk back to the parking area.

User Groups: Hikers and dogs. Dogs must be under control. No bikes, horses, or wheelchair facilities.

Permits: No backcountry permit is needed, but a permit is required for day use or overnight parking at any White Mountain National Forest trailhead. Permits are available at several area stores and from the national forest at a cost of $5 for seven consecutive days or $20 per year. A $3 one-day permit can be purchased at self-service stations at national forest trailheads, but the pass is good only for the trailhead at which it's purchased.

Maps: A waterproof area trail map is available from the Appalachian Mountain Club (Carter Range–Evans Notch/North Country–Mahoosuc, $9.95). For a topographic area map, request Carter Dome from the USGS.

Directions: From the Appalachian Mountain Club Pinkham Notch Visitor Center, drive north on Route 16 approximately four miles to the parking turnout for the Nineteen-Mile Brook Trail on the right (a mile north of the Mount Washington Auto Road).

GPS Coordinates: 44.3021 N, 71.2208 W

Contact: White Mountain National Forest Headquarters, 71 White Mountain Drive, Campton, NH 03246, 603/536-6100, TDD for hearing impaired 603/536-3665, www.fs.fed.us/r9/white.

28 WILDCAT MOUNTAIN
8.5 mi/5.5 hr

in Pinkham Notch in the White Mountain National Forest

The summit of this 4,000-foot peak is wooded and uninteresting, but the walk along Nineteen-Mile Brook and the view from the top of the cliffs overlooking Carter Notch and the Carter Range—reached via a short spur trail just below Wildcat Mountain's 4,422-foot summit—make this hike very worthwhile. Because this end of Wildcat Mountain does not tend to lure many hikers, you might have that viewpoint to yourself. This hike climbs nearly 3,000 feet and coincides in portions with the Appalachian Trail.

From Route 16, the Nineteen-Mile Brook Trail ascends very gently toward Carter Notch, paralleling the wide, rock-strewn streambed and crossing two tributaries. Just 0.2 mile before the trail drops down into the notch—and 3.5 miles from Route 16—turn right onto the Wildcat Ridge Trail, also the white-blazed Appalachian Trail. The next 0.7 mile is a relentless climb up the steep, rocky east face of Wildcat Mountain; footing here is loose even in summer and often dangerously icy in winter. Upon reaching more level ground, shortly before topping the mountain's long summit ridge, watch for the spur trail branching left that leads about 30 feet to the top of the cliffs overlooking Carter Notch. Return to the parking area the way you came—and on the descent, if you still have energy to burn, the half-mile detour from the Nineteen-Mile Brook Trail junction down into Carter Notch is well worth the effort.

User Groups: Hikers and dogs. No bikes, horses, or wheelchair facilities.

Permits: No backcountry permit is needed, but a permit is required for day use or overnight parking at any White Mountain National Forest trailhead. Permits are available at several area stores and from the national forest at a cost of $5 for seven consecutive days

or $20 per year. A $3 one-day permit can be purchased at self-service stations at national forest trailheads, but the pass is good only for the trailhead at which it's purchased.

Maps: A waterproof trail map is available from the Appalachian Mountain Club (Presidential Range map or the Carter Range–Evans Notch/North Country–Mahoosuc map, $9.95 each). For a topographic area map, request Carter Dome from the USGS.

Directions: From the Appalachian Mountain Club Pinkham Notch Visitor Center, drive north on Route 16 approximately four miles to the parking turnout for the Nineteen-Mile Brook Trail on the right (a mile north of the Mount Washington Auto Road).
GPS Coordinates: 44.3021 N, 71.2208 W

Contact: White Mountain National Forest Headquarters, 71 White Mountain Drive, Campton, NH 03246, 603/536-6100, TDD for hearing impaired 603/536-3665, www.fs.fed.us/r9/white.

29 CARTER NOTCH: WILDCAT RIVER TRAIL
8.6 mi/5 hr

in the White Mountain National Forest north of Jackson

This relatively easy hike accesses spectacular Carter Notch via a trail less traveled than the popular Nineteen-Mile Brook Trail (see the *Mount Hight/Carter Dome/Carter Notch* listing in this chapter) and takes you to the Carter Notch Appalachian Mountain Club hut. The trail nets an elevation gain of about 1,500 feet.

From the parking area, follow the Bog Brook Trail for 0.7 mile. Just after crossing the Wildcat River, which can be difficult at times of high water, the Bog Brook Trail bears right, but you will continue straight ahead onto the Wildcat River Trail. Follow it along the gorgeous river, then away from the river into the woods. It ascends steadily but gently, except for brief, steep pitches, for 3.6 miles from the Bog Brook Trail junction to the Appalachian Mountain Club hut in Carter Notch. After exploring the notch a bit, return the way you came.

User Groups: Hikers and dogs. No bikes, horses, or wheelchair facilities.

Permits: No backcountry permit is needed, but a permit is required for day use or overnight parking at any White Mountain National Forest trailhead. Permits are available at several area stores and from the national forest at a cost of $5 for seven consecutive days or $20 per year. A $3 one-day permit can be purchased at self-service stations at national forest trailheads, but the pass is good only for the trailhead at which it's purchased. Carry cash for camping overnight at the Appalachian Mountain Club hut in Carter Notch.

Maps: A waterproof area trail map is available from the Appalachian Mountain Club (Carter Range–Evans Notch/North Country–Mahoosuc, $9.95). For topographic area maps, request Jackson and Carter Dome from the USGS.

Directions: From Route 16A in Jackson, Route 16B loops through the north end of town, its two endpoints leaving Route 16A very near each other; take the left, or westernmost, endpoint of Route 16B and follow it uphill. Where Route 16B turns sharply right, continue straight ahead onto Carter Notch Road. Three miles after leaving Route 16B, just after a sharp left turn in the road, park at a turnout for the Bog Brook Trail.

GPS Coordinates: 44.2168 N, 71.1968 W

Contact: White Mountain National Forest Headquarters, 71 White Mountain Drive, Campton, NH 03246, 603/536-6100, TDD for hearing impaired 603/536-3665, www.fs.fed.us/r9/white.

30 LOST POND

2 mi/1 hr

in the White Mountain National Forest in Pinkham Notch

While this pond is no more lost than the popular Lonesome Lake on the other side of the Whites is lonesome, this is a nice short hike that's flat and offers opportunities for wildlife-viewing and a unique view of Mount Washington. The out-and-back route follows the Appalachian Trail (AT).

From the Appalachian Mountain Club Visitor Center, cross Route 16 and follow the white-blazed Appalachian Trail/Lost Pond Trail, less than 0.8 mile before reaching the pond. Immediately you will see signs of beaver activity—probably dams and a lodge—and, if you're lucky, a moose will be grazing in the swampy area to the left. About halfway around the pond, look across to a fine view of Washington above the still water. Return the way you came. Or for a little extra adventure, keep following the AT until it comes to a junction and turns to follow Wildcat Ridge Trail. You are now just minutes from the 70-foot tall Glen Ellis Falls, which can be reached by turning right (west) and crossing the Ellis River on the way toward Route 16; in spring and early summer, crossing the Ellis River between this trail junction and Route 16 can be difficult and dangerous. You can also reach some nice views of this valley and Mount Washington by turning left at this junction and climbing less than a mile up the Wildcat Ridge Trail. This hike returns the way you came.

User Groups: Hikers and dogs. No bikes, horses, or wheelchair facilities.

Permits: No backcountry permit is needed, but a permit is required for day use or overnight parking at any White Mountain National Forest trailhead. Permits are available at several area stores and from the national forest at a cost of $5 for seven consecutive days or $20 per year. A $3 one-day permit can be

purchased at self-service stations at national forest trailheads, but the pass is good only for the trailhead at which it's purchased.

Maps: Two waterproof area trail maps available from the Appalachian Mountain Club show this hike (Presidential Range map and Carter Range–Evans Notch/North Country–Mahoosuc map, $9.95 each). For topographic area maps, request Mount Washington, Carter Dome, Jackson, and Stairs Mountain from the USGS.

Directions: The hike begins from the Appalachian Mountain Club Visitor Center on Route 16 in Pinkham Notch, at the base of Mount Washington, 12 miles south of the junction of Route 16 and U.S. 2 in Gorham and about 8 miles north of Jackson. The trailhead is across the highway from the visitors center. GPS Coordinates: 44.2565 N, 71.2523 W

Contact: White Mountain National Forest Headquarters, 71 White Mountain Drive, Campton, NH 03246, 603/536-6100, TDD for hearing impaired 603/536-3665, www. fs.fed.us/r9/white. Appalachian Mountain Club Pinkham Notch Visitor Center, P.O. Box 298, Gorham, NH 03581, 603/466-2721, www.outdoors.org.

31 GLEN ELLIS FALLS
0.6 mi/0.75 hr 🏃2 ⛰8

in the White Mountain National Forest south of Pinkham Notch

BEST (

Here's a scenic, short walk that's ideal for young children and enjoyable for adults. The trail descends steeply at times, but there are rock steps and a handrail. (Children will definitely need a steady hand of an adult to hold onto on the way down.) From the parking area, follow the wide gravel trail through a tunnel under Route 16. The trail descends steeply at times, but there are rock steps and a handrail. Continue along a well-worn path to the waterfall, a 70-foot tall wall of water that makes a single, sheer drop

before continuing on along the Glen Ellis River. Return the way you came. This is a popular walk with tourists and it's especially spectacular in late spring, when water flow is heaviest.

Special note: If you're coming from Lost Pond or Wildcat Mountain to see the falls (see the *Lost Pond* and *Carter Notch: Wildcat River Trail* listings in this chapter), be aware that the Wildcat River Trail makes a crossing of the Ellis River near Route 16 that can be treacherous in times of high water and unsafe for young children.

User Groups: Hikers and dogs. Not suitable for bikes, horses, or skis. No wheelchair facilities.

Permits: No backcountry permit is needed, but a permit is required for day use or overnight parking at any White Mountain National Forest trailhead. Permits are available at several area stores and from the national forest at a cost of $5 for seven consecutive days or $20 per year. A $3 one-day permit can be purchased at self-service stations at national forest trailheads, but the pass is good only for the trailhead at which it's purchased.

Maps: Two waterproof area trail maps available from the Appalachian Mountain Club show this hike (Presidential Range map and Carter Range–Evans Notch/North Country–Mahoosuc map, $9.95 each). For topographic area maps, request Mount Washington, Carter Dome, Jackson, and Stairs Mountain from the USGS.

Directions: The trail begins at a parking lot for Glen Ellis Falls off Route 16, less than a mile south of the Appalachian Mountain Club Visitor Center in Pinkham Notch. GPS Coordinates: 44.2456 N, 71.2533 W

Contact: White Mountain National Forest Headquarters, 71 White Mountain Drive, Campton, NH 03246, 603/536-6100, TDD for hearing impaired 603/536-3665, www. fs.fed.us/r9/white. Appalachian Mountain Club Pinkham Notch Visitor Center, P.O. Box 298, Gorham, NH 03581, 603/466-2721, www.outdoors.org.

32 ZEALAND NOTCH/ WILLEY RANGE

17 mi/2–3 days

In the White Mountain National Forest southeast of Twin Mountain

Along the northeastern edge of the Pemigewasset Wilderness, this 17-mile loop passes through spectacular Zealand Notch and traverses the Willey Range, with a pair of 4,000-footers, lots of rugged terrain, and limited views marking this lesser known corner of the Whites. Best spread out over 2–3 days, the cumulative elevation gained is less than 3,000 feet.

From the Zealand Road parking lot, follow the Zealand Trail south, paralleling the Zealand River. At 2.3 miles, the A-Z Trail enters from the left; you will return on that trail. The Zealand Trail reaches a junction with the Twinway and the Ethan Pond Trail at 2.5 miles (the Appalachian Mountain Club's Zealand Falls hut lies 0.2 mile uphill on the Twinway). This hike bears left onto the Ethan Pond Trail, which runs for two miles to the opposite end of the notch, passing numerous overlooks through the trees. Reaching the Thoreau Falls Trail at 4.6 miles, bear right and follow it for 0.1 mile to Thoreau Falls, which tumbles more than 100 feet down through several steps. Backtrack and turn right (east) on the Ethan Pond Trail, which follows level ground for 2.5 miles to the side path leading left less than 0.1 mile to Ethan Pond and the shelter just above the pond.

A mile beyond the junction, turn left (north) onto the Willey Range Trail, which soon begins a steep and sustained climb of 1.1 miles up 4,285-foot Mount Willey, where there are some views from just below the summit. The trail continues north, dropping into a saddle, then ascending to the 4,340-foot summit of Mount Field—named for Darby Field, the first known person to climb Mount Washington—1.4 miles from Willey's summit. Field is wooded with no views. Just beyond the summit, the Avalon Trail branches right, but stay left with the Willey Range Trail, descending steadily to the A-Z Trail, 0.9 mile from the summit of Field. Turn left (west), descending easily for 2.7 miles to the Zealand Trail. Turn right (north) and walk 2.5 miles back to the Zealand Road parking lot.

The Appalachian Mountain Club (AMC) operates the Zealand Falls hut year-round. The Zealand Falls hut is on the Twinway, 0.2 mile from the junction of the Zealand, Twinway, and Ethan Pond Trails and 2.7 miles from the end of Zealand Road. Contact the AMC for information on cost and reservations.

The AMC also operates the first-come, first-served Ethan Pond shelter. A caretaker collects the $8 per person nightly fee late spring–fall. The Ethan Pond shelter is located just off the Ethan Pond Trail, 7.3 miles from the Zealand Road parking lot along this hike's route.

User Groups: Hikers and dogs. No bikes, horses, or wheelchair facilities.

Permits: No backcountry permit is needed, but a permit is required for day use or overnight parking at any White Mountain National Forest trailhead. Permits are available at several area stores and from the national forest at a cost of $5 for seven consecutive days or $20 per year. A $3 one-day permit can be purchased at self-service stations at national forest trailheads, but the pass is good only for the trailhead at which it's purchased.

Maps: Two waterproof area trail maps are available from the Appalachian Mountain Club (Franconia–Pemigewasset Range map and Crawford Notch–Sandwich Range/ Moosilauke–Kinsman map, $9.95 each). For a topographic area map, request Crawford Notch from the USGS.

Directions: From the junction of U.S. 3 and U.S. 302 in Twin Mountain, drive east on U.S. 302 for 2.3 miles and turn right onto Zealand Road. Continue 3.5 miles to a parking lot at the end of the road. Zealand Road is not maintained in winter; the winter parking lot is on U.S. 302, immediately east of Zealand Road.

GPS Coordinates: 44.2221 N, 71.4780 W
Contact: White Mountain National Forest Headquarters, 71 White Mountain Drive, Campton, NH 03246, 603/536-6100, TDD for hearing impaired 603/536-3665, www.fs.fed.us/r9/white. Appalachian Mountain Club Pinkham Notch Visitor Center, P.O. Box 298, Gorham, NH 03581, 603/466-2721, www.outdoors.org.

33 MOUNT HALE
4.6 mi/2.5 hr

in the White Mountain National Forest southeast of Twin Mountain

This climb to the top of Mount Hale (4,054 ft.) offers a net elevation gain of approximately 2,300 feet. Compared to some of New Hampshire's other 4,000-footers, this might seem gentle, but don't assume this hike is a walk in the park: The Hale Brook Trail is a rugged, relentlessly steep 2.3 miles to the summit, passing cascades along the brook, including rocky sections that grow slick in the wet season. At the rapidly disappearing clearing atop Hale (the former site of a firetower is quickly being reclaimed by forest), you do get some views of the Sugarloafs to the north, the Presidential Range to the northeast, Zealand Notch to the southeast, and North and South Twin to the southwest. One curiosity about Hale is that rocks near its summit are magnetized and will interfere with a magnetic compass.

From the parking lot on Zealand Road, pick up the Hale Brook Trail (marked) heading southwest. Within the first half mile, the trail crosses over a cross-country ski trail and then rises at a steady pace until a crossing with Hale Brook at 0.8 mile. The trail continues to ascend, heading up the steep slope and re-crossing Hale Brook at 1.3 miles. Switchbacks in the trail help to reduce the grade somewhat and at 1.7 miles, another small brook is crossed. The trail heads almost due south before swinging to the right to ascend the wooded summit from

the east. This hike returns by descending the same trail, but another option is to create a loop of eight or nine miles—depending on whether you shuttle two vehicles—by descending on the Lend-a-Hand Trail from Hale's summit for 2.7 miles to the Twinway. Turn left on the Twinway, passing the Appalachian Mountain Club's Zealand Falls hut in 0.1 mile and reaching the Zealand Trail 0.3 mile farther. Turn left (north) on the Zealand Trail and follow its fairly flat course 2.5 miles back to Zealand Road. Unless you've shuttled a second vehicle to the Zealand Trail parking area, walk just over a mile down the road back to the parking area for the Hale Brook Trail.

You can make an enjoyable two-day outing of this loop—a great one for families—with a stay in the Zealand Falls hut. The Appalachian Mountain Club operates the Zealand Falls hut year-round. The Zealand Falls hut is on the Twinway, 0.2 mile from the junction of the Zealand, Twinway, and Ethan Pond Trails and 2.7 miles from the end of Zealand Road.

User Groups: Hikers and dogs. No bikes, horses, or wheelchair facilities.

Permits: No backcountry permit is needed, but a permit is required for day use or overnight parking at any White Mountain National Forest trailhead. Permits are available at several area stores and from the national forest at a cost of $5 for seven consecutive days or $20 per year. A $3 one-day permit can be purchased at self-service stations at national forest trailheads, but the pass is good only for the trailhead at which it's purchased.

Maps: A waterproof area trail map is available from the Appalachian Mountain Club (Franconia–Pemigewasset Range, $9.95). For a topographic area map, request Crawford Notch from the USGS.

Directions: From the junction of U.S. 3 and U.S. 302 in Twin Mountain, drive east on U.S. 302 for 2.3 miles and turn right onto Zealand Road. Continue 2.4 miles to a parking lot on the right. The winter parking lot is on U.S. 302, 0.1 mile east of Zealand Road. Zealand Road is not maintained in winter.

GPS Coordinates: 44.2367 N, 71.4867 W

Contact: White Mountain National Forest Headquarters, 71 White Mountain Drive, Campton, NH 03246, 603/536-6100, TDD for hearing impaired 603/536-3665, www.fs.fed.us/r9/white. Appalachian Mountain Club Pinkham Notch Visitor Center, P.O. Box 298, Gorham, NH 03581, 603/466-2721, www.outdoors.org.

34 ZEALAND NOTCH

7.6 mi/5 hr   🏃2 ⛰9

In the White Mountain National Forest southeast of Twin Mountain

Partly due to the convenience provided by the Appalachian Mountain Club's Zealand Falls hut, but also simply because of its splendor, Zealand Notch ranks as one of the most-visited spots in the White Mountains year-round. Although the trail tends to be muddy and has a lot of slippery, exposed roots, this is a nice hike in summer and fall—and fairly easy, gaining only about 500 feet in elevation.

From the end of Zealand Road, follow the Zealand Trail south, paralleling the Zealand River. At 2.3 miles, the A-Z Trail diverges left. Continuing on the Zealand Trail, you reach the junction with the Twinway and the Ethan Pond Trail at 2.5 miles. The AMC's Zealand Falls hut lies 0.2 mile to the right on the Twinway (adding 0.4 mile to this hike's distance). This hike continues straight ahead on the Ethan Pond Trail and soon enters the narrow passageway of Zealand Notch. After about a mile, the trail breaks out of the woods and traverses a shelf across the boulder field left behind by an old rockslide; from this perch, the views of Zealand Notch are spectacular. Cross this open area to where the Ethan Pond Trail reenters the woods near the junction with the Zeacliff Trail, 1.3 miles from the Twinway/Zealand Trail junction. Return the way you came.

Special note: For the ambitious or those with more time because they are spending a night at the Zealand Falls hut, hiking all the way to Thoreau Falls would add 1.6 miles round-trip to this hike. Continue on the Ethan Pond Trail beyond the Zeacliff Trail junction for 0.7 mile, then bear right onto the Thoreau Falls Trail. In another 0.1 mile, the trail reaches the top of the falls, which drops more than 100 feet through several steps and creates a very impressive cascade of ice in winter.

The Appalachian Mountain Club operates the Zealand Falls hut year-round. The Zealand Falls hut is on the Twinway, 0.2 mile from the junction of the Zealand, Twinway, and Ethan Pond Trails and 2.7 miles from the end of Zealand Road.

User Groups: Hikers and dogs. No bikes, horses, or wheelchair facilities.

Permits: No backcountry permit is needed, but a permit is required for day use or overnight parking at any White Mountain National Forest trailhead. Permits are available at several area stores and from the national forest at a cost of $5 for seven consecutive days or $20 per year. A $3 one-day permit can be purchased at self-service stations at national forest trailheads, but the pass is good only for the trailhead at which it's purchased.

Maps: A waterproof area trail map is available from the Appalachian Mountain Club (Franconia–Pemigewasset Range, $9.95). For a topographic area map, request Crawford Notch from the USGS.

Directions: From the junction of U.S. 3 and U.S. 302 in Twin Mountain, drive east on U.S. 302 for 2.3 miles and turn right onto Zealand Road. Continue 3.5 miles to a parking lot at the end of the road. The winter parking lot is on U.S. 302, 0.1 mile east of Zealand Road. Zealand Road is not maintained in winter. GPS Coordinates: 44.2221 N, 71.4780 W

Contact: White Mountain National Forest Headquarters, 71 White Mountain Drive, Campton, NH 03246, 603/536-6100, TDD for hearing impaired 603/536-3665, www.fs.fed.us/r9/white. Appalachian Mountain Club Pinkham Notch Visitor Center, P.O.

Box 298, Gorham, NH 03581, 603/466-2721, www.outdoors.org.

35 ZEALAND NOTCH/ TWINS LOOP

16.1 mi one-way/2 days 4 9

in the White Mountain National Forest south of Twin Mountain

It does require shuttling cars between trail-heads, but with superb views, lots of relatively easy terrain, and a reasonable distance to cover in two days, this moderately difficult 16-mile trek is a fairly popular weekend loop for backpackers. Taking you high above Zealand Notch to the summits of Zealand Mountain (4,260 ft.), Mount Guyot (4,580 ft.), South Twin Mountain (4,902 ft.), and North Twin Mountain (4,761 ft.), this hike nets an elevation gain of approximately 3,500 feet; portions of the route coincide with the Appalachian Trail.

From the Zealand Road parking lot, follow the relatively easy Zealand Trail south for 2.5 miles to its junction with the Ethan Pond Trail and the Twinway. Turn right onto the Twin-way, which coincides with the white-blazed Appalachian Trail (AT), climbing 0.2 mile to the Appalachian Mountain Club's Zealand Falls hut. Beyond the hut, the AT/Twinway passes nice cascades and the Lend-a-Hand Trail junction and cliimbs high above Zealand Notch. Where the trail takes a right turn at 3.9 miles into this trip, a short side path loops out to the Zeacliff overlook, with a spectacular view of Zealand Notch and mountains—from Carrigain to the south to Mount Washington and the Presidential Range to the northeast.

Just 0.1 mile farther up the AT/Twinway, the Zeacliff Trail departs to the left, descending steeply into the notch. This hike continues along the AT/Twinway, which traverses more level terrain on Zealand Mountain, passing a spur trail to Zeacliff Pond at 4.4 miles. After a short climb above the pond, the trail passes

a side path at 5.6 miles that leads right on a flat 0.1-mile spur to the summit of 4,260-foot Zealand Mountain. The AT/Twinway then dips and climbs again to the flat, open summit of Mount Guyot, with views in every direction. Passing over the summit, the AT/Twinway reaches another junction at 8.1 miles. The AT/Twinway bears right and the Bondcliff Trail diverges left (south); the Guyot campsite, a logical stop for the night, is 0.8 mile away along the Bondcliff Trail. (The 1.6 miles round-trip to the campsite is figured into this hike's total distance.)

Back on the AT/Twinway heading northwest, the trail traverses easy terrain, then climbs more steeply on the final short stretch up South Twin Mountain, 8.9 miles into this trek and, at 4,902 feet, the highest point on this trip and the eighth-highest mountain in New Hampshire. The views span much of the Pemigewasset Wilderness and stretch to the Presidential Range. Turn north off the AT/Twinway onto the North Twin Spur, descending into a saddle, then climbing to the wooded and viewless summit of North Twin Mountain (4,761 ft.), 1.3 miles from South Twin's summit and 10.2 miles into this trek. Turn right onto the North Twin Trail, soon emerging from the trees onto open ledges with one of the best views of the White Mountains on this trip. The trail descends, quite steeply for long stretches, for two miles to the Little River; it then swings left and follows an old railroad bed along the river for more than two miles to the parking area where your second vehicle awaits.

The Appalachian Mountain Club (AMC) operates the Zealand Falls hut year-round; it is on the Twinway, 0.2 mile from the junction of the Zealand, Twinway, and Ethan Pond Trails and 2.7 miles from the end of Zealand Road.

The AMC also operates the first-come, first-served Guyot campsite, with a shelter and several tent platforms, located just off the Bondcliff Trail 0.8 mile from the Twinway on Mount Guyot. A caretaker collects the $8 per person nightly fee late spring–fall.

User Groups: Hikers and dogs. No bikes, horses, or wheelchair facilities.

Permits: No backcountry permit is needed, but a permit is required for day use or overnight parking at any White Mountain National Forest trailhead. Permits are available at several area stores and from the national forest at a cost of $5 for seven consecutive days or $20 per year. A $3 one-day permit can be purchased at self-service stations at national forest trailheads, but the pass is good only for the trailhead at which it's purchased.

Maps: A waterproof area trail map is available from the Appalachian Mountain Club (Franconia–Pemigewasset Range, $9.95). For topographic area maps, request Mount Washington, Bethlehem, South Twin Mountain, and Crawford Notch from the USGS.

Directions: You will need to shuttle two vehicles for this trip. To reach this hike's endpoint from the junction of U.S. 302 and U.S. 3 in Twin Mountain, drive south on U.S. 3 for 2.5 miles and turn left onto Haystack Road (Fire Road 304). Or from I-93 north of Franconia Notch State Park, take Exit 35 for U.S. 3 north and continue about 7.5 miles, then turn right onto Fire Road 304. Follow Fire Road 304 to its end and a parking area at the trailhead. Leave one vehicle there. To reach the start of this hike from the junction of U.S. 3 and U.S. 302 in Twin Mountain, drive east on U.S. 302 for 2.3 miles and turn right onto Zealand Road. Continue 3.5 miles to a parking lot at the end of the road. The AMC-run hiker shuttle bus also provides service in this area and may be able to provide transportation for the return trip.

Zealand Road is not maintained in winter; the winter parking lot is on U.S. 302 immediately east of Zealand Road.

GPS Coordinates: 44.2221 N, 71.4780 W

Contact: White Mountain National Forest Headquarters, 71 White Mountain Drive, Campton, NH 03246, 603/536-6100, TDD for hearing impaired 603/536-3665, www.fs.fed.us/r9/white. Appalachian Mountain Club Pinkham Notch Visitor Center, P.O. Box 298, Gorham, NH 03581, 603/466-2721, www.outdoors.org. For route information and to make reservations for the AMC-run hiker shuttle bus, call 603/466-2727.

36 NORTH TWIN MOUNTAIN
8.6 mi/6 hr   👥4 ▲9

in the White Mountain National Forest south of Twin Mountain

Although it is the 12th-highest mountain in New Hampshire at 4,761 feet, North Twin lies sufficiently out of the way and attracts far fewer hikers than nearby Franconia Ridge and Zealand Notch. But the climb is worth it for both the solitude and the scenery. From open ledges just below the summit, nice views are had south to the Pemigewasset Wilderness, east toward the Presidential Range, and west to Franconia. The vertical ascent is about 2,800 feet.

Leaving from the parking area at the end of Fire Road 304, the North Twin Trail heads southeast on an old railroad bed for its first two miles. The trail then turns sharply west (right), crosses the Little River—a daunting ford when the water is high—and makes a steep and sustained ascent of the mountain's east side. A little more than four miles from the trailhead, the trail abruptly breaks from the scrub forest to finally reach the summit ledges. Just a few hundred feet farther lies the true summit, which is wooded. Hike back the same way. For a scenic ridge walk to a summit with somewhat better views, from the top of North Twin, follow the North Twin Spur Trail to the 4,902-foot summit of South Twin Mountain, adding 2.6 miles round-trip to this hike's distance.

User Groups: Hikers and dogs. No bikes, horses, or wheelchair facilities.

Permits: No backcountry permit is needed, but a permit is required for day use or overnight parking at any White Mountain National Forest trailhead. Permits are available

at several area stores and from the national forest at a cost of $5 for seven consecutive days or $20 per year. A $3 one-day permit can be purchased at self-service stations at national forest trailheads, but the pass is good only for the trailhead at which it's purchased.

Maps: A waterproof trail map is available from the Appalachian Mountain Club (Franconia–Pemigewasset Range, $9.95). For topographic area maps, request Bethlehem and South Twin Mountain from the USGS.

Directions: From the junction of U.S. 302 and U.S. 3 in Twin Mountain, drive south on U.S. 3 for 2.5 miles and turn left onto Haystack Road/Fire Road 304, which may be marked only by a faded post reading "USFS 304." Or from I-93 north of Franconia Notch State Park, take Exit 35 for U.S. 3 north and continue about 7.5 miles; then turn right onto Fire Road 304. Follow Fire Road 304 to its end and a parking area at the trailhead for the North Twin Trail.

GPS Coordinates: 44.2394 N, 71.5493 W

Contact: White Mountain National Forest Headquarters, 71 White Mountain Drive, Campton, NH 03246, 603/536-6100, TDD for hearing impaired 603/536-3665, www.fs.fed.us/r9/white.

37 GALEHEAD MOUNTAIN
10.2 mi/5 hr

in the White Mountain National Forest south of Twin Mountain

Galehead Mountain, despite being an official 4,000-footer, attracts few hikers because trees cover its 4,024-foot summit, blocking any views. There is a good view of the tight valley of Twin Brook and a ridge of South Twin Mountain, however, from an overlook on the Frost Trail halfway between the Galehead hut and the summit. For visitors to the Galehead hut, the summit demands no more than a fairly easy one-mile hike—one that promises an opportunity for some quiet. This hike's elevation gain is about 2,400 feet; portions of the route coincide with the Appalachian Trail.

From the parking area, follow the Gale River Trail, a wide and relatively flat path, until right before it crosses the north branch of the Gale River—over a wooden footbridge—at about 1.5 miles. For more than a mile beyond that bridge, the trail parallels the river, one of this 10-mile hike's most appealing stretches. It then makes a second river crossing on rocks, which could be difficult in high water. Four miles from the trailhead, the Gale River Trail ends at a junction with the Garfield Ridge Trail, which coincides with the Appalachian Trail (AT). Bear left on the white-blazed AT/Garfield Ridge Trail and follow it another 0.6 mile to its junction with the Twinway. Turn right onto the Twinway for the Galehead hut (the Appalachian Trail also turns to coincide with the Twinway). Behind the hut, pick up the Frost Trail, which leads 0.5 mile to the Galehead's wooded summit; stop about halfway up and take the short side path to the scenic overlook. Descend the same way you came. For a longer hike combining Galehead and Mount Garfield, see the *Mount Garfield* listing in this chapter.

The Appalachian Mountain Club operates the Galehead hut, where a crew prepares meals and guests share bunkrooms and bathrooms. The hut lies at the western end of the trail called the Twinway, about 100 feet from the junction of the Twinway and the Garfield Ridge Trail.

User Groups: Hikers and dogs. No bikes, horses, or wheelchair facilities.

Permits: No backcountry permit is needed, but a permit is required for day use or overnight parking at any White Mountain National Forest trailhead. Permits are available at several area stores and from the national forest at a cost of $5 for seven consecutive days or $20 per year. A $3 one-day permit can be purchased at self-service stations at national forest trailheads, but the pass is good only for the trailhead at which it's purchased.

Maps: A waterproof area trail map is available from the Appalachian Mountain Club (Franconia–Pemigewasset Range, $9.95). For topographic area maps, request South Twin Mountain and Bethlehem from the USGS.
Directions: From I-93 north of Franconia Notch State Park, take Exit 35 for U.S. 3 north. Drive about 4.8 miles and then turn right onto the dirt Fire Road 25 at a sign for the Gale River Trail. Or from the junction of U.S. 3 and U.S. 302 in Twin Mountain, drive south on U.S. 3 for 5.3 miles and turn left on Fire Road 25. Follow Fire Road 25 for 1.3 miles and turn right onto Fire Road 92. Continue 0.3 mile to a parking area on the left for the Gale River Trail.
GPS Coordinates: 44.2347 N, 71.6085 W
Contact: White Mountain National Forest Headquarters, 71 White Mountain Drive, Campton, NH 03246, 603/536-6100, TDD for hearing impaired 603/536-3665, www.fs.fed.us/r9/white. Appalachian Mountain Club Pinkham Notch Visitor Center, P.O. Box 298, Gorham, NH 03581, 603/466-2721, www.outdoors.org.

38 MOUNT GARFIELD
10 mi/5 hr   🏃3 ⛰9

in the White Mountain National Forest south of Twin Mountain

Holding down the northwest corner of the Pemigewasset Wilderness in the White Mountains, the craggy, 4,500-foot summit of Garfield offers views in all directions, taking in Franconia Ridge to the southwest, the wooded mound of Owl's Head directly south, the Bonds and Mount Carrigain to the southeast, the valley of the Ammonoosuc River to the north, and Galehead Mountain, as well as the long ridge comprising North and South Twin Mountains, due east. When weather permits, you will see the peaks of the Presidential Range poking above the Twins. The hike up the Garfield Trail, while fairly

long and gaining nearly 3,000 feet in elevation, never gets very steep or exposed, portions of the route coincide with the Appalachian Trail.

From the parking area, follow the Garfield Trail, which for a short time parallels Spruce Brook on its steady ascent through the woods. The path is wide and obvious. At 4.8 miles, the trail terminates at a junction with the Garfield Ridge Trail, which is part of the white-blazed Appalachian Trail (AT). To the left (east) on the AT/Garfield Ridge Trail, it's 0.2 mile to the spur trail to the Garfield Ridge campsite. The summit lies 0.2 mile to the right (west), where you'll find the foundation of an old fire tower. Descend the same way you came.

Special note: Mount Garfield and Galehead Mountain (see the *Galehead Mountain* listing in this chapter) can be combined on a loop of 13.5 miles, in which they are linked by hiking 2.7 miles along the Garfield Ridge Trail between the Garfield Trail and the Gale River Trail. The best way to do the loop is to begin on the Gale River Trail and descend the Garfield Trail; that way you will ascend, rather than descend, the often slick, steep, and rocky stretch of the Garfield Ridge Trail east of Mount Garfield. The Gale River Trail and Garfield Trail both begin on Fire Road 92, 1.6 miles apart (a distance not figured into the 13.5-mile loop).

The Appalachian Mountain Club operates the Garfield Ridge campsite (a shelter and seven tent platforms), reached via a 200-yard spur trail off the Garfield Ridge Trail, 0.2 mile east of its junction with the Garfield Trail. A caretaker collects the $8 per person nightly fee late spring–fall.
User Groups: Hikers and dogs. No bikes, horses, or wheelchair facilities.
Permits: No backcountry permit is needed, but a permit is required for day use or overnight parking at any White Mountain National Forest trailhead. Permits are available at several area stores and from the national forest at a cost of $5 for seven consecutive days or $20 per year. A $3 one-day permit can be

purchased at self-service stations at national forest trailheads, but the pass is good only for the trailhead at which it's purchased.

Maps: A waterproof area trail map is available from the Appalachian Mountain Club (Franconia–Pemigewasset Range, $9.95). For topographic area maps, request South Twin Mountain and Bethlehem from the USGS.

Directions: From I-93 north of Franconia Notch State Park, take Exit 35 for U.S. 3 north, continue about 4.5 miles, and then turn right on the dirt Fire Road 92. Or from the junction of U.S. 3 and U.S. 302 in Twin Mountain, drive south on U.S. 3 for 5.6 miles and turn left on Fire Road 92. Follow Fire Road 92 for 1.3 miles to a parking area on the right for the Garfield Trail.

GPS Coordinates: 44.2283 N, 71.6342 W

Contact: White Mountain National Forest Headquarters, 71 White Mountain Drive, Campton, NH 03246, 603/536-6100, TDD for hearing impaired 603/536-3665, www. fs.fed.us/r9/white. Appalachian Mountain Club Pinkham Notch Visitor Center, P.O. Box 298, Gorham, NH 03581, 603/466-2721, www.outdoors.org.

39 ETHAN POND/ THOREAU FALLS

10.4 mi/5.5 hr   🏃3 ⛰9

in the White Mountain National Forest between Zealand Notch and Crawford Notch

BEST (

This moderate day hike—much of it following a flat section of the Appalachian Trail—begins at one of New Hampshire's most spectacular notches and takes in a popular backcountry pond and towering waterfall. With a short, easy detour off this route, you can also take in a second notch. The total elevation gained on this hike is about 1,200 feet.

From the parking area in Crawford Notch State Park, follow the white blazes of the Appalachian Trail, which coincides here with the Ethan Pond Trail. After crossing railroad tracks, the trail begins a steady climb. At 0.2 mile, in a stand of tall birch trees, the trail passes a junction with the Ripley Falls Trail on the left (a worthwhile side trip of 0.2 mile; see the *Ripley Falls* listing in this chapter). At 1.6 miles, a junction is reached with the Willey Range Trail; turn left (west) with the white blazes to stay on the AT/Ethan Pond Trail, which soon flattens out. A mile farther, turn right onto the side path leading about 0.1 mile to scenic Ethan Pond and the Appalachian Mountain Club's Ethan Pond shelter. Back on the AT/Ethan Pond Trail, continue west on flat ground for another 2.5 miles, then turn left onto the Thoreau Falls Trail for the 0.1-mile walk to the waterfall. Hike back along the same route.

The Appalachian Mountain Club operates the Ethan Pond shelter, located just off the Ethan Pond Trail, 2.6 miles from U.S. 302 in Crawford Notch. A caretaker collects the $6 per person nightly fee late spring–fall.

User Groups: Hikers and dogs. No bikes, horses, or wheelchair facilities.

Permits: No backcountry permit is needed, but a permit is required for day use or overnight parking at any White Mountain National Forest trailhead. Permits are available at several area stores and from the national forest at a cost of $5 for seven consecutive days or $20 per year. A $3 one-day permit can be purchased at self-service stations at national forest trailheads, but the pass is good only for the trailhead at which it's purchased.

Maps: Two waterproof area trail maps available from the Appalachian Mountain Club cover this hike (Franconia–Pemigewasset Range map and Crawford Notch–Sandwich Range/Moosilauke–Kinsman map, $9.95 each). For a topographic area map, request Crawford Notch from the USGS.

Directions: From the Crawford Notch Appalachian Mountain Club Highland Center, continue south on U.S. 302 for approximately 3.9 miles. At a sign for Ripley Falls, turn right onto a paved road. Drive 0.3 mile and park at the end of the road.

GPS Coordinates: 44.1670 N, 71.3860 W
Contact: White Mountain National Forest Headquarters, 71 White Mountain Drive, Campton, NH 03246, 603/536-6100, TDD for hearing impaired 603/536-3665, www.fs.fed.us/r9/white. Appalachian Mountain Club Pinkham Notch Visitor Center, P.O. Box 298, Gorham, NH 03581, 603/466-2721, www.outdoors.org.

⁴⁰ MOUNT AVALON
3.6 mi/1.5 hr 🏃‍♂️2 ⛰9

in the White Mountain National Forest and Crawford Notch State Park north of Bartlett and south of Twin Mountain

Named for a rugged hill it was thought to resemble in the Avalon region of Newfoundland, Canada, from various spots on Mount Avalon's 3,442-foot-high summit, you'll get views of the Whites in virtually every direction. A good summit climb for beginners and families, this hike has a moderate 1,400 feet net elevation gain.

From the parking area, cross the railroad tracks behind the visitors center and pick up the Avalon Trail heading southwest. At about 0.2 mile, turn left onto the Cascade Loop Trail, which passes scenic Beecher and Pearl cascades and rejoins the Avalon Trail about a half mile from the parking lot. (The cascades are a worthy destination for an easy hike of a mile; Beecher, an impressive flumelike cascade above a gorge, lies just 0.3 mile from the trailhead and Pearl is a short distance farther.) Turning left to rejoin the Avalon Trail, follow it another 0.8 mile to a junction with the A-Z Trail; bear left, staying on the Avalon, which grows very steep and rocky for the next half mile. Then turn left onto a spur trail that climbs 100 yards to Avalon's craggy summit. Follow the same route back.
User Groups: Hikers and leashed dogs. No bikes, horses, or wheelchair facilities.
Permits: Parking and access are free.

Maps: Two waterproof area trail maps are available from the Appalachian Mountain Club (Franconia–Pemigewasset Range map and the Crawford Notch–Sandwich Range/Moosilauke–Kinsman map, $9.95 each). For a topographic area map, request Crawford Notch from the USGS.
Directions: To reach the Appalachian Mountain Club Highland Center at Crawford Notch, from Twin Mountain, follow U.S. 302 for approximately 10 miles to the Highland Center, located on the right. Ample parking is available.
GPS Coordinates: 44.2178 N, 71.4110 W
Contact: White Mountain National Forest Headquarters, 71 White Mountain Drive, Campton, NH 03246, 603/536-6100, TDD for hearing impaired 603/536-3665, www.fs.fed.us/r9/white.

⁴¹ MOUNT WILLARD
2.8 mi/2 hr 🏃‍♂️1 ⛰9

in Crawford Notch State Park north of Bartlett and south of Twin Mountain

BEST (

The view from the cliffs of Mount Willard (2,865 ft.) is widely considered one of the best in the White Mountains for the relatively minor effort—a gradual ascent of less than 900 feet—required to reach it. Nestled at the top of Crawford Notch and not far from the bustling Appalachian Mountain Club Highland Center, scenic Mount Willard is one of the most popular hikes in the region. Come in late September for a bit more solitude and the chance to have a front row seat for a vivid show of fall color. Crawford Notch may be off-the-beaten path for most leaf peepers, but heavy deciduous forest cover along the lower elevations here yields gorgeous autumn foliage.

From the parking area, cross the railroad tracks behind the visitors center and pick up the Avalon Trail. Within 100 yards, turn left onto the Mount Willard Trail, which ascends at a moderate grade. At 1.2 miles, a side path on the left leads 0.2 mile downhill to the Hitchcock Flume, a dramatic gorge worn into the mountainside by erosion. From that trail junction, it's just another 0.2 mile of flat walking on the Mount Willard Trail to Willard's wide summit. Open ledges afford excellent views from high above the notch, with the Webster Cliffs to the east (left) and the Willey Slide directly south (straight ahead). As you take time to explore, look closely at the ground for the unmistakable prints of the snowshoe hare. Like people, these animals flock to Mount Willard's summit. Hike back the same way.

User Groups: Hikers and leashed dogs. No bikes, horses, or wheelchair facilities.

Permits: Parking and access are free.

Maps: Three waterproof area trail maps available from the Appalachian Mountain Club show this hike (Franconia–Pemigewasset Range map, Presidential Range map, and Crawford Notch–Sandwich Range/Moosilauke–Kinsman map, $9.95 each). For a topographic area map, request Crawford Notch from the USGS.

Directions: To reach the Appalachian Mountain Club Highland Center at Crawford Notch, from Twin Mountain, follow U.S. 302 for approximately 10 miles to the Highland Center, located on the right. Ample parking is available.

GPS Coordinates: 44.2178 N, 71.4110 W

Contact: White Mountain National Forest Headquarters, 71 White Mountain Drive, Campton, NH 03246, 603/536-6100, TDD for hearing impaired 603/536-3665, www.fs.fed.us/r9/white.

42 MOUNTS PIERCE AND EISENHOWER

10.8 mi/6 hr   🏃4 ⛰10

In the White Mountain National Forest and Crawford Notch State Park

The Crawford Path is reputedly the oldest continuously maintained footpath in the country, dating back to 1819, when Abel Crawford and his son Ethan Allen Crawford cut the first section. It's also the easiest route onto the high ridge of the Presidential Range—the road sits at 2,000 feet, and the trail breaks out above the trees in less than three miles. Once on the ridge, you'll have sweeping views of the Whites; the 4,760-foot Mount Eisenhower itself is one of the more distinctive summits in the southern Presidentials. This can, however, be a difficult trail to follow down in foul weather, particularly when it comes to finding your way back into the woods on Mount Pierce. The vertical ascent is more than 2,700 feet.

From the parking lot, the Crawford Connector spur leads 0.2 mile to the Crawford Path. Less than a half mile up the Crawford Path, watch for a short side trail to Gibbs Falls, a pleasant detour if you have the time. After emerging from the woods nearly three miles from the trailhead, the Crawford Path joins the Webster Cliffs Trail and together the trails head south 0.1 mile to the summit of 4,312-foot Mount Pierce. Turning back down the Crawford Path from Pierce makes a six-mile round-trip. This hike follows the Crawford Path—which from here coincides with the Appalachian Trail—north another two miles to the Eisenhower Loop Trail, then 0.4 mile up the loop trail to the Eisenhower summit, which has excellent views in every direction. To the north rises the Northeast's tallest peak, 6,288-foot Mount Washington. Stretching northwest from Washington are the northern Presidentials. The distinct hump in the ridge between Eisenhower and Washington is Mount Monroe. To the east you can see the Montalban Ridge running south from Washington—which includes Mount Isolation, a rocky high point about midway along the ridge—and beyond the ridge into western Maine. To the southwest are the peaks and valleys of the Pemigewasset Wilderness, with Mount Carrigain the tallest among them. And in the distance, more west than south, rises Franconia Ridge, including Mounts Lincoln and Lafayette, as well as Flume and Liberty. Hike back along the same route.

User Groups: Hikers and dogs. No bikes, horses, or wheelchair facilities. This trail should not be attempted in winter except by hikers experienced in mountaineering and prepared for severe winter weather, and is not suitable for skis.

Permits: No backcountry permit is needed, but a permit is required for day use or overnight parking at any White Mountain National Forest trailhead. Permits are available at several area stores and from the national forest at a cost of $5 for seven consecutive days or $20 per year. A $3 one-day permit can be purchased at self-service stations at national forest trailheads, but the pass is good only for the trailhead at which it's purchased.

Maps: A waterproof area trail map showing this hike is available from the Appalachian Mountain Club (Presidential Range, $9.95). For topographic area maps, request Crawford Notch and Stairs Mountain from the USGS.

Directions: From the Appalachian Mountain Club Highland Center on U.S. 302 in Crawford Notch, turn left onto U.S. 302 and drive north for less than 0.1 mile to a right turn for Mount Clinton Road. Follow the road only a short distance to the trailhead parking area.

GPS Coordinates: 44.2200 N, 71.4100 W

Contact: White Mountain National Forest Headquarters, 71 White Mountain Drive, Campton, NH 03246, 603/536-6100, TDD for hearing impaired 603/536-3665, www. fs.fed.us/r9/white. The Appalachian Mountain Club Pinkham Notch Visitor Center has up-to-date weather and trail information about the Whites; call 603/466-2725.

43 ELEPHANT HEAD
0.6 mi/0.5 hr

in Crawford Notch State Park

From the north end of Saco Lake in Crawford Notch, gaze south toward the short but prominent cliff at the far end of the pond. The mass of gray rock striped with white quartzite bears an uncanny resemblance to the head and trunk of an elephant. A short, easy hike along the Webster-Jackson Trail takes you to this natural marvel.

Leaving the parking area just south of the Appalachian Mountain Club Highland Center, cross U.S. 302 to the Webster-Jackson Trail (leaving from the east side of the road). The blue-blazed trail quickly enters the woods and after just 0.1 mile, comes to the side path for the Elephant Head Trail. Turn right onto the spur and continue 0.2 mile to the top of the cliff, with fine views over the notch. Return the way you came.

User Groups: Hikers and leashed dogs. No bikes, horses, or wheelchair facilities.

Permits: Parking and access are free.

Maps: Two waterproof area trail maps from the Appalachian Mountain Club cover this hike (Presidential Range map and Franconia–Pemigewasset Range map, $9.95 each). For a topographic area map, request Crawford Notch from the USGS.

Directions: From the Appalachian Mountain Club Highland Center in Crawford Notch, drive south on U.S. 302, 0.3 to the parking turnout on the left.

GPS Coordinates: 44.2151 N, 71.4080 W

Contact: White Mountain National Forest Headquarters, 71 White Mountain Drive, Campton, NH 03246, 603/536-6100, TDD for hearing impaired 603/536-3665, www. fs.fed.us/r9/white.

44 WEBSTER CLIFFS
9.4 mi/5.5 hr

in the White Mountain National Forest and Crawford Notch State Park north of Bartlett and south of Twin Mountain

This rugged, 9.4-mile hike along a particularly scenic stretch of the Appalachian Trail (AT) follows the brink of the Webster Cliffs high above Crawford Notch before eventually reaching the summits of Mount Webster (3,910 ft.) and the show stopping Mount Jackson (4,052 ft.), an open summit with fine views in every direction. The elevation gain is about 2,700 feet.

From the parking area, cross U.S. 302 to find a sign for the Appalachian Trail/Webster Cliffs Trail. The white-blazed trail ascends steadily with good footing at first, then grows steeper and rockier. The first good view comes within two miles, from a wide, flat ledge overlooking the notch and White Mountains to the south and west.

For a round-trip hike of just four miles, this ledge makes a worthwhile destination. But from there, you can see the next open ledge, just 0.2 mile farther and a little higher along the ridge, beckoning you onward. The trail continues past several outlooks along the cliffs with sweeping views of the Whites, including the Willey Range across Crawford Notch and Mount Chocorua, the prominent horned peak to the southeast. At 3.3 miles, the AT passes over Mount Webster's 3,910-foot partly wooded but craggy summit, with excellent views of the notch and mountains from Chocorua to Mount Carrigain and the Saco River Valley. Descending slightly off Webster, the trail crosses relatively flat and boggy terrain, then slabs up to the open summit of Jackson, 4.7 miles from the trailhead. Head back the same way.

User Groups: Hikers and dogs. No bikes, horses, or wheelchair facilities. This trail should not be attempted in winter except by hikers experienced in mountaineering and prepared for severe winter weather.

Permits: Parking and access are free.

Maps: Three waterproof area trail maps from the Appalachian Mountain Club cover this hike (Franconia–Pemigewasset Range map, Presidential Range map, and the Crawford Notch–Sandwich Range/Moosilauke–Kinsman map, $9.95 each). For a topographic area map, request Crawford Notch from the USGS.

Directions: From the Crawford Notch Appalachian Mountain Club Highland Center, continue south on U.S. 302 for approximately 3.9 miles. At a sign for Ripley Falls, turn right onto a paved road. Drive 0.3 mile and park at the end of the road.

GPS Coordinates: 44.1670 N, 71.3860 W

Contact: White Mountain National Forest Headquarters, 71 White Mountain Drive, Campton, NH 03246, 603/536-6100, TDD for hearing impaired 603/536-3665, www.fs.fed.us/r9/white. New Hampshire Division of Parks and Recreation, Bureau of Trails, P.O. Box 1856, Concord, NH 03302-1856, 603/271-3254.

45 MOUNT ISOLATION TRAVERSE
20 mi one-way/2 days

in the White Mountain National Forest north of Jackson and east of Crawford Notch State Park

In the heart of the Dry River Wilderness, south of Mount Washington, Mount Isolation's baldpate lies too far from any road for most day hikers—which translates into a true sense of isolation. If you have the urge to get away from it all, but with a rugged backpack trek to a scenic 4,000-footer that requires shuttling cars between trailheads, this two-day traverse could be for you. The total elevation gain to Isolation's summit is about 3,000 feet.

From the parking area off Route 16, follow the Rocky Branch Trail west for 3.7 miles to the Rocky Branch, an aptly named tributary of the Saco River. Cross the stream and turn right (north) on the Isolation Trail, passing a shelter and eventually swinging west in a climb onto the Montalban Ridge. Approximately 2.6 miles out from the Rocky Branch, the trail comes to a junction with the Davis Path. Turn left (south) on the Davis Path and find a place to camp that is well off the trail. Leave your backpack behind for the one-mile hike south on the Davis Path to the short but steep spur trail to Mount Isolation's barren summit (4,005 ft.). You'll have terrific views west and north to the southern Presidentials and Mount Washington, and to the southwest and south of the sprawling Whites. Return to your campsite.

On day two, hike north 0.3 mile on the Davis Path to where the Isolation Trail turns west (left) toward the valley of the Dry River; be careful, because this trail junction is easily overlooked. In about 2.5 miles, turn left (south) on the Dry River Trail, paralleling the broad, boulder-choked river and crossing countless mountain brooks feeding into it. When the trees are bare, you get some fine views of Mount Washington directly upriver. It's nearly five miles from the Isolation Trail junction to U.S. 302.

There is a lean-to shelter (Rocky Branch shelter 2) at the junction of the Rocky Branch Trail and Isolation Trail that is slated to be dismantled as soon as it needs major maintenance.

User Groups: Hikers and dogs. No bikes, horses, or wheelchair facilities. This trail should not be attempted in winter except by hikers experienced in mountaineering and prepared for severe winter weather.

Permits: No backcountry permit is needed, but a permit is required for day use or overnight parking at any White Mountain National Forest trailhead. Permits are available at several area stores and from the national forest at a cost of $5 for seven consecutive days or $20 per year. A $3 one-day permit can be purchased at self-service stations at national forest trailheads, but the pass is good only for the trailhead at which it's purchased.

Maps: A waterproof area trail map is available from the Appalachian Mountain Club (Presidential Range, $9.95). For topographic area maps, request Jackson and Stairs Mountain from the USGS.

Directions: You will need to shuttle two vehicles. Leave one at the roadside turnout at the Dry River Trailhead on U.S. 302, 0.3 mile north of the Dry River Campground and 4.5 miles south of the Appalachian Mountain Club Highland Center in Crawford Notch. Then drive south on U.S. 302 to Glen, turn left onto Route 16 north, and drive 8.1 miles to a large parking lot on the left for the Rocky Branch Trail.

GPS Coordinates: 44.2038 N, 71.2408 W

Contact: White Mountain National Forest Headquarters, 71 White Mountain Drive, Campton, NH 03246, 603/536-6100, TDD for hearing impaired 603/536-3665, www.fs.fed.us/r9/white. The Appalachian Mountain Club Pinkham Notch Visitor Center has up-to-date weather and trail information about the Whites; call 603/466-2725.

46 THE BALDIES LOOP

9.7 mi/7 hr   🥾5 ⛰10

in the White Mountain National Forest near North Chatham

BEST (

As their names suggest, the pair of 3,500-foot peaks called the Baldies mimic higher mountains with their craggy summits, four miles of open ridge, and some of the best views east of Mount Washington. This rugged hike is not to be underestimated. Besides its length of almost 10 miles and some 3,300 feet of vertical ascent, it climbs steep exposed ledges on the way up South Baldface that may make some hikers uncomfortable. The Baldies can also attract harsh conditions—winds encountered here are often strong enough to make standing difficult. Although it's probably the most popular hike in the Evans Notch area, this loop still sees less boot traffic than other parts of the Whites.

From the parking area, walk 50 yards north on Route 113 and cross the road to the start of the Baldface Circle Trail. It's a wide, easy trail for 0.7 mile to Circle Junction, where a side trail leads right 0.1 mile to Emerald Pool, a highly worthwhile detour that adds 0.2 mile to this hike (see the *Emerald Pool* listing in this chapter). From Circle Junction, this hike bears left at a sign for South Baldface and, climbing steadily, the trail reaches the South Baldface shelter 2.5 miles from the road. Beyond the lean-to, the trail hits all the prominent ledges visible from the road and for nearly a half mile winds up them, requiring steep scrambling. A bit more than three miles from the road, the trail reaches the level shoulder of South Baldface, where the Baldface Knob Trail leads left (south) to Baldface Knob and Eastman Mountain. Stay on the Circle Trail; from here, you'll get your first view into the broad glacial cirque, or ravine, bounded by North and South Baldface and the Bicknell Ridge. The Circle Trail then continues a half mile west—and 500 feet up—to the 3,569-foot summit of South Baldface. The summit views extend to much of the White Mountains to the west and south, including Mounts Washington, Carrigain, and Chocorua. To the north rise the Mahoosuc Range and a long chain of mountains reaching far into Maine. To the east lies a landscape of lakes and low hills, most prominently the long, low ridge of Pleasant Mountain.

Continue northwest on the Circle Trail another 1.2 miles, dropping into the woods and then ascending to the 3,591-foot summit of North Baldface, where the views are equally awesome. Descend north off North Baldy via the Circle Trail, and continue nearly a mile to the signed junction with the Bicknell Ridge Trail. Turn right (east) on Bicknell, a scenic alternative to completing the Circle Trail loop. The Bicknell descends an open ridge for about a mile before entering the forest and reaching its lower junction with the Circle Trail

in 2.5 miles, at a stream crossing. Follow the Circle Trail another 0.7 mile to Circle Junction. Turn left and the trail returns 0.7 mile back to the road.

User Groups: Hikers and dogs. No bikes, horses, or wheelchair facilities.

Permits: No backcountry permit is needed, but a permit is required for day use or overnight parking at any White Mountain National Forest trailhead. Permits are available at several area stores and from the national forest at a cost of $5 for seven consecutive days or $20 per year. A $3 one-day permit can be purchased at self-service stations at national forest trailheads, but the pass is good only for the trailhead at which it's purchased.

Maps: A trail map is available from the Chatham Trails Association (Map of Cold River Valley and Evans Notch, $6). This hike is also covered on a waterproof area trail map available from the Appalachian Mountain Club (Carter Range–Evans Notch/North Country–Mahoosuc, $9.95). For a topographic area map, request Chatham from the USGS.

Directions: The trail begins near a large parking lot on the east side of Route 113, 2.7 miles north of the northern junction of Routes 113 and 113B in North Chatham. GPS Coordinates: 44.2385 N, 71.0169 W

Contact: White Mountain National Forest Headquarters, 71 White Mountain Drive, Campton, NH 03246, 603/536-6100, TDD for hearing impaired 603/536-3665, www.fs.fed.us/r9/white. Chatham Trails Association, P.O. Box 605, Center Conway, NH 03813, http://chathamtrails.org.

47 EMERALD POOL

1.6 mi/1 hr

in the White Mountain National Forest near North Chatham

BEST (

The aptly named and gorgeous Emerald Pool is a deep hole of verdant water just below the narrow gorge and falls along Charles Brook.

It's a flat, easy walk to the pool, making this a good hike for young children.

From the parking area, walk 50 yards north on Route 113 and cross the road to the start of the Baldface Circle Trail. Follow the wide, easy trail for 0.7 mile to Circle Junction, where a side trail leads right 0.1 mile to Emerald Pool. As pretty as it is to look at, it's even better to take a dip in the inviting water, a popular local swimming hole in the summer months. Return the same way.

User Groups: Hikers and dogs. No bikes, horses, or wheelchair facilities.

Permits: No backcountry permit is needed, but a permit is required for day use or overnight parking at any White Mountain National Forest trailhead. Permits are available at several area stores and from the national forest at a cost of $5 for seven consecutive days or $20 per year. A $3 one-day permit can be purchased at self-service stations at national forest trailheads, but the permit is good only for the trailhead at which it's purchased.

Maps: A trail map is available from the Chatham Trails Association (Map of Cold River Valley and Evans Notch, $6). A waterproof area trail map showing this hike is available from the Appalachian Mountain Club (Carter Range–Evans Notch/North Country–Mahoosuc, $9.95). For a topographic area map, request Chatham from the USGS.

Directions: The trail begins near a large parking lot on the east side of Route 113, 2.7 miles north of the northern junction of Routes 113 and 113B in North Chatham.
GPS Coordinates: 44.2385 N, 71.0169 W

Contact: White Mountain National Forest Headquarters, 71 White Mountain Drive, Campton, NH 03246, 603/536-6100, TDD for hearing impaired 603/536-3665, www.fs.fed.us/r9/white. Chatham Trails Association, P.O. Box 605, Center Conway, NH 03813, http://chathamtrails.org.

48 MOUNT LAFAYETTE: SKOOKUMCHUCK TRAIL

10 mi/6 hr   🏃4 ⛰10

in the White Mountain National Forest north of Franconia Notch State Park

Compared to other routes up popular Mount Lafayette (5,260 ft.), the Skookumchuck is less traveled, a bit longer than some, and ascends more gradually. Still, it's 10 miles round-trip, and you will gain more than 3,500 feet in elevation. Views from the top of the Lafayette summit, part of the Franconia Ridge, make the long trek worth it. At the summit you are rewarded with a panorama spanning the peaks and valleys of the Pemigewasset Wilderness all the way to the Presidential Range, Vermont's Green Mountains, and, on a very clear day, New York's Adirondacks. This trail offers a nice winter outing on snowshoes, but turn around before reaching the Garfield Ridge Trail if you're not prepared for severe cold and wind. This is also a great hike for seeing woodland wildflowers in May.

From the parking lot, pick up the Skookumchuck Trail, which is sporadically marked with blue blazes (the trail corridor is fairly obvious). It contours southward around the west slope of a hill called Big Bickford Mountain, crossing an overgrown logging road a few times. Upon reaching Skookumchuck Brook at a little over a mile (Skookumchuck means "rapid water" in some Native American dialects), the trail turns east to climb steadily along the brook for more than a half mile. It then leaves the brook at 1.8 miles and begins to ascend a steep mountainside, passing through beautiful birch forest. Ascending into subalpine forest, you get your first views through the trees of the upper slopes of Lafayette. Shortly after breaking out of the forest, the Skookumchuck terminates at the Garfield Ridge Trail at 4.3 miles. Turn right (south) and follow the Garfield Ridge Trail another 0.7 mile along the exposed ridge to the summit of Lafayette. Return the way you came.

User Groups: Hikers and dogs. No bikes, horses, or wheelchair facilities. This trail should not be attempted in winter except by hikers experienced in mountaineering and prepared for severe winter weather.

Permits: No backcountry permit is needed, but a permit is required for day use or overnight parking at any White Mountain National Forest trailhead. Permits are available at several area stores and from the national forest at a cost of $5 for seven consecutive days or $20 per year. A $3 one-day permit can be purchased at self-service stations at national forest trailheads, but the pass is good only for the trailhead at which it's purchased.

Maps: Two waterproof area trail maps available from the Appalachian Mountain Club show this hike (Franconia–Pemigewasset Range map and Crawford Notch–Sandwich Range/Moosilauke–Kinsman map, $9.95 each). For a topographic area map, request Franconia from the USGS.

Directions: In Franconia Notch, the Skookumchuck Trail begins at a parking lot on U.S. 3, about 0.6 mile north of Exit 35 off I-93. GPS Coordinates: 44.1944 N, 71.6807 W

Contact: White Mountain National Forest Headquarters, 71 White Mountain Drive, Campton, NH 03246, 603/536-6100, TDD for hearing impaired 603/536-3665, www.fs.fed.us/r9/white.

49 CANNON MOUNTAIN: KINSMAN RIDGE TRAIL

4.4 mi/3 hr

in Franconia Notch State Park north of Lincoln and south of Franconia

Cannon Mountain (4,077 ft.) stands out at the north end of spectacular Franconia Notch because of the 1,000-foot cliff on its east face. That cliff was once the home of the Old Man of the Mountain, the famous stone profile that suddenly gave way to gravity in

2003. The "Great Stone Face" may be gone from the mountain, but this moderate hike of 4.4 miles round-trip, climbing 2,100 feet in elevation, still leads to the excellent views from Cannon's scenic summit.

From the tramway parking lot, follow the Kinsman Ridge Trail through a picnic area and briefly along a ski area trail before entering the woods. The trail ascends at a moderate grade, passing a short side path at 1.5 miles that leads to open ledges and a nice view across the notch to Franconia Ridge. The Kinsman Ridge Trail swings right, soon climbing more steeply to the summit, where there is an observation platform and the summit tramway station. To the east, the views extend to Mounts Lafayette and Lincoln. To the west, you can see Vermont's Green Mountains and New York's Adirondacks on a clear day. Head back along the same route.

User Groups: Hikers and leashed dogs. No bikes, horses, or wheelchair facilities. This trail should not be attempted in winter except by hikers prepared for severe winter weather, and is not suitable for skis.

Permits: Parking and access are free.

Maps: Two waterproof area trail maps available from the Appalachian Mountain Club show this hike (Franconia–Pemigewasset Range map and Crawford Notch–Sandwich Range/Moosilauke–Kinsman map, $9.95 each). For a topographic area map, request Franconia from the USGS.

Directions: From Lincoln, follow I-93 north for about 10 miles to Franconia Notch. The hike begins from the tramway parking lot at Exit 34B off I-93, at the north end of the notch. Look for a sign for the Kinsman Ridge Trail.

GPS Coordinates: 44.1684 N, 71.6861 W

Contact: White Mountain National Forest Headquarters, 71 White Mountain Drive, Campton, NH 03246, 603/536-6100, TDD for hearing impaired 603/536-3665, www.fs.fed.us/r9/white. Franconia Notch State Park, Franconia, NH 03580, 603/745-8391, www.franconianotchstatepark.com.

50 CANNON MOUNTAIN: HI-CANNON TRAIL
5.6 mi/3.5 hr   🏃4 ⛰9

in Franconia Notch State Park north of Lincoln
and south of Franconia

The most rigorous trail on Cannon Mountain (4,077 ft.), the Hi-Cannon's route is so steep in sections that hikers are required to climb a 15-foot tall ladder just to stay on trail. A net climb of 2,300 feet, the views from open ledges along the way and the panoramic tableau that awaits at Canonn's summit make this calf burner worth the effort.

From the Lafayette Campground parking lot, pick up the Lonesome Lake Trail at the trail marker and follow it through the campground, ascending steadily toward Lonesome Lake. At 0.4 mile, turn right onto the Hi-Cannon Trail (look for the trail marker at the well-defined trail junction). Hi-Cannon at first climbs steadily through a series of switchbacks, but at 1.2 miles from the campground, the trail suddenly becomes increasingly vertical and rugged on its way up a ridge. Pass a fine overlook with views towards Franconia Notch at 1.6 miles and, a few yards later, climb up a ladder to negotiate a cliff-like rock slab. Tall hikers and those carrying tall frame packs should be mindful of a rock overhang hovering overhead at the top of the ladder. Continuing on, still on rocky, somewhat open terrain, at 2.4 miles from the campground, turn right on the Kinsman Ridge Trail and follow it 0.4 mile to Cannon's summit, with good views in every direction, most spectacularly toward Franconia Ridge (see the *Cannon Mountain: Kinsman Ridge Trail* listing in this chapter for more information). Return the way you came.

User Groups: Hikers and leashed dogs. No bikes, horses, or wheelchair facilities. This trail should not be attempted in winter and is not suitable for skis.

Permits: Parking and access are free.

Maps: Two waterproof trail maps showing this hike are available from the Appalachian Mountain Club (Franconia–Pemigewasset Range map and Crawford Notch–Sandwich Range/Moosilauke–Kinsman map, $9.95 each). For a topographic area map, request Franconia from the USGS Map.

Directions: From Lincoln, follow I-93 north for approximately 10 miles to enter Franconia Notch. At signs for the Lafayette Place Campground, park in one of the large parking lots on the east side of I-93 (for southbound vehicles, another parking lot is on the west side of the highway). From the east side parking lot, hikers can cross under the highway to the Lafayette Place Campground on the west side, where the trail begins.

GPS Coordinates: 44.1419 N, 71.6860 W

Contact: Franconia Notch State Park, Franconia, NH 03580, 603/745-8391, www.franconianotchstatepark.com. White Mountain National Forest Headquarters, 71 White Mountain Drive, Campton, NH 03246, 603/536-6100, TDD for hearing impaired 603/536-3665, www.fs.fed.us/r9/white.

51 LONESOME LAKE
3.2 mi/2 hr   🏃2 ⛰10

in Franconia Notch State Park north of Lincoln
and south of Franconia

Lonesome Lake's name gives a newcomer to Franconia Notch no forewarning of the crowds that flock to this scenic mountain tarn. Nonetheless, if you accept the likelihood of sharing this beautiful spot with dozens of other visitors, the view from the lake's southwest corner across its crystal waters to Mounts Lafayette and Lincoln on Franconia Ridge has no comparison. The trail to Lonesome Lake passes through extensive boggy areas, which, combined with heavy foot traffic, can make for a muddy hike. It ascends about 1,000 feet in elevation.

From the parking lot, pick up the Lonesome Lake Trail, which crosses Lafayette Place Campground and ascends at a moderate grade for 1.2 miles to the northeast corner of the lake. Turn left (south) on the Cascade Brook Trail, following it nearly 0.3 mile to the south end of the lake. Turn right on the Fishin' Jimmy Trail, crossing the lake's outlet and reaching a small beach area where people often swim. The Appalachian Mountain Club hut lies a short distance off the lake, in the woods. Bear right off the Fishin' Jimmy Trail onto the Around-Lonesome-Lake Trail, which heads north along the lake's west shore, crossing boggy areas on boardwalks. In 0.3 mile, turn right (east) on the Lonesome Lake Trail and follow it 1.4 miles back to the campground.

The Appalachian Mountain Club (AMC) operates the Lonesome Lake hut on the Fishin' Jimmy Trail near Lonesome Lake; contact the AMC for reservation and rate information.

User Groups: Hikers and leashed dogs. No bikes, horses, or wheelchair facilities.

Permits: Parking and access are free.

Maps: Two waterproof area trail maps available from the Appalachian Mountain Club show this hike (Franconia–Pemigewasset Range map and Crawford Notch–Sandwich Range/Moosilauke–Kinsman map, $9.95 each). For a topographic area map, request Franconia from the USGS.

Directions: From Lincoln, follow I-93 north for approximately 10 miles to reach Franconia Notch. At signs for the Lafayette Place Campground, park in one of the large parking lots on the east side of I-93 (for southbound vehicles, another parking lot is on the west side of the highway). From the east side parking lot, hikers can cross under the highway to the Lafayette Place Campground on the west side, where the trail begins.

GPS Coordinates: 44.1419 N, 71.6860 W

Contact: White Mountain National Forest Headquarters, 71 White Mountain Drive, Campton, NH 03246, 603/536-6100, TDD for hearing impaired 603/536-3665, www.fs.fed.us/r9/white. Franconia Notch State Park, Franconia, NH 03580, 603/745-8391, www.franconianotchstatepark.com. Appalachian Mountain Club Pinkham Notch Visitor Center, P.O. Box 298, Gorham, NH 03581, 603/466-2721, www.outdoors.org.

52 NORTH AND SOUTH KINSMAN

11.1 mi/8 hr

in the White Mountain National Forest and Franconia Notch State Park north of Lincoln and south of Franconia

Rising high above Franconia Notch, opposite the 5,000-foot peaks of Lafayette and Lincoln, Kinsman Mountain's two distinct peaks offer good views of the notch. But the more popular attractions on this 11.1-mile hike are the 1.5 miles of falls and cascades along Cascade Brook and the views across Lonesome Lake to Franconia Ridge. Many hikers, especially families with young children, explore only as far as the brook—a refreshing place on a hot summer day. Most of the stream crossings on this hike utilize rocks or downed trees, and can be difficult at times of high water. Also, heavily used trails in the area are often wet and muddy, making rocks and exposed roots slick and footing difficult. This hike ascends about 2,500 feet in elevation; portions of the route coincide with the Appalachian Trail.

You can begin this hike on either side of I-93. From the parking lot on the northbound side of I-93, follow the signs to the Basin, passing beneath I-93 and crossing a footbridge over the Pemigewasset River. Beyond the bridge, the trail bends right; within 100 feet, bear left at a sign for the Basin-Cascades Trail. From the parking lot on the southbound side, follow the walkway south to the Basin. Turn right on the bridge over the Pemigewasset and watch for the Basin-Cascades Trail branching left. Hikers from either parking lot will converge at this trailhead near the Basin, a natural stone bowl carved out by the Pemigewasset River and a popular spot for tourists. Follow the Basin-Cascades Trail just 0.1 mile before the Basin-Cascades Trail meets the Cascade Brook Trail.

From this junction to the summit of 4,356-foot South Kinsman, the hike coincides with the white-blazed Appalachian Trail (AT). Turn right (northwest) on the AT/Cascade Brook Trail, immediately crossing the brook on stones or a downed tree. A half mile farther, the Kinsman Pond Trail bears left and crosses Cascade Brook; however, you should bear right and continue roughly north on the AT/Cascade Brook Trail another mile to a junction with the Fishin' Jimmy Trail at the south end of Lonesome Lake. Turn left (west) with the AT onto the Fishin' Jimmy Trail, crossing a log bridge over the lake's outlet to a beachlike area popular for swimming. There's an outstanding view across Lonesome Lake to Franconia Ridge and Mounts Lafayette and Lincoln and Little Haystack (from left to right). Stay on the AT/Fishin' Jimmy Trail, passing the Appalachian Mountain Club's Lonesome Lake hut, which sits back in the woods just above the beach area. The trail rises and falls, passing over the hump separating Lonesome Lake from the upper flanks of Kinsman Mountain. After crossing a feeder stream to Cascade Brook, the trail ascends steeply, often up rock slabs into which wooden steps have been drilled in places. Two miles from Lonesome Lake, the Fishin' Jimmy Trail terminates at Kinsman Junction.

From the junction, follow the AT straight (west) onto the Kinsman Ridge Trail, climbing steep rock. Reach the wooded summit of 4,293-foot North Kinsman 0.4 mile from the junction; a side path leads 20 feet from the summit cairn to an open ledge with a sweeping view eastward. Continue south on the AT/Kinsman Ridge Trail, descending past two open areas with good views. The trail drops into the saddle between the two peaks, then ascends steadily to the broad, flat summit of South Kinsman, nearly a mile from North Kinsman's summit. From various spots on South Kinsman's summit, you have views toward Franconia Ridge, North Kinsman, and Moosilauke to the south.

Backtrack to North Kinsman and descend to Kinsman Junction. Turn right (south) on the Kinsman Pond Trail, reaching the Appalachian Mountain Club shelter at Kinsman Pond in 0.1 mile. The trail follows the eastern shore of this scenic mountain tarn, below the summit cone of North Kinsman. It then hooks southeast into the forest, leading steadily downhill and making four stream crossings; this stretch of trail may be poorly marked, wet, and difficult to follow. It reaches the AT/Cascade Brook Trail 2.5 miles from Kinsman Junction, right after crossing Cascade Brook. Bear right (southeast) onto the AT/Cascade Brook Trail, following it a half mile. Immediately after crossing Cascade Brook again, turn left onto the Basin-Cascades Trail, which leads a mile back to the Basin.

The Appalachian Mountain Club (AMC) operates the Kinsman Pond campsite, with a shelter and three tent platforms, located along the Kinsman Pond Trail, 0.1 mile from Kinsman Junction and 4.5 miles from the Basin. A caretaker collects the $8 per person nightly fee during the warmer months. The AMC also operates the Lonesome Lake hut, where a crew prepares meals and guests share bunkrooms and bathrooms; contact the AMC for reservation and rate information.

User Groups: Hikers and dogs. No bikes, horses, or wheelchair facilities. This trail should not be attempted in winter except by hikers experienced in mountaineering and prepared for severe winter weather.

Permits: Parking and access are free.

Maps: Two waterproof area trail maps available from the Appalachian Mountain Club show this hike (Franconia–Pemigewasset Range map and Crawford Notch–Sandwich Range/Moosilauke–Kinsman map, $9.95 each). For topographic area maps, request Franconia and Lincoln from the USGS.

Directions: From Lincoln, follow I-93 north for 10 miles into Franconia Notch; take the exit at the sign for the Basin. Park in one of the large parking lots on the east side of I-93 (for southbound vehicles, another parking lot is on the west side of the highway). From the east side parking lot, hikers can cross under the highway to the west side, where the trail begins. This hike begins in Franconia Notch State Park, but much of it lies within the White Mountain National Forest.

GPS Coordinates: 44.1199 N, 71.6826 W

Contact: White Mountain National Forest Headquarters, 71 White Mountain Drive, Campton, NH 03246, 603/536-6100, TDD for hearing impaired 603/536-3665, www.fs.fed.us/r9/white. Franconia Notch State Park, Franconia, NH 03580, 603/745-8391, www.franconianotchstatepark.com. Appalachian Mountain Club Pinkham Notch Visitor Center, P.O. Box 298, Gorham, NH 03581, 603/466-2721, www.outdoors.org.

53 FRANCONIA NOTCH: PEMI TRAIL

5.5 mi one-way/2.5 hr

in Franconia Notch State Park north of Lincoln and south of Franconia

The Pemi Trail offers an easy and scenic 5.5-mile, one-way walk (a shuttling of cars is suggested) through Franconia Notch, with periodic views of the cliffs and peaks flanking the notch.

From the parking area, the trail follows the west shore of Profile Lake, with excellent views across the water to Eagle Cliff on Mount Lafayette. When the light is right, you can distinguish a free-standing rock pinnacle in a gully separating two major cliffs on this shoulder of Lafayette. Known as the Eaglet, this pinnacle is a destination for rock climbers and has been a nesting site in spring for peregrine falcons, which you might see flying around in spring. After crossing the paved bike path through the notch just south of Profile Lake and a second time just north of Lafayette Place Campground, the Pemi Trail follows a campground road along the west bank of the Pemigewasset River, then

leaves the campground and parallels the river all the way to the water-sculpted rock at the Basin. It crosses the Basin-Cascades Trail, meets the Cascade Brook Trail, crosses east beneath I-93, and finishes at the parking lot immediately north of the Flume. Return the way you came or find the second car you left earlier waiting in the lot.

User Groups: Hikers and leashed dogs. No bikes, horses, or wheelchair facilities.

Permits: Parking and access are free.

Maps: Obtain the free map of Franconia Notch State Park, available at the state park or from the New Hampshire Division of Parks and Recreation. Two waterproof area trail maps available from the Appalachian Mountain Club show this hike (Franconia–Pemigewasset Range map and Crawford Notch–Sandwich Range/Moosilauke–Kinsman map, $9.95 each). For topographic area maps, request Franconia and Lincoln from the USGS.

Directions: This one-way trail requires a shuttling of cars. From Lincoln, follow I-93 north for about 10 miles to Franconia Notch. Leave one car at the parking area off I-93, immediately north of the Flume (the end of the Pemi Trail). The hike begins from the tramway parking lot at Exit 34B off I-93, at the northern end of the notch.

GPS Coordinates: 44.1003 N, 71.6827 W

Contact: Franconia Notch State Park, Franconia, NH 03580, 603/745-8391, www.franconianotchstatepark.com.

54 MOUNT LAFAYETTE: OLD BRIDLE PATH

8 mi/6 hr

in the White Mountain National Forest and Franconia Notch State Park north of Lincoln and south of Franconia

This eight-mile hike provides the most direct and popular route to the 5,260-foot summit of Mount Lafayette, the sixth-highest peak in the White Mountains. The elevation gain is about 3,500 feet, ranking this hike among the most difficult in New England, though it does not present the exposure of hikes like Mount Washington's Huntington Ravine. It is also a fairly well-traveled route in winter, often with a packed snow trough that makes footing a bit easier. The Appalachian Mountain Club's Greenleaf hut offers a scenic location for making this hike a two-day trip and a way to catch the sunset high up the mountain. (See the *Mounts Lincoln and Lafayette* listing in this chapter for more description of the views from the Old Bridle Path, Greenleaf Trail, and Lafayette's summit.)

From the parking lot on the east side of I-93, follow the Falling Waters Trail and Old Bridle Path for 0.2 mile. Where the Falling Waters Trail turns sharply right, continue straight ahead on the Old Bridle Path. It climbs fairly easily at first through mostly deciduous forest, then grows steeper as it ascends the prominent west ridge of Lafayette. Once on the crest of that ridge, you'll get great views from a few open ledges of the summits of Lafayette to the left and Mount Lincoln (5,089 ft.) to the right of Lafayette. At 2.9 miles from the trailhead, the Old Bridle Path terminates at the Greenleaf Trail and Greenleaf hut. From there, follow the Greenleaf Trail as it dips down into a shallow basin, passes through subalpine forest, and soon emerges onto the rocky, open west slope of Lafayette, climbing another 1.1 miles and 1,000 feet in elevation to Lafayette's summit. The views from the summit take in most of the White Mountains and the North Country as well as Vermont's Green Mountains to the west. Return the way you came.

The Appalachian Mountain Club (AMC) operates the Greenleaf hut at the junction of the Greenleaf Trail and Old Bridle Path; contact the AMC for reservation and rate information.

User Groups: Hikers and leashed dogs. No bikes, horses, or wheelchair facilities. This trail should not be attempted in winter except by hikers experienced in mountaineering and prepared for severe winter weather.

Permits: Parking and access are free.

Maps: Two waterproof area trail maps available from the Appalachian Mountain Club show this hike (Franconia–Pemigewasset Range map and Crawford Notch–Sandwich Range/Moosilauke–Kinsman map, $9.95 each). For a topographic area map, request Franconia from the USGS.

Directions: From Lincoln, follow I-93 north for approximately 10 miles to reach Franconia Notch. At the signs for the Lafayette Place Campground, park in the large parking lot on the east side of I-93, where the trail begins. For southbound vehicles, another parking lot is located on the west side of the highway. From the west side parking lot, hikers can walk under the highway to the east lot and trailhead.

GPS Coordinates: 44.1411 N, 71.6818 W

Contact: White Mountain National Forest Headquarters, 71 White Mountain Drive, Campton, NH 03246, 603/536-6100, TDD for hearing impaired 603/536-3665, www.fs.fed.us/r9/white. Franconia Notch State Park, Franconia, NH 03580, 603/745-8391, www.franconianotchstatepark.com. Appalachian Mountain Club Pinkham Notch Visitor Center, P.O. Box 298, Gorham, NH 03581, 603/466-2721, www.outdoors.org.

55 MOUNTS LINCOLN AND LAFAYETTE

8.8 mi/6.5 hr   👤5   ⛰10

in the White Mountain National Forest and Franconia Notch State Park north of Lincoln and south of Franconia

BEST (

For many New England hikers, this 8.8-mile loop over the sixth- and seventh-highest peaks in New Hampshire becomes a favorite hike revisited many times over the years. With nearly two miles of continuous, exposed ridgeline high above the forest connecting Mounts Lincoln (5,089 ft.) and Lafayette (5,260 ft.), this hike lures hundreds of people on warm weekends in summer and fall. The views from Franconia Ridge encompass most of the White Mountains, spanning the peaks and valleys of the Pemigewasset Wilderness all the way to the Presidential Range, Vermont's Green Mountains, and, on a very clear day, New York's Adirondacks. The Falling Waters Trail passes several waterfalls and cascades and the Old Bridle Path follows a long shoulder of Mount Lafayette over some open ledges that offer excellent views of Lincoln and Lafayette. This rugged climb offers a net elevation gain of 3,600 feet; portions of the route coincide with the Appalachian Trail (AT).

From the parking lot on the east side of I-93, follow the Falling Waters Trail, which coincides for 0.2 mile with the Old Bridle Path, then turns sharply right and crosses Walker Brook on a bridge. The trail climbs steadily and steeply, crossing Dry Brook at 0.7 mile, which could be difficult in high water. Over the ensuing mile, it passes several cascades and waterfalls, including Cloudland Falls, with a sheer drop of 80 feet, and makes two more crossings of the brook.

Continue up the Falling Waters Trail, emerging above the trees about 0.1 mile before reaching the Appalachian Trail/Franconia Ridge Trail at the summit of Little Haystack Mountain, 3.2 miles from the trailhead. Turn left (north) on the open ridge, following the cairns and white blazes of the AT/Franconia Ridge Trail. Briefly following easy ground, the trail then climbs steeply to the summit of Lincoln, 0.7 mile from Haystack. It then passes over a subsidiary summit of Lincoln immediately to the north, dropping into a saddle before making the long ascent of Mount Lafayette, 0.9 mile from Lincoln's summit. This highest point on the ridge, predictably, tends to be the windiest and coldest spot as well, although there are sheltered places in the rocks on the summit's north side. Turn left (west) and descend the Greenleaf Trail, much of it over open terrain, for 1.1 miles to the Appalachian Mountain Club's Greenleaf hut. Just beyond the hut, bear left onto the

Old Bridle Path, descending southwest over the crest of a long ridge before reentering the woods and eventually reaching the parking lot, 2.9 miles from the hut.

Special note: Under most conditions, it's desirable to hike this loop in the direction described here because the steep sections of the Falling Waters Trail are easier to ascend than descend, especially when the trail is wet. But if you're doing the hike on a day with cold wind, consider reversing the direction; the wind generally comes from the northwest, and reversing this hike's direction would put it at your back while atop Franconia Ridge, rather than in your face.

The Appalachian Mountain Club (AMC) operates the Greenleaf hut at the junction of the Greenleaf Trail and Old Bridle Path; contact the AMC for reservation and rate information.

User Groups: Hikers and leashed dogs. No bikes, horses, or wheelchair facilities. This trail should not be attempted in winter except by hikers experienced in mountaineering and prepared for severe winter weather.

Permits: Parking and access are free.

Maps: Two waterproof area trail maps showing this hike are available from the Appalachian Mountain Club (Franconia–Pemigewasset Range map and Crawford Notch–Sandwich Range/Moosilauke–Kinsman map, $9.95 each). For a topographic area map, request Franconia from the USGS.

Directions: From Lincoln, follow I-93 north for approximately 10 miles to reach Franconia Notch. At the signs for the Lafayette Place Campground, park in the large parking lot on the east side of I-93, where the trail begins. For southbound vehicles, another parking lot is located on the west side of the highway. From the west side parking lot, hikers can walk under the highway to the east lot and trailhead.

GPS Coordinates: 44.1411 N, 71.6818 W

Contact: White Mountain National Forest Headquarters, 71 White Mountain Drive, Campton, NH 03246, 603/536-6100, TDD

for hearing impaired 603/536-3665, www.
fs.fed.us/r9/white. Franconia Notch State
Park, Franconia, NH 03580, 603/745-8391,
www.franconianotchstatepark.com. Appalachian Mountain Club Pinkham Notch Visitor
Center, P.O. Box 298, Gorham, NH 03581,
603/466-2721, www.outdoors.org.

56 FRANCONIA NOTCH LOOP
14 mi/9 hr or 1-2 days 🏃5 ⛰10

in the White Mountain National Forest and
Franconia Notch State Park north of Lincoln
and south of Franconia

Making the most of the skywalk effect atop
Franconia Ridge, this 14-mile loop heads
south on the ridge to bag Mount Lafayette
(5,260 ft.), Mount Lincoln (5,089 ft.), Little
Haystack Mountain (4,760 ft.), and Mount
Liberty (4,459 ft.). While this loop can be
done in a day by fit hikers, you might want
to make an overnight trip of it, staying either
in the Greenleaf hut or at the Liberty Springs
campsite. Either place gives you a great high-
elevation base from which to catch the sunset
and then get back up to the ridge the next
morning to see the sun burst majestically over
the White's eastern peaks. The cumulative
elevation gained on this hike is about 4,700
feet; portions of the route coincide with the
Appalachian Trail.

From the parking lot on the east side of
I-93, follow the Falling Waters Trail and the
Old Bridle Path for 0.2 mile to where the trails
split; then continue straight ahead on the Old
Bridle Path. An easy climb at first, the trail
pushes steeply for 2.9 miles to reach a junction with the Greenleaf Trail at the Greenleaf hut. From the hut, continue east on the
Greenleaf Trail as it dips down into a shallow
basin, passes through subalpine forest, and
soon emerges onto the rocky, open west slope
of Lafayette, climbing another 1.1 miles and
more than 1,000 feet in elevation to Lafayette's
summit, with open views in all directions.

Turn right (south) on the Franconia Ridge
Trail, which coincides with the Appalachian
Trail (AT), and hike the rugged, open, and in
places narrow Franconia Ridge for only one
mile before reaching the 5,089-foot summit of
Mount Lincoln. It's then another 0.7 mile to
the summit of Little Haystack (4,760 ft.).

Continuing south on the AT/Franconia
Ridge Trail, the path soon drops into subalpine forest—although the forest cover is thin
and the ridge narrow enough that you can
see through the trees and know how abruptly
the earth drops off to either side. At 1.8 miles
past Little Haystack, the AT departs the
Franconia Ridge Trail, turning right (west)
to follow the Liberty Spring Trail. Continue
south on the Franconia Ridge Trail another
0.3 mile, climbing less than 300 feet to the
rocky summit of Mount Liberty for excellent,
360-degree views encompassing the Whites,
the Pemigewasset Wilderness, the Green
Mountains to the west, and on a clear day,
as far west as New York's Adirondacks.

From Liberty's summit, backtrack 0.3 mile
to the Liberty Spring Trail and descend it.
Within 0.3 mile you'll reach the Liberty Spring
campsite, where you can spend the night if
backpacking. From the campsite, descend the
Liberty Spring Trail another 2.6 miles to the
blue-blazed Whitehouse Trail (it coincides
with the Franconia Notch Bike Path). Cross
the Pemigewasset River on a bridge, and just
beyond the bridge turn right onto the Pemi
Trail. Walk under the highway, then stay to
the right (north) on the Pemi Trail and follow
it nearly a mile to the Basin, where the Pemigewasset River has carved impressive natural
bowls and cascades into the granite bedrock.
From the Basin, you can stay on the Pemi
Trail, or follow the paved bike path, about
two miles farther to the parking lot on the
west side of the highway at Lafayette Place
Campground. If you parked on the east side of
the highway, you can walk under the highway
to that parking lot.

The Appalachian Mountain Club (AMC)
operates the Greenleaf hut at the junction of

the Greenleaf Trail and Old Bridle Path; contact the AMC for current reservation and rate information. The AMC also manages the Liberty Spring campsite, with 12 tent platforms, located along the Liberty Spring Trail, 2.6 miles from the Whitehouse Trail and 0.3 mile from the Franconia Ridge Trail. A caretaker collects the $8 per person nightly fee during the warmer months.

User Groups: Hikers and leashed dogs. No bikes, horses, or wheelchair facilities. This trail should not be attempted in winter except by hikers experienced in mountaineering and prepared for severe winter weather.

Permits: Parking and access are free.

Maps: Two waterproof area trail maps showing this hike are available from the Appalachian Mountain Club (Franconia–Pemigewasset Range map and Crawford Notch–Sandwich Range/Moosilauke–Kinsman map, $9.95 each). For a topographic area map, request Franconia from the USGS.

Directions: From Lincoln, follow I-93 north for approximately 10 miles to reach Franconia Notch. At the signs for the Lafayette Place Campground, park in the large parking lot on the east side of I-93, where the trail begins. For southbound vehicles, another parking lot is located on the west side of the highway. From the west side parking lot, hikers can walk under the highway to the east lot and trailhead.

GPS Coordinates: 44.1411 N, 71.6818 W

Contact: White Mountain National Forest Headquarters, 71 White Mountain Drive, Campton, NH 03246, 603/536-6100, TDD for hearing impaired 603/536-3665, www.fs.fed.us/r9/white. Franconia Notch State Park, Franconia, NH 03580, 603/745-8391, www.franconianotchstatepark.com. Appalachian Mountain Club Pinkham Notch Visitor Center, P.O. Box 298, Gorham, NH 03581, 603/466-2721, www.outdoors.org.

57 FRANCONIA NOTCH BIKE PATH

8.5 mi one-way/3.5 hr

in the White Mountain National Forest and Franconia Notch State Park north of Lincoln and south of Franconia

The Franconia Notch Bike Path runs like a stream, north/south for about 8.5 miles through Franconia Notch, providing a paved route for exploring one of the most spectacular notches in New England. Popular with families, it's great for cycling, walking, wheelchair hiking, running, snowshoeing, and cross-country skiing. With several access points, you can do as much of the path as you like. Much of it is in the forest, but there are numerous views of the surrounding peaks from the path. The path is accessible for wheelchairs provided the user can manage the few short, but somewhat steep, hills that mark the route.

The elevation begins at about 1,700 feet at the Skookumchuck trailhead, rises to around 2,000 feet at the base of Cannon Mountain and Profile Lake, then drops to about 1,100 feet at the Flume; going north to south on the path is easier, especially from anywhere south of Profile Lake. Scenic points along the path include the Flume, a natural cleavage in the mountainside; the Basin, where the still-small Pemigewasset River pours through natural bowls in the bedrock; a view of Cannon Cliff from a spot immediately north of Profile Lake; and the truck-sized boulder, estimated to weigh between 20 and 30 tons, lying right beside the paved path north of Lafayette Place campground, deposited there by a rockslide off Cannon Cliff in 1997.

User Groups: Hikers, leashed dogs, bikes, horses, and wheelchairs. In-line skating is prohibited.

Permits: Parking and access are free within Franconia Notch State Park, but the Skookumchuck Trail parking lot lies within the White Mountain National Forest, and a permit is required for day use or overnight parking. Permits are available at several area stores and from the national forest at a cost of $5 for seven consecutive days or $20 per year. A $3 one-day permit can be purchased at self-service stations at national forest trailheads, but the pass is good only for the trailhead at which it's purchased.

Maps: A waterproof area trail map is available from the Appalachian Mountain Club (Franconia–Pemigewasset Range, $9.95). For topographic area maps, request Franconia and Lincoln from the USGS.

Directions: The bike path can be accessed from several points. Its northern end is at the parking lot for the Skookumchuck Trail, on U.S. 3 about 0.6 mile north of Exit 35 off I-93 in Franconia. Its southern end is at the Flume, reached via the exit for the Flume off I-93 in Franconia Notch. Other access points in Franconia Notch include the Cannon Mountain parking lot at Exit 2, the Profile Lake parking lot, the Lafayette Place Campground, and the Basin parking lot.

GPS Coordinates: 44.1003 N, 71.6827 W

Contact: White Mountain National Forest Headquarters, 71 White Mountain Drive, Campton, NH 03246, 603/536-6100, TDD for hearing impaired 603/536-3665, www.fs.fed.us/r9/white. Franconia Notch State Park, Franconia, NH 03580, 603/745-8391, www.franconianotchstatepark.com.

58 MOUNTS FLUME AND LIBERTY

9.8 mi/7 hr   4 ⛰ 9

In the White Mountain National Forest and Franconia Notch State Park north of Lincoln and south of Franconia

If these two summits were located almost anywhere else in the region, this loop hike would enjoy enormous popularity. But the 5,000-footers to the north, Lafayette and Lincoln, are what captures the attention of most hikers venturing onto the sweeping Franconia

Ridge. Many people who call the Lafayette-Lincoln Loop (see the *Mounts Lincoln and Lafayette* listing in this chapter) their favorite hike in the Whites have never enjoyed the uninterrupted views from the rocky summits of 4,325-foot Flume or 4,459-foot Liberty: Franconia Notch, west to Mount Moosilauke and the Green Mountains, and a grand sweep of peaks to the east all the way to the Presidential Range. This hike's cumulative elevation gain is nearly 2,500 feet.

From the parking lot, take the blue-blazed Whitehouse Trail north for nearly a mile (it coincides briefly with the Franconia Notch Bike Path). Pick up the white-blazed Liberty Spring Trail—a part of the Appalachian Trail—heading east. Within a half mile, signs mark where the Flume Slide Trail branches right. From that junction to the slide, the trail is somewhat overgrown, marked very sporadically with light-blue blazes and can be hard to follow. It grows steep on the upper part of the slide, and you will scramble over rocks that can be very slick when wet. (For a less exposed route to the summit of Mount Liberty, go up and down the Liberty Spring Trail.)

At 3.3 miles from where the Flume Slide Trail left the Liberty Spring Trail, it hits the ridge crest and reaches a junction. Turn left onto the Osseo Trail, which leads a short distance to Mount Flume's open summit. Continue north over the summit on the Franconia Ridge Trail (look for the marker), dipping into the saddle between the peaks, then climbing to Liberty's summit a mile past the top of Flume. Another 0.3 mile beyond the summit, turn left onto the Liberty Spring Trail and descend for 2.9 miles to the Whitehouse Trail, following it back to the parking lot.

The Appalachian Mountain Club operates the Liberty Spring campsite, with 12 tent platforms, located along the Liberty Spring Trail, 2.6 miles from the Whitehouse Trail and 0.3 mile from the Franconia Ridge Trail. A caretaker collects the $8 per person nightly fee during the warmer months.

User Groups: Hikers and leashed dogs. No

bikes, horses, or wheelchair facilities. This trail should not be attempted in winter except by hikers experienced in mountaineering and prepared for severe winter weather and is not suitable for skis.

Permits: Parking and access are free. This hike begins in Franconia Notch State Park, but much of it lies within the White Mountain National Forest.

Maps: Two waterproof area trail maps available from the Appalachian Mountain Club show this hike (Franconia–Pemigewasset Range map and Crawford Notch–Sandwich Range/Moosilauke–Kinsman map, $9.95 each). For topographic area maps, request Franconia and Lincoln from the USGS.

Directions: From Lincoln, follow I-93 north for approximately 10 miles into Franconia Notch. Follow the signs for the Flume exit and then follow signs leading to ample trailhead parking for the Whitehouse Trail and the Appalachian Trail.

GPS Coordinates: 44.1114 N, 71.6821 W

Contact: Franconia Notch State Park, Franconia, NH 03580, 603/745-8391, www.franconianotchstatepark.com. White Mountain National Forest Headquarters, 71 White Mountain Drive, Campton, NH 03246, 603/536-6100, TDD for hearing impaired 603/536-3665, www.fs.fed.us/r9/white. Appalachian Mountain Club Pinkham Notch Visitor Center, P.O. Box 298, Gorham, NH 03581, 603/466-2721, www.outdoors.org.

59 PEMIGEWASSET WILDERNESS TRAVERSE

19.5 mi one-way/10-12 hr or 1-2 days

🏃3 ⛰10

In the White Mountain National Forest between U.S. 302 near Twin Mountain and Route 112 east of Lincoln

BEST

The Pemigewasset Wilderness is the sprawling roadless area of mountains and wide valleys in the heart of the White Mountains. A federally designated wilderness area, the Pemi harbors spectacular big-mountain hikes such as Mount Carrigain (see *Mount Carrigain* listing in this chapter), but this traverse follows the wooded valleys of the Pemi. Much of it is relatively easy hiking along routes once followed by the railroads of 19th-century logging companies. A climb of only about 1,000 feet in elevation, this hike is best broken up into a two-day backpacking trip.

From the summer parking lot at the end of Zealand Road, pick up the blue-blazed Zealand Trail, a winding walk through the forest on fairly flat ground, with some short, steep steps. At 2.5 miles, the trail comes to a junction. To the right, the Twinway leads 0.2 mile uphill to the Appalachian Mountain Club's Zealand Falls hut. This hike continues straight ahead onto the Ethan Pond Trail, which coincides with the Appalachian Trail (AT). The Ethan Pond Trail contours along the west slope of Whitewall Mountain.

About 1.3 miles past the Zealand Trail, the AT/Ethan Pond Trail emerges from the forest onto the open scar of an old rockslide on Whitewall, in the middle of Zealand Notch. Above loom the towering cliffs of the mountain; below, the rockslide's fallout, a broad boulder field. Across the notch rises Zealand Mountain, and straight ahead, to the south, stands Carrigain. The trail crosses the rockslide for about 0.2 mile, then reenters the woods. At 2.1 miles past the Zealand Trail, bear right onto the Thoreau Falls Trail, following easy terrain for 0.1 mile to Thoreau Falls, which tumbles more than 100 feet and forms an impressive cascade of ice in winter. The trail crosses the stream immediately above the brink of the falls. Be careful here in any season, but especially in winter, and do not assume that any snow or ice bridge is safe.

Once across the stream, the trail climbs steeply, angling across a wooded hillside, then dropping just as steeply down the other side. At 4.7 miles from the Ethan Pond Trail, the trail crosses a bridge over the east branch of the Pemigewasset River. Just 0.4 mile past the bridge, turn right (west) onto the Wilderness

Trail, which is the easiest trail on this route. The Wilderness Trail crosses the river again in 0.9 mile, on a 180-foot suspension bridge, then parallels the river for the remaining 5.4 flat miles to the Lincoln Woods parking lot on the Kancamangus Highway (the last three miles of the trail are also called the Lincoln Woods Trail).

The Appalachian Mountain Club (AMC) operates the Zealand Falls hut year-round; it is on the Twinway, 0.2 mile from the junction of the Zealand, Twinway, and Ethan Pond Trails and 2.7 miles from the end of Zealand Road. Contact the AMC for information on cost and reservations. The Franconia Brook campsite (16 tent platforms), operated by the White Mountain National Forest, costs $8 per person and is open only during summer and fall; the campsite is reached by hiking the trail known as East Branch Road for three miles from the Lincoln Woods trailhead. On this hike, you would reach this campsite by turning left (south) from the Wilderness Trail onto the Cedar Brook Trail right before the second bridge crossing of the east branch of the Pemigewasset River; following the Cedar Brook Trail west for a little more than a half mile; then turning right onto the East Branch Road, which is overgrown and may be easily overlooked. Camping in the forest is legal, provided you remain at least 200 feet from a trail and a quarter mile from established camping areas such as Guyot campsite.

User Groups: Hikers and dogs. No bikes, horses, or wheelchair facilities. This trail should not be attempted in winter except by hikers experienced in mountaineering and prepared for severe winter weather.

Permits: No backcountry permit is needed, but a permit is required for day use or overnight parking at any White Mountain National Forest trailhead. Permits are available at several area stores and from the national forest at a cost of $5 for seven consecutive days or $20 per year. A $3 one-day permit can be purchased at self-service stations at national forest trailheads, but the pass is good only for the trailhead at which it's purchased.

Maps: A waterproof area trail map is available from the Appalachian Mountain Club (Franconia–Pemigewasset Range, $9.95). For topographic area maps, request Bethlehem, Mount Washington, South Twin Mountain, Crawford Notch, Mount Osceola, and Mount Carrigain from the USGS.

Directions: You need to shuttle two vehicles for this one-way traverse. To go north to south, as described here, leave one vehicle in the Lincoln Woods parking lot, where there is a White Mountain National Forest ranger station. The lot is off the Kancamagus Highway (Route 112), five miles east of the McDonald's in Lincoln and just east of the bridge where the Kancamagus crosses the east branch of the Pemigewasset River. The Wilderness Trail— also known for its initial three miles as the Lincoln Woods Trail—begins here. To reach the start of this hike, from the junction of U.S. 3 and U.S. 302 in Twin Mountain, drive east on U.S. 302 for 2.3 miles and turn right onto Zealand Road, then continue 3.5 miles to a parking lot at the end of the road. Zealand Road is not maintained in winter.

GPS Coordinates: 44.2221 N, 71.4780 W

Contact: White Mountain National Forest Headquarters, 71 White Mountain Drive, Campton, NH 03246, 603/536-6100, TDD for hearing impaired 603/536-3665, www. fs.fed.us/r9/white. Appalachian Mountain Club Pinkham Notch Visitor Center, P.O. Box 298, Gorham, NH 03581, 603/466-2721, www.outdoors.org.

60 ARETHUSA FALLS

2.8 mi/1.5 hr

in Crawford Notch State Park north of Bartlett and south of Twin Mountain

With a thundering drop of nearly 200 feet, Arethusa Falls is the tallest waterfall in New

Hampshire. It's unusual name comes from a poem by Percy Bysshe Shelley that tells the tale of the beautiful Arethusa, a nymph who is transformed into a fountain. A climb of approximately 900 feet, this fairly easy hike and its watery, scenic payoff rank the falls as among the region's most frequently visited natural wonders.

From the far end of the lower parking lot, you can pick up a connector trail to the upper lot. There, follow the Arethusa Falls Trail (marked) for 0.1 mile to a left turn onto the Bemis Brook Trail, which parallels the Arethusa Trail for a half mile and eventually rejoins it. Bemis Brook Trail is more interesting for the short cascades it passes—Bemis Falls and Coliseum Falls—as well as Fawn Pool. After reaching the Arethusa Trail again, turn left and continue uphill another 0.8 mile to the base of the magnificent falls. Taking in the powerful cascade, you will probably notice the views would be even better on the other side of Bemis Brook. Crossing the brook can be very difficult under high water conditions and should not be attempted by children. Return the way you came.

User Groups: Hikers and leashed dogs. No bikes, horses, or wheelchair facilities.

Permits: Parking and access are free.

Maps: Two waterproof area trail maps available from the Appalachian Mountain Club cover this hike (Franconia–Pemigewasset Range map and Crawford Notch–Sandwich Range/Moosilauke–Kinsman map, $9.95 each). For topographic area maps, request Crawford Notch and Stairs Mountain from the USGS.

Directions: From the Appalachian Mountain Club Highland Center in Crawford Depot, follow U.S. 302 south for 5.2 miles to a sign for Arethusa Falls. Turn right onto the paved road and park in the lower lot immediately on the right, or drive 0.2 mile and park at the end of the road.

GPS Coordinates: 44.1478 N, 71.3693 W

Contact: White Mountain National Forest Headquarters, 71 White Mountain Drive, Campton, NH 03246, 603/536-6100, TDD for hearing impaired 603/536-3665, www.fs.fed.us/r9/white.

61 RIPLEY FALLS

1 mi/0.75 hr

in Crawford Notch State Park north of Bartlett and south of Twin Mountain

As Avalanche Brook races out of the Pemigewasset Wilderness towards the lowland of Crawford Notch, it stops long enough to tumble down an impressive 100-foot sheer granite face known as Ripley Falls. An easy walk from the trailhead at any time of year, the falls tend to be at their picturesque best in late spring and early summer when the brook swells with runoff.

From the railroad tracks at the end of the access road and parking area, pick up the Ethan Pond Trail, which coincides here with the white-blazed Appalachian Trail (AT). As the easy, wide trail climbs steadily uphill, it passes through an area of tall birch trees at 0.2 mile and then reaches a fork. The Ethan Pond Trail/AT bears right, but go left onto the Ripley Falls Trail. Continue 0.3 mile to the cascading falls and then return the way you came.

Special note: It is possible to reach soaring Arethusa Falls (see the *Arethusa Falls* listing in this chapter) from Ripley Falls by continuing on the Arethusa-Ripley Falls Trail for another 2.3 miles (adding 4.6 miles round-trip and 400 feet in elevation gain to this hike).

User Groups: Hikers and dogs. No bikes, horses, or wheelchair facilities.

Permits: Parking and access are free.

Maps: Two waterproof area trail maps available from the Appalachian Mountain Club cover this hike (Franconia–Pemigewasset Range map and Crawford Notch–Sandwich Range/Moosilauke–Kinsman map, $9.95 each). For a topographic area map, request Crawford Notch from the USGS.

Directions: From the Appalachian Mountain Club Highland Center in Crawford Depot, drive south on U.S. 302 for 3.9 miles to a sign for Ripley Falls. Turn right and drive 0.3 mile to parking at the end of the road.

GPS Coordinates: 44.1669 N, 71.3863 W

Contact: White Mountain National Forest Headquarters, 71 White Mountain Drive, Campton, NH 03246, 603/536-6100, TDD for hearing impaired 603/536-3665, www.fs.fed.us/r9/white. New Hampshire Division of Parks and Recreation, Bureau of Trails, P.O. Box 1856, Concord, NH 03302-1856, 603/271-3254.

62 STAIRS MOUNTAIN
9.2 mi/5 hr   🏃4 ⛰️8

in the White Mountain National Forest north of Bartlett

Stairs Mountain is so named because of its Giant Stairs, a pair of steplike ledges on the 3,463-foot mountain's south end. From the cliffs atop the Giant Stairs, you get wide views of the wild backcountry of the Saco River valley. A net climb of approximately 2,100 feet, this hike can be done in a day or can be split up over two days with a stay on one of the shelters near this route.

From the end of Jericho Road, follow the Rocky Branch Trail north a flat two miles to the Rocky Branch Shelter 1, where there is a lean-to and a tent site. Just beyond it, the Stairs Col Trail turns left (west) and ascends steadily for nearly two miles, passing below the Giant Stairs and through Stairs Col to the Davis Path. Turn right (north) on the Davis Path and follow it for less than a half mile to a side path leading right for about 0.2 mile to the summit cliffs above the Giant Stairs. Return the way you came. To spend the night before heading back, retrace your steps on the Davis Path and pass the junction with the Stairs Col Trail, staying south on the Davis Path for another 0.3 mile to the Resolution Shelter.

User Groups: Hikers and dogs. No bikes, horses, or wheelchair facilities.

Permits: No backcountry permit is needed, but a permit is required for day use or overnight parking at any White Mountain National Forest trailhead. Permits are available at several area stores and from the national forest at a cost of $5 for seven consecutive days or $20 per year. A $3 one-day permit can be purchased at self-service stations at national forest trailheads, but the pass is good only for the trailhead at which it's purchased.

Maps: A waterproof area trail map showing this hike is available from the Appalachian Mountain Club (Crawford Notch–Sandwich Range/Moosilauke–Kinsman, $9.95). For topographic area maps, request North Conway West, Bartlett, and Stairs Mountain from the USGS.

Directions: From the junction of Route 16 and U.S. 302 in Glen, drive west on U.S. 302 for one mile and turn right onto Jericho Road/Rocky Branch Road. Follow the road, which is paved for about a mile and then becomes gravel for the remaining five miles. At the end of the road is a parking area and the Rocky Branch trailhead.

GPS Coordinates: 44.1388 N, 71.2664 W

Contact: White Mountain National Forest Headquarters, 71 White Mountain Drive, Campton, NH 03246, 603/536-6100, TDD for hearing impaired 603/536-3665, www.fs.fed.us/r9/white. The Appalachian Mountain Club Pinkham Notch Visitor Center has up-to-date weather and trail information about the Whites; call 603/466-2725.

63 THE WILDERNESS/ LINCOLN WOODS TRAIL
10.8 mi/5 hr   🏃2 ⛰️8

in the White Mountain National Forest, east of Lincoln

This scenic hike along the east branch of the Pemigewasset River is virtually flat for its entire distance—making it a pleasant walk in the wilderness, rather than a grueling climb. Some visitors only go the nearly three miles out to the first bridge, over Franconia Brook, and return. This description covers the 5.4 miles out to the suspension bridge over the east branch of the Pemi at the junction with the Thoreau Falls Trail.

From the visitors center parking lot, take the bridge over the east branch of the Pemigewasset River, then turn right onto the Lincoln Woods Trail—the name given in recent years to the first three miles of what was formerly known entirely as the Wilderness Trail. Following an old railroad grade, the trail is wide, level, and shady as it runs parallel to the river (Pemigewasset is Abenaki for "swiftly moving," an apt name for this river, especially in late spring/early summer). At 2.6 miles, pass a side path leading 0.8 mile to Black Pond Trail and at 2.7 miles, reach a side path on the left leading 0.4 mile to Franconia Falls, a worthwhile detour (no wheelchair facilities). Staying on the Lincoln Woods, the trail crosses a footbridge over Franconia Brook and at 2.9 miles, officially enters the Pemigewasset Wilderness. Now called the Wilderness Trail and still following the river, the trail continues straight ahead, passing a junction with the Bondcliff Trail at 4.7 miles. The trail soon crosses Black Brook on a bridge near an old logging railroad bridge and from there, it's just another 0.7 mile to the suspension bridge over the Pemi's east branch (at the junction with the Thoreau Falls Trail). Return the way you came.

Special note: You can make a loop of about the same distance from the Lincoln Woods trailhead by starting out on the Pemi East Side Trail, also leaving from the visitors center parking lot, but staying on the east side of the river. Within four miles, you'll turn left (east) onto the Cedar Brook Trail; follow it about a half mile, cross the bridge over the east branch of the Pemi River, then turn left (west) and follow the Wilderness Trail back to the trailhead.

The Franconia Brook campsite (16 tent platforms), operated by the White Mountain National Forest, costs $8 per person and is open only during summer and fall. The campsite is reached by hiking the trail known as East Branch Road for three miles from the Lincoln Woods trailhead. On this hike, you would reach this campsite from the Wilderness Trail by crossing the bridge over the east branch of the Pemigewasset River and turning right (west) onto the Cedar Brook Trail. From there, follow the Cedar Brook Trail west for a little more than a half mile before turning right onto the East Branch Road, which is overgrown and may be easily overlooked. Follow East Branch Road to the campground.

User Groups: Hikers and dogs. The Lincoln Woods Trail is accessible for wheelchairs for approximately the first half mile; as the wide path continues, old railroad ties surface and the route becomes uneven. No bikes or horses.

Permits: No backcountry permit is needed, but a permit is required for day use or overnight parking at any White Mountain National Forest trailhead. Permits are available at several area stores and from the national forest at a cost of $5 for seven consecutive days or $20 per year. A $3 one-day permit can be purchased at self-service stations at national forest trailheads, but the pass is good only for the trailhead at which it's purchased.

Maps: Two waterproof area trail maps available from the Appalachian Mountain Club show this hike (Franconia–Pemigewasset Range map and Crawford Notch–Sandwich Range/Moosilauke–Kinsman map, $9.95 each). For a topographic area map, request the Mount Osceola map from the USGS.

Directions: Drive to the large parking lot at Lincoln Woods along the Kancamagus Highway/Route 112, five miles east of the McDonald's in Lincoln, and just east of the bridge where the Kancamagus crosses the east branch of the Pemigewasset River. The Wilderness Trail—also known for its initial three miles as the Lincoln Woods Trail—begins here.

GPS Coordinates: 44.0643 N, 71.5904 W

Contact: White Mountain National Forest Headquarters, 71 White Mountain Drive, Campton, NH 03246, 603/536-6100, TDD for hearing impaired 603/536-3665, www.fs.fed.us/r9/white.

64 MOUNT CARRIGAIN
10 mi/7 hr

in the White Mountain National Forest southwest of Crawford Notch State Park

The tallest peak in this corner of the Whites, 4,700-foot Carrigain offers one of the finest—and unquestionably unique—views in these mountains from the observation tower on its summit. On a clear day, the panorama takes in Mount Washington and the Presidential Range, the vast sweep of peaks across the Pemigewasset Wilderness to Franconia Ridge, Moosilauke to the west, and the peaks above Waterville Valley and the distinctive horn of Chocorua to the south. Although 10 miles round-trip, with a vertical ascent of about 3,300 feet, this hike grows steep only for the ascent to the crest of Signal Ridge, which itself has spectacular views, including one toward the cliffs of Mount Lowell to the east.

From the parking area, pick up the marked Signal Ridge Trail. At first following Whiteface Brook as it tumbles along in a series of picturesque cascades, at 0.6 mile, the trail veers away from the brook and at 1.7 miles from the road, passes a junction with the Carrigain Notch Trail (just before a crossing of the Carrigain Brook). From here, the trail grows increasingly steep and changes direction several times; most of the hike's elevation is gained in the final 1.5-mile push to the summit. Finally reaching the open terrain of Signal Ridge at about 4.5 miles out, enjoy the many excellent views, particularly east across Carrigain Notch to Mount Lowell's cliffs. The ridge ascends easily to the summit observation tower. Return the same way you came.

User Groups: Hikers and dogs. No bikes, horses, or wheelchair facilities.

Permits: No backcountry permit is needed, but a permit is required for day use or overnight parking at any White Mountain National Forest trailhead. Permits are available at several area stores and from the national forest at a cost of $5 for seven consecutive days or $20 per year. A $3 one-day permit can be purchased at self-service stations at national forest trailheads, but the pass is good only for the trailhead at which it's purchased.

Maps: Two waterproof area trail maps available from the Appalachian Mountain Club show this hike (Franconia–Pemigewasset Range map and Crawford Notch–Sandwich Range/Moosilauke–Kinsman map, $9.95 each). For topographic area maps, request Mount Carrigain and Bartlett from the USGS.

Directions: From U.S. 302, 10.7 miles south of the visitor information center in Crawford Notch and 10.3 miles north of the junction of U.S. 302 and Route 16 in Glen, turn south onto Sawyer River Road/Fire Road 34. Follow it for two miles to the Signal Ridge Trail on the right, just before a bridge over Whiteface Brook. There is parking on the left, just past the brook. Sawyer River Road/Fire Road 34 is usually closed to vehicles once snow arrives. GPS Coordinates: 44.0704 N, 71.3841 W

Contact: White Mountain National Forest Headquarters, 71 White Mountain Drive, Campton, NH 03246, 603/536-6100, TDD for hearing impaired 603/536-3665, www.fs.fed.us/r9/white.

65 MOUNT STANTON
3 mi/2 hr

in the White Mountain National Forest between Bartlett and Glen

At just 1,716 feet above sea level, Mount Stanton offers open ledges with good views and the feel of a big mountain climb for relatively little work—just three miles and 1,000 feet of elevation gain. These factors make it a good hike for children or for a day when bad weather keeps you off the big mountains. The trail does have a few moderately steep stretches, but they are neither sustained nor very difficult; fit people could easily run up the path for a quick workout.

From the roadside trailhead marker, the moderately ascending trail curves in an almost serpentine-shaped route, heading west, north, east, north, and then west again all within its first mile. As the trail nears the Mount Stanton summit, you will see the open ledges to the left (south). Venture out on the ledges and you are on the brink of a 500-foot sheer drop, atop a cliff called White's Ledge (a wonderful technical rock climb for those with experience). You might see rock climbers reaching the top at this popular climbing area; be careful not to kick stones over the edge. The ledges offer broad views of the Saco River Valley. Follow the same route back.

User Groups: Hikers and dogs. No bikes, horses, or wheelchair facilities.

Permits: Parking and access are free.

Maps: A waterproof area trail map is available from the Appalachian Mountain Club (Crawford Notch–Sandwich Range/Moosilauke–Kinsman, $9.95). For a topographic area map, request North Conway West from the USGS.

Directions: From the junction of U.S. 302 and Highway 16 in Glen, drive on U.S. 302 west toward Bartlett for about two miles. Just before the covered bridge, turn right onto Covered Bridge Lane (there is a small sign high on a tree). Follow the paved road 0.2 mile and bear right onto Oak Ridge Drive. Almost immediately, make a sharp right turn onto Hemlock Drive, which is a dirt road for a short distance before becoming paved, and continue for 0.3 mile. Park by the trail sign on the road. The trail begins just uphill on the left side of the driveway near the trail sign.

GPS Coordinates: 44.0960 N, 71.2120 W

Contact: White Mountain National Forest Headquarters, 71 White Mountain Drive, Campton, NH 03246, 603/536-6100, TDD for hearing impaired 603/536-3665, www.fs.fed.us/r9/white.

66 MOUNT MOOSILAUKE: BEAVER BROOK TRAIL

7.6 mi/5.5 hr

in the White Mountain National Forest west of North Woodstock

A 4,802-foot massif in the southwest corner of the White Mountains, Mount Moosilauke is the western most of the range's 4,000-footers. Passing numerous cascades and scaling rough terrain on its way to an alpine summit with views spanning much of the White Mountains and west to the Green Mountains in Vermont and New York's Adirondacks, the Beaver Brook Trail is a steep, scenic trek to Moosilauke's top with a net climb of approximately 3,000 feet. The Beaver Brook Trail coincides with the Appalachian Trail (AT) for its entire length.

Leaving from the parking area on Route 112, the white-blazed AT/Beaver Brook Trail immediately pushes southwest in a sharp, sustained uphill climb as it runs parallel to the tumbling cascades of Beaver Brook; rock and wood steps, and iron rings help with the ascent. Leaving the brook near the one-mile mark, the trail levels out somewhat, passing a Dartmouth Outing Club shelter at 1.5 miles. And then at 1.9 miles, the relentless climb begins again as the trail skirts the edge of Joblidunk Ravine and runs just below the wooded shoulder known as Mount Blue (4,529 ft.). Emerging from the trees, the AT/Beaver Brook Trail comes to a junction with the Benton Trail. Here the AT/Beaver Brook Trail turns left, coinciding with the southbound Benton Trail for a nearly flat 0.4-mile walk to the summit. Hike back the way you came.

Special note: By shuttling two vehicles to the trailheads, this hike can be combined with the Glencliff Trail for a traverse of

Moosilauke via the Appalachian Trail (see the *Mount Moosilauke: Glencliff Trail* listing in this chapter).

User Groups: Hikers and dogs. No bikes, horses, or wheelchair facilities.

Permits: No backcountry permit is needed, but a permit is required for day use or overnight parking at any White Mountain National Forest trailhead. Permits are available at several area stores and from the national forest at a cost of $5 for seven consecutive days or $20 per year. A $3 one-day permit can be purchased at self-service stations at national forest trailheads, but the pass is good only for the trailhead at which it's purchased.

Maps: A waterproof area trail map is available from the Appalachian Mountain Club (Crawford Notch–Sandwich Range/Moosilauke–Kinsman, $9.95). For a topographic area map, request Mount Moosilauke from the USGS.

Directions: The Beaver Brook Trail, which coincides with the Appalachian Trail, begins from a parking lot along Route 112 at the height of land in Kinsman Notch, 6.2 miles west of North Woodstock and 4.8 miles south of the junction of Routes 112 and 116. GPS Coordinates: 44.0394 N, 71.7921 W

Contact: White Mountain National Forest Headquarters, 71 White Mountain Drive, Campton, NH 03246, 603/536-6100, TDD for hearing impaired 603/536-3665, www.fs.fed.us/r9/white.

67 MOUNT MOOSILAUKE: GLENCLIFF TRAIL

7.8 mi/5.5 hr

in the White Mountain National Forest north of Warren

The Glencliff Trail, a section of the white-blazed Appalachian Trail, offers a scenic, but steep route to the 4,802-foot summit of Mount Moosilauke, where an extensive alpine area offers panoramic views stretching across much of the White Mountains and west to

Vermont's Green Mountains and New York's Adirondacks. Leaving from Benton State Forest and taking a northeasterly approach to the pinnacle of the Moosilauke massif, this hike gains about 3,300 feet in elevation.

From the parking lot, follow the white blazes of the Appalachian Trail (AT) past a gate and along an old farm road. Entering the woods at 0.4 mile, immediately pass a small side path leading left to a Dartmouth College cabin (not open to the public) and a junction with the Hurricane Trail to the right. The AT/Glencliff Trail ascends steadily but at a moderate grade for the next two miles, then grows very steep as it rises into the mountain's krummholz, the scrub conifers that grow in the subalpine zone. At three miles, a spur path leads right (south) 0.2 mile to Moosilauke's craggy south peak, a worthwhile detour. This hike continues, meeting up almost immediately with the Moosilauke Carriage Road. Here, the AT/Glencliff Trail turns left (north) and follows the wide carriage road over easy ground along the open ridge—with great views—on its gentle ascent to the summit at 3.9 miles. Return the way you came. (For a full traverse of Moosilauke via the Appalachian Trail, see the *Mount Moosilauke: Beaver Brook Trail* listing.)

User Groups: Hikers and dogs. No bikes, horses, or wheelchair facilities. This trail should not be attempted in winter except by hikers experienced in mountaineering and prepared for severe winter weather, and is not suitable for skis.

Permits: No backcountry permit is needed, but a permit is required for day use or overnight parking at any White Mountain National Forest trailhead. Permits are available at several area stores and from the national forest at a cost of $5 for seven consecutive days or $20 per year. A $3 one-day permit can be purchased at self-service stations at national forest trailheads, but the pass is good only for the trailhead at which it's purchased.

Maps: A waterproof area trail map is available from the Appalachian Mountain Club (Crawford Notch–Sandwich Range/

Moosilauke–Kinsman, $9.95). For a topographic area map, request Mount Moosilauke from the USGS.

Directions: From Route 25 in Glencliff Village, turn onto High Street, just past the sign for the Glencliff Home for the Elderly. Drive 1.2 miles to a dirt parking lot on the right. GPS Coordinates: 43.9980 N, 71.8820 W

Contact: White Mountain National Forest Headquarters, 71 White Mountain Drive, Campton, NH 03246, 603/536-6100, TDD for hearing impaired 603/536-3665, www.fs.fed.us/r9/white.

68 MOUNT OSCEOLA
6.4 mi/4 hr   👫3 ⛰9

in the White Mountain National Forest north of Waterville Valley and east of Lincoln

One of the easiest 4,000-footers in New Hampshire to hike—with a vertical ascent of only about 2,000 feet—Osceola's summit ledges, rising 4,340 feet above sea level, give a sweeping view to the south and southeast of Waterville Valley and Mount Tripyramid, and northeast to the Pemigewasset Wilderness and the Presidential Range.

From the parking area on Tripoli Road, follow the Mount Osceola Trail as it ascends the mountain's Breadtray Ridge over somewhat rocky footing. A moderate climb with numerous switchbacks, the trail reaches a ledge overlook with a view of Sandwich Mountain at 2.1 miles and crosses a small brook at 2.3 miles. The switchbacks continue for the next mile as the trail ascends the ridge and reaches the summit ledges at 3.2 miles. To reach 4,156-foot East Osceola, follow the trail for one more mile, adding two miles and approximately 1.5 hours to this hike's distance and time. This hike returns along the same route.

User Groups: Hikers and dogs. No bikes, horses, or wheelchair facilities.

Permits: No backcountry permit is needed, but a permit is required for day use or overnight parking at any White Mountain National Forest trailhead. Permits are available at several area stores and from the national forest at a cost of $5 for seven consecutive days or $20 per year. A $3 one-day permit can be

© JACQUELINE TOURVILLE

Mount Osceola

purchased at self-service stations at national forest trailheads, but the pass is good only for the trailhead at which it's purchased.

Maps: Two waterproof area trail maps available from the Appalachian Mountain Club show this hike (Franconia–Pemigewasset Range map and Crawford Notch–Sandwich Range/Moosilauke–Kinsman map, $9.95 each). For topographic area maps, request Mount Osceola and Waterville Valley from the USGS.

Directions: From I-93, take Exit 31 for Tripoli Road. Drive east on Tripoli Road for seven miles to a parking lot on the left for the Mount Osceola Trail. Tripoli Road is generally not maintained in winter.

GPS Coordinates: 43.9834 N, 71.5588 W

Contact: White Mountain National Forest Headquarters, 71 White Mountain Drive, Campton, NH 03246, 603/536-6100, TDD for hearing impaired 603/536-3665, www. fs.fed.us/r9/white.

69 GREELEY PONDS NORTH
4.4 mi/2 hr 👫2 ⛰8

In the White Mountain National Forest on the Kancamagus Highway/Route 112 between Lincoln and Conway

This fairly flat 4.4-mile hike offers the shortest and easiest route to the Greeley Ponds, two pool-like bodies of water nestled at the bottom of Mad River Notch. With an elevation gain of only a few hundred feet, this is a pleasant hike for beginners and a fun one for kids—especially if you spot a moose or two taking a dip at these favorite watering holes.

From the parking area along the Kancamangus Highway, follow the Greeley Ponds Trail as it winds southward through a mixed deciduous and conifer forest. At 1.3 miles, the Mount Osceola Trail diverges to the right (east), soon to climb steeply up East Osceola and Osceola, a worthwhile side trip. This

hike continues south on the Greeley Ponds Trail for nearly another half mile to the upper Greeley Pond, which sits in a scenic basin below the dramatic cliffs of East Osceola. Continuing another half mile on the trail brings you to the lower pond. Return the way you came.

Camping and fires are prohibited within the Greeley Ponds Scenic Area, the boundary of which is marked by a sign along the trail.

User Groups: Hikers and dogs. No bikes, horses, or wheelchair facilities.

Permits: No backcountry permit is needed, but a permit is required for day use or overnight parking at any White Mountain National Forest trailhead. Permits are available at several area stores and from the national forest at a cost of $5 for seven consecutive days or $20 per year. A $3 one-day permit can be purchased at self-service stations at national forest trailheads, but the pass is good only for the trailhead at which it's purchased.

Maps: Two waterproof area trail maps from the Appalachian Mountain Club show this hike (Franconia–Pemigewasset Range map and Crawford Notch–Sandwich Range/Moosilauke–Kinsman map, $9.95 each). For topographic area maps, request the Mount Osceola, Mount Carrigain, Mount Tripyramid, and Waterville Valley maps from the USGS.

Directions: The hike begins at a small parking area along the Kancamagus Highway/Route 112, 9.9 miles east of the McDonald's on Route 112 in Lincoln (Exit 32 off I-93), 3.4 miles west of the sign at Kancamagus Pass and 25.6 miles west of the junction of Routes 112 and 16 in Conway.

GPS Coordinates: 44.0317 N, 71.5168 W

Contact: White Mountain National Forest Headquarters, 71 White Mountain Drive, Campton, NH 03246, 603/536-6100, TDD for hearing impaired 603/536-3665, www. fs.fed.us/r9/white.

70 GREELEY PONDS SOUTH
7.4 mi/4 hr

in Waterville Valley in the White Mountain National Forest

This popular 7.4-mile round-tripper from Waterville Valley leads to the two scenic Greeley Ponds on a route that is longer and with a bit more climb to it than the approach to the ponds from the north (see the *Greeley Ponds North* listing in the chapter). The total vertical ascent on this hike is about 700 feet.

From the parking lot on West Branch Road, follow the Livermore Trail for 0.25 mile, turning left at the sign for the Greeley Ponds Trail. (If you are here in winter, the trail is not groomed but is often packed and tracked by snowshoers and skiers, making it a good destination for a cold weather trek.) Flat at first and running parallel to the Mad River, the wide, well worn path passes a number of trail junctions in its first two miles as it makes its way into the notch. With the cliffs of Mount Osceola towering to the left and Mount Kancamagus looming to the right, the trail grows considerably steeper in the last 0.1 mile before reaching the lower Greeley Pond. After passing a short path that leads to different viewing points along the pond (a worthwhile detour), the trail crosses over the Mad River to its left bank. From here, it's another 0.5 mile to the upper pond. Return the way you came.

Camping and fires are prohibited within the Greeley Ponds Scenic Area, the boundary of which is marked by a sign along the trail.

User Groups: Hikers and dogs. No bikes, horses, or wheelchair facilities.

Permits: No backcountry permit is needed, but a permit is required for day use or overnight parking at any White Mountain National Forest trailhead. Permits are available at several area stores and from the national forest at a cost of $5 for seven consecutive days or $20 per year. A $3 one-day permit can be purchased at self-service stations at national

forest trailheads, but the pass is good only for the trailhead at which it's purchased.

Maps: Two waterproof area trail maps from the Appalachian Mountain Club show this hike (Franconia–Pemigewasset Range map and Crawford Notch–Sandwich Range/Moosilauke–Kinsman map, $9.95 each). For topographic area maps, request the Mount Osceola, Mount Carrigain, Mount Tripyramid, and Waterville Valley maps from the USGS.

Directions: From I-93 in Campton, take Exit 28 onto Route 49 east. Drive about 11.4 miles into Waterville Valley and turn right onto Valley Road, which is still Route 49. Just 0.4 mile farther, turn left onto West Branch Road, in front of the Osceola Library. Drive another 0.7 mile and turn right into the parking lot, just before the bridge.

GPS Coordinates: 43.9654 N, 71.5138 W

Contact: White Mountain National Forest Headquarters, 71 White Mountain Drive, Campton, NH 03246, 603/536-6100, TDD for hearing impaired 603/536-3665, www.fs.fed.us/r9/white.

71 CATHEDRAL LEDGE
0.1 mi/0.25 hr

in Echo Lake State Park west of North Conway

This is less of a hike than it is an easy, five-minute walk to the top of Cathedral Ledge, a sheer, 400-foot cliff with breathtaking views of North Conway and the surrounding mountains. Popular with tourists when the access road is open late spring–autumn, the lookout is protected by a fence to keep visitors from wandering too close to the brink. Cathedral is one of New Hampshire's most popular rock-climbing areas, so you're likely to see climbers pulling over the top of the cliff right in front of you. Obviously, you should not throw anything off the cliff, given the likelihood of there being people below.

From the parking circle at the end of the access road, look for the Cathedral Ledge sign

Cathedral Ledge

marker and follow the wide, obvious path as it leads a short distance through the woods to the top of the cliff. From this perch high above Echo Lake State Park, views take in Echo Lake almost directly below, the town of North Conway, and due east to the ski slopes of Cranmore Mountain and surrounding hills. Return the same way.

User Groups: Hikers and leashed dogs. No bikes, horses, or wheelchair facilities.

Permits: Parking and access are free.

Maps: Although no map is necessary for this hike, it is shown on the Crawford Notch–Sandwich Range/Moosilauke–Kinsman map, available from the Appalachian Mountain Club ($9.95, waterproof). For a topographic map of the area, request North Conway West from the USGS.

Directions: From Route 16 in North Conway in front of the Eastern Slope Inn, turn west at traffic lights onto River Road. Continue 1.5 miles and turn left at a sign for Cathedral Ledge. Follow the road for more than a mile

to its end at a circle near the cliff top. The access road is not maintained in winter and is blocked by a gate.

GPS Coordinates: 44.0628 N, 71.1672 W

Contact: New Hampshire Division of Parks and Recreation, P.O. Box 1856, 172 Pembroke Rd., Concord, NH 03302, 603/271-3556, camping reservations 603/271-3628, www.nhstateparks.org.

7.2 DIANA'S BATH

1.6 mi/1 hr 　　　　🏃1 ⛰9

in the White Mountain National Forest west of North Conway

BEST (

A bathtub fit for a goddess, Diana's Bath is a series of crashing cascades and swirling potholes formed by the rushing water of Lucy Brook. In spring, the water roars through in a can't-miss spectacle. But when levels drop somewhat in the heat of summer, the curiously circular potholes—the result of glacial erosion—transform into a number of surprisingly warm and very popular swimming holes. The trail to Diana's Bath is flat and accessible, making this a good destination for wheelchair hikers and others in need of a level walking surface.

From the fully accessible parking area, follow the level walkway 0.8 mile to Diana's Bath. Reaching the bath, different viewing points along the path lead to a 20-foot waterfall (definitely at its best in spring) as well as close-up looks at the cascades, naturally forming waterspouts, and the potholes. Future Forest Service plans for this path include the installation of an all-access vault style toilet at the trailhead and an extension of the walkway to more viewing points.

User Groups: Hikers, dogs, and wheelchairs. No bikes or horses.

Permits: No backcountry permit is needed, but a permit is required for day use or overnight parking at any White Mountain National Forest trailhead. Permits are available at several area stores and from the national forest at a cost of $5 for seven consecutive days or $20 per year. A $3 one-day permit can be purchased at self-service stations at national forest trailheads, but the pass is good only for the trailhead at which it's purchased.

Maps: A waterproof trail map is available from the Appalachian Mountain Club (Crawford Notch–Sandwich Range/Moosilauke–Kinsman, $9.95). For a topographic area map, request North Conway West from the USGS.

Directions: From Route 16 in North Conway, turn west at the traffic lights in front of the Eastern Slope Inn onto River Road. Continue about 2.2 miles to a large parking area on the left for Diana's Bath.

GPS Coordinates: 44.0716 N, 71.1701 W

Contact: White Mountain National Forest Headquarters, 71 White Mountain Drive, Campton, NH 03246, 603/536-6100, TDD for hearing impaired 603/536-3665, www.fs.fed.us/r9/white.

73 NORTH MOAT MOUNTAIN
8.4 mi/6 hr   🏃3 ⛰9

in the White Mountain National Forest west of North Conway

North Moat (3,196 ft.) is one of the finest summit hikes you can make in the White Mountains without going up a big peak. From North Moat on a clear day, the views extend due north as far as Mount Washington. A popular climb for visitors to the resort town of North Conway, this 8.4-mile round-trip nets an elevation gain of nearly 2,700 feet.

From the parking area for Diana's Bath on the left (west) side of the road, strike out on the North Moat Trail heading almost due west. A flat, well-trod path running parallel to Lucy Brook, at 1.5 miles, the trail takes a sharp left to begin the climb to the North Moat summit (the Attitash Trail continues straight ahead). It's a steady climb under forest cover for much of the way. The trail grows truly steep only in its last 0.5-mile push to

the rocky summit. Enjoy views east to the village of North Conway and north to the Saco River valley, Wildcat Mountain, and the soaring Mount Washington. Return the way you came.

User Groups: Hikers and dogs. No bikes, horses, or wheelchair facilities.

Permits: No backcountry permit is needed, but a permit is required for day use or overnight parking at any White Mountain National Forest trailhead. Permits are available at several area stores and from the national forest at a cost of $5 for seven consecutive days or $20 per year. A $3 one-day permit can be purchased at self-service stations at national forest trailheads, but the pass is good only for the trailhead at which it's purchased.

Maps: A waterproof trail map is available from the Appalachian Mountain Club (Crawford Notch–Sandwich Range/Moosilauke–Kinsman map, $9.95). For a topographic area map, request North Conway West from the USGS.

Directions: From Route 16 in North Conway, turn west at the traffic lights in front of the Eastern Slope Inn onto River Road. Continue about 2.2 miles to a large parking area on the left for Diana's Baths. The trail begins on the west side of the parking area.

GPS Coordinates: 44.0716 N, 71.1701 W

Contact: White Mountain National Forest Headquarters, 71 White Mountain Drive, Campton, NH 03246, 603/536-6100, TDD for hearing impaired 603/536-3665, www.fs.fed.us/r9/white.

74 ROCKY GORGE
0.5 mi/0.5 hr   🏃1 ⛰8

in the White Mountain National Forest on the Kancamagus Highway

This wheelchair-accessible trail leads to a dramatic gorge and picturesque pond formed by the aptly named Swift River. Rocky Gorge scenic area is also a popular picnic area and rest stop for travelers on the Kancamagus Highway. From the parking area, follow the paved path to a bridge just below the Swift River gorge. Across the bridge, the path narrows as it winds along the edge of the gorge to another viewing area (depending on ability, this may not be suitable for all wheelchair hikers). The path continues up a small ridge at an 8 percent grade to the top, where it crosses the Nanamocomuck Trail, then descends in a short section of 14 percent grade before arriving at Falls Pond and a hardened viewing area near the water's edge. There are benches for resting along the trail from the parking area to the pond. The total distance of the trail to Falls Pond is approximately 1,300 feet. Return the way you came.

Note: A second choice is to proceed from the parking lot and, instead of crossing the bridge, continuing on the hardened gravel trail as it follows the river. The level trail runs for approximately 1,000 feet before ending at a widened area with a beautiful view upstream back to the bridge. Return the way you came.

User Groups: Hikers, dogs, and wheelchairs. No bikes or horses.

Permits: No backcountry permit is needed, but a permit is required for day use or overnight parking at any White Mountain National Forest trailhead. Permits are available at several area stores and from the national forest at a cost of $5 for seven consecutive days or $20 per year. A $3 one-day permit can be purchased at self-service stations at national forest trailheads, but the pass is good only for the trailhead at which it's purchased.

Maps: Two waterproof area trail maps available from the Appalachian Mountain Club show this hike (Franconia–Pemigewasset Range map and Crawford Notch–Sandwich Range/Moosilauke–Kinsman map, $9.95 each). For a topographic area map, request Mount Tripyramid from the USGS.

Directions: The hike begins at the Rocky Gorge Scenic Area parking lot along the Kancamagus Highway/Route 112, 26 miles

east of Lincoln and approximately 10 miles west of the junction of Routes 16 and 112 (Kancamangus Highway) in Conway.

GPS Coordinates: 44.0072 N, 71.2753 W

Contact: White Mountain National Forest Headquarters, 71 White Mountain Drive, Campton, NH 03246, 603/536-6100, TDD for hearing impaired 603/536-3665, www.fs.fed.us/r9/white.

75 SABBADAY FALLS
0.8 mi/0.75 hr 👫1 ⛰10

in the White Mountain National Forest on the Kancamagus Highway

BEST (

The early explorers of the Passaconaway Valley reached Sabbaday Falls on a Sunday, and thereafter the spectacular falls became a popular destination on the Sabbath. Formed by the gouging action of rocks and sand released by glacial melt-off 10,000 years ago, the roaring falls drop twice through a narrow gorge so perfect in its geometry it seems the work of engineers. Below the gorge, Sabbaday Brook settles quietly, if briefly, in a clear pool. This easy hike is a great one for young children.

From the picnic area, follow the wide gravel and dirt Sabbaday Brook Trail, which parallels the rocky brook. The trail ascends very little over its first 0.3 mile to where a side path to the falls leads left. With the sound of rushing water growing thunderous, the path loops past the lower pool and above the gorge, crossing a bridge with nice views of the falls and back down to the pool; a handrail is located all along this stretch of the trail. Ascending a series of steps as it turns away from the gorge, the path rejoins the Sabbaday Brook Trail. Turn right to return to the parking area.

User Groups: Hikers and dogs. No bikes, horses, or wheelchair facilities.

Permits: No backcountry permit is needed, but a permit is required for day use or overnight parking at any White Mountain

National Forest trailhead. Permits are available at several area stores and from the national forest at a cost of $5 for seven consecutive days or $20 per year. A $3 one-day permit can be purchased at self-service stations at national forest trailheads, but the pass is good only for the trailhead at which it's purchased.

Maps: Two waterproof area trail maps available from the Appalachian Mountain Club show this hike (Franconia–Pemigewasset Range map and Crawford Notch–Sandwich Range/Moosilauke–Kinsman map, $9.95 each). For a topographic area map, request Mount Tripyramid from the USGS.

Directions: The hike begins at the Sabbaday Falls parking area along the Kancamagus Highway/Route 112, 19.9 miles east of the McDonald's on Route 112 in Lincoln, 6.6 miles east of the sign at Kancamagus Pass, and 15.6 miles west of the junction of Routes 112 and 16 in Conway.
GPS Coordinates: 43.9973 N, 71.3925 W
Contact: White Mountain National Forest Headquarters, 71 White Mountain Drive, Campton, NH 03246, 603/536-6100, TDD for hearing impaired 603/536-3665, www.fs.fed.us/r9/white.

🔢 MOUNT TRIPYRAMID
11 mi/7 hr

In the White Mountain National Forest east of Waterville Valley

Tripyramid's three wooded summits offer little in the way of compelling views, but the challenging scramble up and down Tripyramid's two rockslides and the fact that North Tripyramid (4,180 ft.) and Middle Tripyramid (4,140 ft.) are both official 4,000-footers are enough to make this a popular draw for hikers on the lookout for a more rugged mountain experience. The loop hike to all three summits ascends about 3,000 feet over its length and involves some exposed scrambling, especially

going up the north slide; it is not for the faint of heart or anyone not in good shape.

From the parking area, walk around the gate onto Livermore Road (also called the Livermore Trail), an old logging road that rises steadily 2.6 miles to the south end of the Mount Tripyramid Trail. To add extra flavor to this hike, mountain bike this stretch and stash your bike in the woods near the Mount Tripyramid trailhead. Turning right onto the Mount Tripyramid Trail from Livermore Road, the path begins its ascent up the mountain's exposed and steep north side. At 0.5 mile out from Livermore Road, the trail reaches the bottom of the slide and the real climb begins. Gaining 1,200 feet in elevation over the next 0.5 mile, the trail becomes almost vertical as it traverses the rock slabs; footing here can be treacherous when the rocks are wet or icy. Leveling out somewhat after such a strenuous push, the trail reaches North Tripyramid at 1.2 miles, with limited views. Stay on the narrow path as it leaves the summit, passing a junction with the Sabbaday Brook Trail 0.5 mile past the north peak and reaching Middle Tripyramid (4,140 ft.) 0.3 mile farther. A pair of outlooks just off the trail offer decent views. The trail continues to South Peak (4,090 ft.), which is wooded. Just beyond that peak, bear right to descend the steep south slide. Rocks here are loose and footing can be tricky. At the end of the slide, the trail enters the woods again and follows Slide Brook past nice pools to the Livermore Trail, 2.5 miles from South Peak. Turn right and hike (or bike) 3.6 miles back to the parking area.

User Groups: Hikers and dogs on the Mount Tripyramid Trail; hikers, dogs, and bikes on the Livermore Trail. No horses or wheelchair facilities. The Mount Tripyramid Trail should not be attempted in winter except by hikers experienced in mountaineering and prepared for severe winter weather.

Permits: No backcountry permit is needed, but a permit is required for day use or overnight parking at any White Mountain National Forest trailhead. Permits are available

at several area stores and from the national forest at a cost of $5 for seven consecutive days or $20 per year. A $3 one-day permit can be purchased at self-service stations at national forest trailheads, but the pass is good only for the trailhead at which it's purchased.

Maps: Two waterproof area trail maps available from the Appalachian Mountain Club show this hike (Franconia–Pemigewasset Range map and Crawford Notch–Sandwich Range/Moosilauke–Kinsman map, $9.95 each). For topographic area maps, request Mount Tripyramid and Waterville Valley from the USGS.

Directions: From I-93 in Campton, take Exit 28 onto Route 49 east. Drive about 11.4 miles into Waterville Valley and turn right onto Valley Road, which is still Route 49 east. Just 0.4 mile farther, turn left onto West Branch Road, in front of the Osceola Library. Drive another 0.7 mile and turn right (before the bridge) into the parking lot at the start of the Livermore Trail (also called the Livermore Road). In the winter months, you can ski or snowshoe up Livermore Trail, which is groomed and tracked for skating or diagonal skiing, without having to pay the trail fee for the cross-country ski touring center in Waterville Valley because Livermore Trail is within the national forest.

GPS Coordinates: 43.9834 N, 71.5588 W

Contact: White Mountain National Forest Headquarters, 71 White Mountain Drive, Campton, NH 03246, 603/536-6100, TDD for hearing impaired 603/536-3665, www.fs.fed.us/r9/white.

77 WELCH AND DICKEY

4.5 mi/3.5 hr

In the White Mountain National Forest southwest of Waterville Valley

BEST (

A delightful hike in July and August, this 4.5-mile loop over Welch (2,605 ft.) and Dickey (2,736 ft.) may best be saved for September or October when views from the mountains' many open ledges simply burst with autumn color. Relatively easy, with just a few brief, steep stretches, it's a good hike for children, entailing only about 1,700 feet of uphill over 4.5 miles.

From the parking area, pick up the Welch Mountain Trail (views are best when hiking this loop counterclockwise). Within a mile, the trail emerges onto open ledges just below the summit of Welch Mountain, with a wide view across the Mad River Valley to Sandwich Mountain. During peak fall foliage season, the vista here will be ablaze with yellow, orange, and red. The trail turns left and ascends another mile to the summit, with broad views in every direction, including Dickey Mountain to the north. Continuing on the trail, you drop steeply into a shallow saddle, then climb up onto Dickey, a half mile from Welch. Watch for a sign pointing to nearby ledges, where there is a good view toward Franconia Notch. From Dickey's summit, follow an arrow onto an obvious trail north, which soon descends steeply to slab ledges above the cliffs of Dickey Mountain, overlooking a beautiful, narrow valley between Welch and Dickey that lights up with color in the fall. The Dickey Mountain Trail continues descending the ridge, re-entering the woods, then reaching the parking area, two miles from Dickey's summit.

User Groups: Hikers and dogs. No bikes, horses, or wheelchair facilities.

Permits: No backcountry permit is needed, but a permit is required for day use or overnight parking at any White Mountain National Forest trailhead. Permits are available at several area stores and from the national forest at a cost of $5 for seven consecutive days or $20 per year. A $3 one-day permit can be purchased at self-service stations at national forest trailheads, but the pass is good only for the trailhead at which it's purchased.

Maps: Two waterproof area trail maps from the Appalachian Mountain Club show this hike (Franconia–Pemigewasset Range map and Crawford Notch–Sandwich Range/

Moosilauke–Kinsman map, $9.95 each). For a topographic area map, request Waterville Valley from the USGS.

Directions: From I-93 in Campton, take Exit 28 onto Route 49 north, toward Waterville Valley. After passing through the traffic lights in Campton, drive another 4.4 miles on Route 49, then turn left onto Upper Mad River Road, immediately crossing the Mad River on Six Mile Bridge. Continue 0.7 mile from Route 49, then turn right onto Orris Road at a small sign reading Welch Mountain Trail. Drive another 0.7 mile to a parking area on the right.

GPS Coordinates: 43.9038 N, 71.5886 W

Contact: White Mountain National Forest Headquarters, 71 White Mountain Drive, Campton, NH 03246, 603/536-6100, TDD for hearing impaired 603/536-3665, www. fs.fed.us/r9/white.

🔢 SANDWICH MOUNTAIN
8.3 mi/5.5 hr

in Waterville Valley in the White Mountain National Forest

At 3,993 feet, Sandwich Mountain is a tad short to attract the same attention among hikers as many of the 4,000-footers in the White Mountains. But from the small area of rocks jutting just above the forest at its summit, you get a wide view from the northwest to the east of most of the White Mountains—certainly more peaks are visible from here than from many of the smaller 4,000-footers in the Whites. This loop over Sandwich Mountain can be done in either direction—the hike in this description follows a clockwise route and nets 2,500 feet in elevation gain.

From the north end of the parking lot, pick up the Drake's Brook Trail. Follow the old logging road for 0.4 mile, bearing right to stay on the trail where a junction is reached with a bike path. The trail then crosses Drake's Brook (difficult during times of high water)

and runs parallel to the brook for the next 2.5 miles before finally swinging to the right and climbing a steep 0.3 mile to a junction with the Sandwich Mountain Trail (SMT). Turn left on the SMT and continue on 1.1 miles to the summit, breaking out of the spruce forest to spectacular views of Waterville Valley in the near foreground, including the peaks surrounding it (from left to right): Tecumseh, Osceola, and Tripyramid, with its south slide visible. To the east, the view encompasses the broad ridge connecting Whiteface, Passaconaway, and Chocorua's bald knob beyond. Massive Mount Moosilauke dominates the horizon to the west. The high Franconia Ridge rises above everything else in the distant northwest. And to the northeast, the biggest peaks in the Whites, Mount Washington and the Presidential Range, are clearly visible. Behind you, look for a somewhat hidden footpath through scrub trees that leads a few feet to a view south toward the Lakes Region. Descend the Sandwich Mountain Trail for 3.9 miles back to the parking area.

User Groups: Hikers and dogs. No bikes, horses, or wheelchair facilities.

Permits: No backcountry permit is needed, but a permit is required for day use or overnight parking at any White Mountain National Forest trailhead. Permits are available at several area stores and from the national forest at a cost of $5 for seven consecutive days or $20 per year. A $3 one-day permit can be purchased at self-service stations at national forest trailheads, but the pass is good only for the trailhead at which it's purchased.

Maps: Two waterproof area trail maps from the Appalachian Mountain Club show this hike (Franconia–Pemigewasset Range map and Crawford Notch–Sandwich Range/ Moosilauke–Kinsman map, $9.95 each). For topographic area maps, request the Waterville Valley and Mount Tripyramid maps from the USGS.

Directions: From Exit 28 off I-93 in Campton, take Route 49 north for about 10.2 miles and turn right into a parking lot for the Drake's Brook and Sandwich Mountain Trails.

GPS Coordinates: 43.9379 N, 71.5116 W
Contact: White Mountain National Forest Headquarters, 71 White Mountain Drive, Campton, NH 03246, 603/536-6100, TDD for hearing impaired 603/536-3665, www.fs.fed.us/r9/white.

79 MOUNT WHITEFACE
8.2 mi/5.5 hr   🏃4 ▲9

in the southern White Mountain National Forest north of Wonalancet

Whiteface, at 4,010 feet, is not among the best-known 4,000-footers in the Whites, but the cliffs just below its summit offer dramatic views of the southern Whites, Mount Washington, and the Lakes Region to the south. Come here in September and early October to see the surrounding woods lit with color. This climb's vertical ascent is approximately 3,800 feet. (For a longer loop linking Whiteface with Passaconaway, see the *Mount Passaconaway* listing in this chapter.)

From the parking lot, walk back to the road and turn right, following the road for 0.3 mile to the Blueberry Ledge trailhead (marked). At first following a single-lane dirt road, the trail crosses a bridge over Wonalancet Brook and continues on to where it enters the woods. Now a footpath, the Blueberry Ledge Trail remains a fairly level trek until reaching slab ledges at 1.5 miles from the parking lot. For the next two miles, the route grows increasingly steep. Good views south to the lakes region begin at 3.6 miles, where the Blueberry Ledge Trail turns sharply right at a slab and the brink of a cliff. This can be a hazardous spot when wet or icy; on a winter hike, you might want the security of roping up and belaying this section. Continue up the Blueberry Ledge Trail for another 0.3 mile; you will pass ledges with terrific views down into the broad glacial cirque known as the Bowl (which is framed by Whiteface and neighboring Mount Passaconaway), east to Mount Chocorua, and

north to Mount Washington. At 3.9 miles, rear right at a trail junction onto the Rollins Trail, following it 0.2 mile to the wooded summit of Whiteface. Descend along the same route.
User Groups: Hikers and dogs. No bikes, horses, or wheelchair facilities.
Permits: No backcountry permit is needed, but a permit is required for day use or overnight parking at any White Mountain National Forest trailhead. Permits are available at several area stores and from the national forest at a cost of $5 for seven consecutive days or $20 per year. A $3 one-day permit can be purchased at self-service stations at national forest trailheads, but the pass is good only for the trailhead at which it's purchased.
Maps: A waterproof area trail map is available from the Appalachian Mountain Club (Crawford Notch–Sandwich Range/Moosilauke–Kinsman, $9.95). For topographic area maps, request Mount Chocorua and Mount Tripyramid from the USGS.
Directions: From Route 113A in Wonalancet, turn north onto Ferncroft Road. Follow it for a half mile and bear right at a sign into the hiker parking lot. Trails in this part of the national forest are accessed through private land; be sure to stay on trails.
GPS Coordinates: 43.9128 N, 71.3653 W
Contact: Wonalancet Out Door Club, HCR 64 Box 248, Wonalancet, NH 03897, www.wodc.org. White Mountain National Forest Headquarters, 71 White Mountain Drive, Campton, NH 03246, 603/536-6100, TDD for hearing impaired 603/536-3665, www.fs.fed.us/r9/white.

80 MOUNT PASSACONAWAY
9.5 mi/6.5 hr   🏃5 ▲8

in the southern White Mountain National Forest north of Wonalancet

Mount Passaconaway (4,060 ft.) is wooded, with no views (unless you're here in winter and standing on several feet of snow to see over the low spruce trees). But there are two nice views near the summit that make this mountain, named for the famed Penacook leader, Chief Passaconaway, worth the effort. The trails are marked with blue blazes and the vertical ascent is about 3,800 feet.

From the parking lot, walk back to the road and turn right, following the road for 0.8 mile straight onto the Dicey's Mill Trail. Soon after entering the woods, the trail crosses into the national forest. It parallels and eventually crosses Wonalancet Brook at 2.3 miles (0.4 mile beyond the Wiggin Trail junction), then begins ascending more steeply. The trail passes the junction with the Rollins Trail, which comes in from the left (west) at 3.7 miles, and then passes the East Loop Trail at 3.9 miles. At around 4.5 miles, you'll get a view toward the peaks above Waterville Valley to the northwest. The junction with the Walden Trail is reached at 4.6 miles; from there, a spur path leads to the right about 50 yards to Passaconaway's summit. Follow the Walden Trail around the summit cone about 100 yards to the best view on this hike, from a ledge overlooking Mount Chocorua to the east and Mount Washington to the north. Continue descending the Walden Trail, dropping steeply to the East Loop, 0.6 mile from the summit spur path. Turn right (west) on the East Loop, which leads 0.2 mile back to the Dicey's Mill Trail. Turn left (south) and follow that trail 3.9 miles back to the Ferncroft Road parking area.

Special note: You can combine Passaconaway and Mount Whiteface on a rugged loop of nearly 12 miles, with more than 4,600 feet of climbing. Hike the Blueberry Ledge Trail up Whiteface, then the Rollins Trail for 2.3 miles over the high ridge connecting the two peaks; there are some views along the Rollins, though much of it is within the subalpine conifer forest. Turn left (north) on the Dicey's Mill Trail and then complete the Passaconaway hike described in this listing.

Camping is permitted on the hardened ground at the former site of the Camp Rich shelter, near the junction of the Rollins and Dicey's Mill Trails. See the Wonalancet Out Door Club website (www.wodc.org) for current information.

User Groups: Hikers and dogs. No bikes, horses, or wheelchair facilities.

Permits: No backcountry permit is needed, but a permit is required for day use or overnight parking at any White Mountain National Forest trailhead. Permits are available at several area stores and from the national forest at a cost of $5 for seven consecutive days or $20 per year. A $3 one-day permit can be purchased at self-service stations at national forest trailheads, but the pass is good only for the trailhead at which it's purchased.

Maps: A waterproof trail map is available from the Appalachian Mountain Club (Crawford Notch–Sandwich Range/Moosilauke–Kinsman, $9.95). For topographic area maps, request Mount Chocorua and Mount Tripyramid from the USGS.

Directions: From Route 113A in Wonalancet, turn north onto Ferncroft Road. Follow it for a half mile and bear right at a sign into the hiker parking lot. Trails in this part of the national forest are accessed through private land; be sure to stay on the path.

GPS Coordinates: 43.9147 N, 71.3659 W

Contact: Wonalancet Out Door Club, HCR 64 Box 248, Wonalancet, NH 03897, www.wodc.org. White Mountain National Forest Headquarters, 71 White Mountain Drive, Campton, NH 03246, 603/536-6100, TDD for hearing impaired 603/536-3665, www.fs.fed.us/r9/white.

81 MOUNT CHOCORUA: BROOK-LIBERTY LOOP

7.4 mi/5 hr   4 ⚠10

in the White Mountain National Forest north of Tamworth and east of Wonalancet

The eye-catching eastern end of the Sandwich Range, Chocorua's distinctive horn-shaped

the great horn of Mount Chocorua

© MATT SINGER

summit cone makes this 3,500-foot peak a natural draw for visitors. Some come just to stand in the parking lot and snap photos of this "mini Alp," but during peak hiking season, Chocorua is one of the most traveled mountains in New Hampshire. The intent of this loop is to get away from the crowds (as much as possible) for a more solitary experience of Chocorua's splendor. This hike climbs about 2,600 feet in elevation.

This hike ascends via the Brook Trail, which is steep, and descends via the Liberty Trail, known as the easiest route on Chocorua. (Hikers looking for a less demanding route could opt to go up and down the Liberty Trail.) From the parking area, walk past the gate and follow the gravel woods road, which the Brook Trail leaves within a half mile. The trail passes a small waterfall along Claybank Brook less than two miles up and after some easy to moderately-difficult hiking, emerges from the woods onto the bare rock of Chocorua's summit cone at three miles. The trail's final 0.6 mile ascends steep slabs and ledges; the Liberty Trail coincides with the Brook Trail for the last 0.2 mile to

the top. Open summit views stretch north to Mount Washington, west across the White Mountains, south to the lakes region, and east over the hills and lakes of western Maine. To descend, follow the two trails down for that 0.2 mile, and then bear left onto the Liberty Trail. It traverses somewhat rocky ground high on the mountain, passing the U.S. Forest Service's Jim Liberty cabin within a half mile. The descent grows more moderate, eventually following an old bridle path back to the parking area, 3.8 miles from the summit.

The U.S. Forest Service maintains the Jim Liberty cabin (which has a capacity of nine) on the Liberty Trail, a half mile below Chocorua's summit; a fee is charged and the water source is unreliable in dry seasons. Contact the White Mountain National Forest for rate and reservation information.

User Groups: Hikers and dogs. No bikes, horses, or wheelchair facilities.

Permits: No backcountry permit is needed, but a permit is required for day use or overnight parking at any White Mountain National Forest trailhead. Permits are available

at several area stores and from the national forest at a cost of $5 for seven consecutive days or $20 per year. A $3 one-day permit can be purchased at self-service stations at national forest trailheads, but the pass is good only for the trailhead at which it's purchased.

Maps: A waterproof area trail map is available from the Appalachian Mountain Club (Crawford Notch–Sandwich Range/Moosilauke–Kinsman, $9.95). For topographic area maps, request Mount Chocorua and Silver Lake from the USGS.

Directions: From the junction of Routes 113 and 113A in Tamworth, drive west on Route 113A for 3.4 miles and turn right onto the dirt Howler's Mill Road. Continue for 1.2 miles and turn left (at trail signs) onto Paugus Road/Fire Road 68. The parking area and trailhead lie 0.8 mile up the road.

GPS Coordinates: 43.9174 N, 71.2932 W

Contact: White Mountain National Forest Headquarters, 71 White Mountain Drive, Campton, NH 03246, 603/536-6100, TDD for hearing impaired 603/536-3665, www.fs.fed.us/r9/white.

82 MOUNT CHOCORUA: PIPER TRAIL

9 mi/6.5 hr   4 ⚠10

In the White Mountain National Forest north of Chocorua and west of Conway

This is the most heavily used route up the popular, 3,500-foot Mount Chocorua, though at nine miles for the round-trip, it is not the shortest. The trail suffers from erosion due to overuse, which can make the footing difficult in places. This hike nets an elevation gain of 2,700 feet.

From the parking area, the trail starts out on easy ground, entering the woods. About two miles out, it crosses the Chocorua River and ascends in switchbacks up the mountainside. At 3.1 miles, a short side path leads to the Camp Penacook shelter and tent sites. The

final half mile of trail passes over open ledges with sweeping views and on to the summit, where the panoramic views take in Mount Washington to the north, New Hampshire's Lakes Region to the south, the hills and lakes of western Maine to the east, and the grand sweep of the White Mountains to the west and northwest. Views here are especially pleasing in early fall. Descend the same trail.

The national forest maintains Camp Penacook, which consists of a lean-to shelter and four tent platforms, 3.1 miles up the Piper Trail and 1.4 miles below Chocorua's summit; there is no fee.

User Groups: Hikers and dogs. No bikes, horses, or wheelchair facilities.

Permits: No backcountry permit is needed, but a permit is required for day use or overnight parking at any White Mountain National Forest trailhead. Permits are available at several area stores and from the national forest at a cost of $5 for seven consecutive days or $20 per year. A $3 one-day permit can be purchased at self-service stations at national forest trailheads, but the pass is good only for the trailhead at which it's purchased.

Maps: A waterproof area trail map is available from the Appalachian Mountain Club (Crawford Notch–Sandwich Range/Moosilauke–Kinsman, $9.95). For topographic area maps, request Mount Chocorua and Silver Lake from the USGS.

Directions: The Piper Trail begins behind the Piper Trail Restaurant and Cabins on Route 16 between the towns of Chocorua and Conway, six miles south of the junction of Route 16 and Route 112/Kancamagus Highway. Follow the dirt road to the right of the store for a quarter mile to the trailhead parking area.

GPS Coordinates: 43.9312 N, 71.2243 W

Contact: White Mountain National Forest Headquarters, 71 White Mountain Drive, Campton, NH 03246, 603/536-6100, TDD for hearing impaired 603/536-3665, www.fs.fed.us/r9/white.

83 MOUNT ISRAEL

4.2 mi/2.5 hr   👥3 ▲8

in the southern White Mountain National Forest northwest of Center Sandwich

Just 2,630 feet high, Mount Israel's summit ledges have nice views of the entire Sandwich Range to the north and Mount Moosilauke to the west. Considering the hike's relatively easy access and the ascent of just 1,600 feet, this should be one of the most popular climbs in the area. But Mount Israel is one scenic summit that is definitely overlooked; you may share the mountain with only a few other hikers, even in peak season.

From the Mead Base Camp parking area, pass to the left of the main Mead Base building and pick up the Wentworth Trail, which is marked by a sign. The trail climbs steadily up the mountain's southern slope, keeping the grade reduced by a number of sweeping switchbacks. At 1.5 miles, the trail reaches a good overlook south to the Lakes Region. Approximately two miles from the start of this hike, the trail emerges at the summit ledges and a wide view of the Sandwich Range (from left to right): Sandwich Mountain, Tripyramid, Whiteface with a cliff near its summit, Passaconaway immediately behind and to the right of Whiteface, and Chocorua far to the right, barely within sight. From a nearby ledge, you can look west to Moosilauke. Descend the way you came.

User Groups: Hikers and dogs. No bikes, horses, or wheelchair facilities.

Permits: No backcountry permit is needed, but a permit is required for day use or overnight parking at any White Mountain National Forest trailhead. Permits are available at several area stores and from the national forest at a cost of $5 for seven consecutive days or $20 per year. A $3 one-day permit can be purchased at self-service stations at national forest trailheads, but the pass is good only for the trailhead at which it's purchased.

Maps: A waterproof trail map is available from the Appalachian Mountain Club (Crawford Notch–Sandwich Range/Moosilauke–Kinsman, $9.95). For topographic area maps, request Squam Mountains and Center Sandwich from the USGS.

Directions: From Route 113 in Center Sandwich, turn onto Grove Street at a sign for Sandwich Notch. At 0.4 mile, bear left on Diamond Ledge Road (don't be deceived by the name of the road bearing right—Mount Israel Road). At 2.5 miles from Route 113, bear right at a sign for Mead Base Camp. Follow that road another mile to its end at Mead Base Camp and parking on the right. GPS Coordinates: 43.8257 N, 71.4838 W

Contact: White Mountain National Forest Headquarters, 71 White Mountain Drive, Campton, NH 03246, 603/536-6100, TDD for hearing impaired 603/536-3665, www.fs.fed.us/r9/white. Squam Lakes Association, P.O. Box 204, Holderness, NH 03245, 603/968-7336, www.squamlakes.org.

84 STINSON MOUNTAIN

3.6 mi/2.5 hr   👥2 ▲8

north of Rumney in the White Mountain National Forest

Tucked away in the very southwestern corner of the White Mountain National Forest is little Stinson Mountain (2,900 ft.), a small mountain with a great summit view of the valley of the Baker River, the state college town of Plymouth, and the surrounding hills. It's a nice spot to catch the sunrise or foliage at its peak. This hike ascends 1,400 feet in a 1.8-mile uphill jaunt.

Follow the Stinson Mountain Trail, which begins quite easily, then grows moderately steep but never very difficult. Within a quarter mile the trail crosses an old logging road and in a half mile it bears right where an old wooden footbridge leads left on a former trail. Although the trail is generally an easy, wide, and obvious path, be careful not to be fooled into these wrong turns. Within a hundred yards of the summit, or 1.8 miles from the trailhead, the trail forks, with both branches leading to the summit ledges. Trees block the view somewhat from the summit, but immediately north of the summit ledges, a side path leads 200 feet to good views of Stinson Lake and the Moosilauke massif. Return the way you came.

User Groups: Hikers and dogs. No bikes, horses, or wheelchair facilities.

Permits: No backcountry permit is needed, but a permit is required for day use or overnight parking at any White Mountain National Forest trailhead. Permits are available at several area stores and from the national forest at a cost of $5 for seven consecutive days or $20 per year. A $3 one-day permit can be purchased at self-service stations at national forest trailheads, but the pass is good only for the trailhead at which it's purchased.

Maps: A waterproof area trail map is available from the Appalachian Mountain Club (Crawford Notch–Sandwich Range/Moosilauke–Kinsman, $9.95). For a topographic area map, request Rumney from the USGS.

Directions: From Route 25 in Rumney Village (3.5 miles north of the traffic circle at Routes 25 and 3A, 2.1 miles north of the Polar Caves Park, 7.7 miles west of I-93 Exit 26, and 4.2 miles south of the junction of Routes 25 and 118), turn at a blinking yellow light onto Main Street. In a mile, the street becomes Stinson Lake Road. At 5.1 miles from Route 25, bear right on Cross Road at a sign for Hawthorne Village. In 0.3 mile, bear right onto a gravel road, then drive another half mile and turn right at a sign for the Stinson Mountain Trail. Drive 0.3 mile farther to parking on the left and a trail sign.

GPS Coordinates: 43.8528 N, 71.7991 W

Contact: White Mountain National Forest Headquarters, 71 White Mountain Drive, Campton, NH 03246, 603/536-6100, TDD for hearing impaired 603/536-3665, www.fs.fed.us/r9/white.

THE LAKES REGION AND SOUTH

© THOMAS L. JEANNE

BEST HIKES

❰ Bird-Watching
Great Bay National Estuarine Research Reserve,
   page 121.

❰ Fall Foliage
Mount Monadnock: White Dot Trail, **page 126.**

❰ Summit Hikes
Mount Cardigan: West Side Loop, **page 115 .**

The sky-high peaks of the northern White Mountains may stand out as the Granite State's star attraction, but for smaller summits in the lower half of New Hampshire – regional favorites such as Monadnock, Cardigan, Kearsarge, Sunapee, Major, and Smarts – the beauty is in the details. This is the land of rolling countryside, lakeside cliffs, and proudly isolated summits. Leaving behind the predominant conifer cover found in the northern part of the state, the deciduous forest of maples, beech, oaks, and birch found so abundantly here provide treks with a backdrop of ever-changing color. Lime green in June and lush blue in summer, the landscape gradually heats up to an autumn fire of red, orange, and golden yellow.

Southern New Hampshire is also home to the state's 18-mile-long seacoast (the shortest stretch of seaboard located within the boundaries of one state). Shoehorned between Massachusetts and Maine, New Hampshire's coastal area offers sandy beaches and rocky shoreline, but the heart of this region is found in the tidal estuaries that form a great inland bay. Hikes around aptly named Great Bay take you to a unique marine environment where fertile fields and freshwater rivers meet salt marshes and coastal tides.

Along the coast, as well as in the rest of the southern and central portions of the state – from hills along the Appalachian Trail in the Upper Connecticut Valley and the scenic Lakes Region to magnificent Mount Monadnock and wooded rambles along the Massachusetts border – access to the outdoors is easy to come by. Almost 85 percent of New Hampshire is forest-covered and state parks, town forests, and private reserves liberally scattered throughout the region offer countless miles of hiking trails, reclaimed railroad tracks, and old logging roads. Two long-distance trails in southern New Hampshire – the 21-mile Wapack Trail and the 50-mile Monadnock-Sunapee Greenway – offer scenic hiking over hills that see far fewer boots than popular corners of the Whites.

Along the Appalachian Trail in New Hampshire (Moose Mountain, Smarts Mountain, and Holt's Ledge in this chapter), dogs must be under verbal or physical restraint at all times. Hikers should carry a leash not longer than 6 feet and be prepared to leash a dog quickly if conditions warrant. Horses, bikes, hunting, and firearms are prohibited. Cross-country skiing and showshoeing are allowed on the Appalachian Trail, though the trail is often too rugged for skiing.

In most state parks and forests, dogs are allowed, but must remain leashed; private reserves and land conservancies often prohibit pets. The woods throughout much of the region are populated by an assortment of deer, beaver, fox, fisher cats, wild turkey, water fowl, and even a few reclusive brown bears and moose. Most state parks and forests allow certain types of hunting in season and hikers will need to take appropriate precautions in the woods at these times. The prime, snow-free hiking season in southern New Hampshire generally runs from April or May through mid-November.

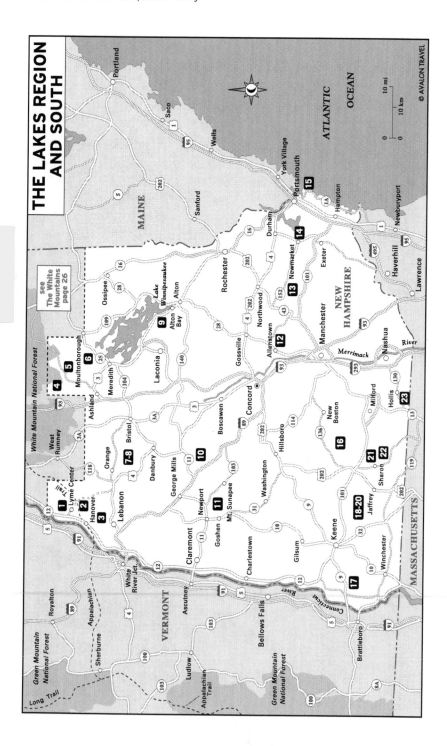

THE LAKES REGION AND SOUTH

© AVALON TRAVEL

❶ SMARTS MOUNTAIN
8.2 mi/3.5 hr

in Lyme

A popular hike for students from nearby Dartmouth College and one of the first summits encountered along the New Hampshire stretch of the northbound Appalachian Trail, Smarts (3,240 ft.) blends a walk in the woods and along the rocky crest of a ridge with a rigorous push to the summit. Though mostly wooded at the top, an abandoned fire tower can still be climbed and is what makes the finish of this hike so spectacular. On a clear day, panoramic views take in the upper Connecticut Valley, the nearby Green Mountains, and north to more rugged peaks (Smarts is actually an isolated southern summit of the White Mountains). From the trailhead, this hike offers a net elevation gain of about 2,100 feet.

Near the entrance to the parking area, pick up the white-blazed Lambert Ridge Trail at the large trail marker (this is also the Appalachian Trail). An unmarked wide path seen at the end of the lot is the Ranger Trail, your route of descent. The hike starts as a slightly steep trek through mixed woods, with several switchbacks helping to reduce the grade. At 0.3 mile, the trail begins the ascent up rocky Lambert Ridge—itself a nice destination for a short hike. For the next 1.3 miles, tree cover thins and views become frequent. The trail then drops slightly, changes direction a few times—watch for white blazes—and ascends the relentlessly steep west slope of Smarts, passing an unmarked junction with the Ranger Trail at 3.5 miles from the parking lot. Here, you will also notice the beech and maple trees giving way to a boreal forest of firs and evergreen (the only boreal forest found this far south in New Hampshire). A half-mile more and you've reached the mountain's flat, wooded summit. Continue on for another 0.1 mile, watching on the left for a spur trail to the fire tower. Another summit spur trail leads to a tent camping site. Return to the parking area by backtracking 0.6 mile to the trail junction and bearing left for the 3.5-mile descent along the more moderately graded Ranger Trail.

A hiker takes in the view from Smarts Mountain.

User Groups: Hikers and dogs. No horses, mountain bikes, or wheelchair facilities.

Permits: Parking and access are free.

Maps: Local trail maps are available from the Dartmouth Outing Club (including a three-color, double-sided map covering a 75-mile section of the AT from Route 12 in Woodstock, VT, to Route 112 in Woodstock, NH, $2). For a topographic map, request Smarts Mountain from the USGS.

Directions: From Route 10 on the Green in Lyme, take Dorchester Road (at the white church), following signs for the Dartmouth Skiway. Two miles from the Green, you'll pass through the village of Lyme Center. Continue for another 1.3 miles and then bear left onto the gravel Lyme-Dorchester Road. Follow for 1.8 miles. Just before an iron bridge over Grant Brook, park in a small lot on the left, at the trailhead.

GPS Coordinates: 43.7971 N, 72.0719 W

Contact: Appalachian Trail Conference, 799 Washington St., P.O. Box 807, Harpers Ferry, WV 25425-0807, 304/535-6331, www.appalachiantrail.org. Dartmouth Outdoor Programs Office, 119 Robinson Hall, Dartmouth College, Hanover, NH 03755, 603/646-2834, www.dartmouth.edu/~doc.

2 HOLT'S LEDGE
2.4 mi/1.5 hr 🏃2 ⛰8

in Lyme

Holt's Ledge, at the top of a tall, rugged cliff, lies at the end of a fairly short and easy walk along the Appalachian Trail. On a clear day, the views from this high perch (2,100 ft.) are expansive: Smarts Mountain, Mount Cube, and Mounts Cardigan and Kearsarge are seen to the north and east; to the south, Vermont's Ascutney rises in the distance. The total elevation gain for this hike is 1,000 feet.

To pick up this stretch of the Appalachian Trail (AT), leave the Dartmouth Skiway parking area and walk 0.1 mile back towards Dorchester Road. Find the white-blazed AT on the left (west) side of the road. Beginning as a gentle ascent south through mixed woods, the trail crosses over a stone wall and a double-rut access road before reaching a trail junction at 0.6 mile. Here, a blue-blazed spur trail leads to the Trapper John shelter, an AT lean-to named for the character on the TV Show *MASH* (Dr. John McIntyre supposedly went to Dartmouth College). Continue on the AT and as the climb becomes a steeper ascent up the hillside, another junction is reached at 1.1 miles. To reach the open ledges, leave the AT and turn left onto an orange-black-orange-blazed side trail leading 0.1 mile to the cliff's scenic overlook. Descend along the same route.

Special Note: Hikers on the ledge will notice a weathered fence at the edge of the cliff. There not only to keep people away from a rather precipitous drop, the fence also protects the privacy of peregrine falcons nesting just below. In the 1970s, pesticide contamination ravaged populations of the majestic bird in New England (exposure to DDT caused falcon eggs to thin and break). Holt's Ledge was one of the first sites in the state where peregrines were successfully reintroduced and today remains one of the region's most popular nesting grounds.

User Groups: Hikers and dogs. No bikes, horses, or wheelchair facilities.

Permits: Parking and access are free.

Maps: Local trail maps are available from the Dartmouth Outing Club (including a three-color, double-sided map covering a 75-mile section of the AT from Route 12 in Woodstock, VT, to Route 112 in Woodstock, NH, $2). For a topographic map, request Smarts Mountain from the USGS.

Directions: From Route 10 on the Green in Lyme, take Dorchester Road (at the white church), following signs for the Dartmouth Skiway. Two miles from the Green, you'll pass through the village of Lyme Center. In another 1.3 miles, bear right at the fork in the road and drive 0.1 mile to the Dartmouth Skiway parking area.

GPS Coordinates: 43.7924 N, 72.1031 W
Contact: Dartmouth Outdoor Programs Office, 119 Robinson Hall, Dartmouth College, Hanover, NH 03755, 603/646-2834, www.dartmouth.edu/~doc.

3 MOOSE MOUNTAIN

4.1 mi/2 hr

in Hanover

Twin-peaked Moose Mountain rises 2,290 feet along the northeastern edge of Hanover, a quaint Upper Valley town and, most notably, the home of Dartmouth College. Passing over the higher of Moose's two summits (south summit), this loop hike uses the Appalachian Trail (AT) for its ascent. For not much effort, surprisingly open views can be had to the east and southeast, taking in Goose Pond (in the foreground) and Clark Pond (in the distance) in the town of Canaan, and Mounts Cardigan and Kearsarge even farther in the distance. The hike to south summit climbs just under 1,000 feet.

From the parking area along Three Mile Road, cross the road heading east and pick up the white-blazed AT at the large sign marker. The trail fords a brook and then crosses the wide, two-track Harris Trail (at 0.4 mile). The AT then begins the ascent of Moose Mountain, climbing at a moderate angle at first, leveling somewhat, then climbing again to the south summit at 1.8 miles. The lack of forest cover here is the result of a plane crash that happened on the mountain over 40 years ago (during the crash recovery effort, bulldozers cleared the summit for use as a helicopter landing). Continue on the trail north across the clearing, following the white blazes another 0.5 mile to a junction with the Clark Pond Loop. Straight ahead the AT continues on to the north summit of Moose Mountain. For this hike, turn left (west) onto the Clark Loop and descend 0.7 mile to reach a gravel road. Take a left and follow the road for about 50

feet. At another junction, turn left (south) onto the Harris Trail and after 0.7 mile reach the junction with the AT. Turn right and follow the AT's white blazes 0.4 mile back to Three Mile Road.

User Groups: Hikers and dogs. No bikes, horses, or wheelchair facilities. This trail is not suitable for skis.

Permits: Parking and access are free.

Maps: Local trail maps are available from the Dartmouth Outing Club (including a three-color, double-sided map covering a 75-mile section of the AT from Route 12 in Woodstock, VT, to Route 112 in Woodstock, NH $2). For topographic area maps, request Hanover and Canaan from the USGS.

Directions: From the center of Hanover, drive straight through the traffic lights (the Dartmouth College Green is to your left) onto East Wheelock Street and follow it 4.3 miles into the Hanover village of Etna. Turn left onto Etna Road, proceed 0.8 mile, and then turn right onto Ruddsboro Road. Continue 1.5 miles and then turn left onto Three Mile Road. Drive another 1.3 miles to a turnout on the left, where the white-blazed Appalachian Trail crosses the road.

The Moose Mountain AT shelter is located 0.2 mile off this loop, as the AT continues to the north summit (2.3 miles from the AT trailhead at Three Mile Road).

GPS Coordinates: 43.7187 N, 72.1752 W
Contact: Dartmouth Outdoor Programs Office, 119 Robinson Hall, Dartmouth College, Hanover, NH 03755, 603/646-2834, www.dartmouth.edu/~doc.

4 SQUAM MOUNTAINS

5.1 mi/3 hr

between Holderness and Center Sandwich

In late summer and early fall, this low mountain range suddenly lights up as its mainly mixed deciduous forest transforms into a colorful palette of reds, oranges, and yellows.

The contrast of fall foliage is especially vivid against the blue backdrop of Sqaum Lake and Lake Winnipesaukee and leaf peepers come from far and wide to take in the sights; peak foliage season typically runs from late September through the third weekend of October. This popular and fairly easy hike takes you to Squam's Mount Morgan (2,200 ft.) and Mount Percival (2,212 ft.) and includes only one short, difficult section—the cliffs on the Mount Morgan Trail—which can be avoided. The vertical ascent is about 1,400 feet.

From the parking area on Route 113, walk around the gate to pick up the yellow-blazed Mount Morgan Trail. Ascend gently along the trail for more than a mile. At 1.5 miles, the climb becomes somewhat steeper and at 1.7 miles, watch for the Crawford-Ridgepole Trail to enter from the left; it then coincides with the Mount Morgan Trail for the next 0.2 mile. Where the two trails split again, the Crawford-Ridgepole bears right for an easier route up Mount Morgan. This hike, however, turns left and continues on the Mount Morgan Trail, immediately scaling low cliffs on a wooden ladder, after which you crawl through a cavelike rock passage and emerge atop the cliffs with an excellent view of the big lakes to the south. Follow the blazes up the slabs to Morgan's open, rocky summit and again enjoy extensive views south. From the summit, follow the marked Crawford-Ridgepole Trail eastward along the Squam Mountains Ridge, a pleasant, relatively level walk filled with blueberry bushes for a quick summer snack. After 0.8 mile, reach the open summit of Mount Percival, which has equally excellent views of Squam and Winnipesaukee Lakes. Descend using the Mount Percival Trail to the southeast (look for a small trail sign nailed to a tree at the base of the summit slabs). Initially very steep, the trail quickly turns into a relatively easy descent of 1.9 miles back to Route 113. Once you reach the road, turn right and walk for 0.3 mile to the parking area.

Special note: Some hikers will find that hiking this loop in the opposite direction, going up the steep section just below the summit of Mount Percival, rather than down it, is much easier on the knees.

User Groups: Hikers and dogs. No bikes, horses, or wheelchair facilities.

Permits: Parking and access are free.

Maps: Squam Lakes trail map is available from the Squam Lakes Association for a modest fee. A waterproof trail map is available from the Appalachian Mountain Club (Crawford Notch–Sandwich Range/Moosilauke–Kinsman, $7.95). For a topographic area map, request Squam Mountains from the USGS.

Directions: From Route 3 in Holderness, follow Route 113 east for 5.5 miles to the marked parking turnout.

GPS Coordinates: 43.7892 N, 71.5486 W

Contact: Squam Lakes Association, P.O. Box 204, Holderness, NH 03245, 603/968-7336, www.squamlakes.org.

⑤ WEST RATTLESNAKE
1.8 mi/1 hr   🏃2 ⛰9

between Holderness and Center Sandwich

The classic movie *On Golden Pond* was filmed along the shores of Squam Lake and this easy hike to a cliff top above the lake offers cinematic views of Squam and the surrounding landscape (net elevation gain 450 feet). From the parking area for the Mount Morgan Trail, cross Route 113 and walk west about 100 feet to the sign marker for the Old Bridle Path. Follow the well-worn, gently-inclining path for almost a mile through the birch-filled woods. At 0.9 mile, where the main trail turns left, follow a side path to the right about 100 feet to the cliffs. At the summit, you may notice rock barriers surrounding Douglas' Knotweed, an endangered plant; avoid walking on the vegetation. Return the way you came.

User Groups: Hikers and dogs. No bikes, horses, or wheelchair facilities.

Permits: Parking and access are free.

Maps: Local trail guide and map are sold by

the Squam Lakes Association for a modest fee. A waterproof trail map is available from the Appalachian Mountain Club (Crawford Notch–Sandwich Range/Moosilauke–Kinsman, $7.95). For a topographic area map, request Squam Mountains Quad from the USGS.

Directions: From Route 3 in Holderness, follow Route 113 east for 5.6 miles to the marked parking turnout.

GPS Coordinates: 43.7892 N, 71.5486 W

Contact: Squam Lakes Association, P.O. Box 204, Holderness, NH 03245, 603/968-7336, www.squamlakes.org.

⑥ EAGLE CLIFF
1.2 mi/45 min

north of Center Harbor

The open ledges of Eagle Cliff rise 800 vertical feet over Squam Lake, providing hikers with a perfect bird's-eye view of this picturesque body of water. A short trek, the climbing is easy until a sharp ascent at the very end forces a steep scramble to the top of the cliff.

From the parking turnout on Bean Road, cross the road to what looks like an unmarked trailhead. Just a few steps down the path (and out of sight from the road) is a small sign reading Eagle Cliff Trail. A pleasant, moderate rise through mixed forest for the first 0.4 mile, the trail suddenly grows into a somewhat steep rock scramble for much of the final 0.2-mile push to Eagle Cliff. Finally reaching the open ledges, the views are dramatic. Sweeping out almost right underneath you is the lake, with the low ridge of the Squam Mountains visible in the distance. Look to the north for views of the southern White Mountains; the most readily identifiable is the horn of Mount Chocorua to the northeast. Hike back along the same route or descend north from the cliff along the much more gently inclined Teedie Trail. The recommended route for this hike (both up and down) when the ground is wet

or icy, Teedie Trail brings you back to Bean Road, next to a private tennis court at the Sandwich-Moltonborough town line, 0.4 mile north from where you parked.

User Groups: Hikers and dogs. Trail is not suitable for bikes or horses. No wheelchair facilities.

Permits: Parking and access are free.

Maps: Local trail guide and map are sold by the Squam Lakes Association for a modest fee. A waterproof trail map is available from the Appalachian Mountain Club (Crawford Notch–Sandwich Range/Moosilauke–Kinsman, $7.95). For a topographic area map, request Squam Mountains Quad from the USGS.

Directions: In Center Harbor, immediately east of the junction of Routes 25 and 25B, turn north off Route 25 onto Bean Road. Follow for five miles, crossing the Sandwich-Moultonborough town line. At 0.4 mile beyond the town line—where the road becomes Squam Lakes Road—look for roadside parking in the southbound turnout. The trail marker is a small sign located downhill from the roadside and is not visible until you start down the path.

GPS: 43.7695 N, 71.4807 W

Contact: Squam Lakes Association, P.O. Box 204, Holderness, NH 03245, 603/968-7336, www.squamlakes.org.

⑦ MOUNT CARDIGAN: WEST SIDE LOOP
3.5 mi/2 hr   2 🏕10

in Cardigan State Park east of Canaan

BEST (

Left bare by a fire in 1855, the 3,121-foot crown of Mount Cardigan, "Old Baldy," affords a 360-degree panoramic view of the Green and White Mountains and of prominent hills to the south, such as Sunapee and Vermont's Mount Ascutney. It's a popular hike: Hundreds of people, many of them children, will climb Cardigan on sunny weekends during the warm months. This easy loop on the west side of the mountain sees the most foot traffic of any of the Cardigan summit routes and offers a vertical gain of about 1,200 feet.

From the parking area, the orange blazes of the West Ridge Trail lead immediately uphill, climbing steadily on a wide and somewhat rocky footpath. At the half-mile mark, the South Ridge Trail enters from the right. Stay to the left on the West Ridge Trail, crossing a small brook on a wooden footbridge and passing by another trail junction. More than a mile from the trailhead, the West Ridge Trail emerges onto the nearly barren upper cone of Mount Cardigan, climbing steep slabs to the summit. The views here are long and unobstructed, but a fire tower at the summit offers even longer views. For the return trip, turn back for about 100 feet on the West Ridge Trail and take a left at a marked junction to follow the white blazes of the Clark Trail. The trail becomes briefly quite steep on slabs that can be a bit hazardous when wet, reaching the tiny ranger's cabin 0.2 mile past Cardigan's summit. Here, turn right and follow the orange blazes of the South Ridge Trail past the cabin, moving in and out of low trees for 0.3 mile to South Peak, with good views to the south and west of the hills of central and western New Hampshire. The South Ridge Trail enters the forest and continues descending, very steeply in spots, for another mile to the West Ridge Trail. Turn left and descend another half mile to the parking lot.

User Groups: Hikers and leashed dogs. No bikes, horses, or wheelchair facilities. Snowshoeing is possible at lower elevations but may be difficult above the tree line due to ice and harsh weather.

Permits: Parking and access are free.

Maps: Free, basic trail maps are available at the trailhead parking lot. A waterproof trail map is available from the Appalachian Mountain Club (Monadnock/Cardigan, $7.95). For a topographic area map, request Mount Cardigan from the USGS.

Directions: From the junction of Routes 4 and 118 in Canaan, drive north on Route 118 for 0.6 mile and then turn right at a sign for Cardigan State Park. Follow that road for 4.1 miles to a large dirt parking lot. The trail begins beside the parking lot. The access road is maintained in winter only to a parking area about 0.6 mile before the summer parking lot.

GPS Coordinates: 43.6515 N, 71.9514 W

Contact: New Hampshire Division of Parks and Recreation, P.O. Box 1856, Concord, NH 03302, 603/271-3254, www.nhstateparks.org. Trails on Mount Cardigan are maintained by the Cardigan Highlanders, P.O. Box 104, Enfield Center, NH 03749, 603/632-5640.

8 MOUNT CARDIGAN: EAST SIDE LOOP

5.2 mi/3.5 hr   🏃3 ⛰10

in Cardigan State Park west of Alexandria

This relatively steep hike up the east side of Cardigan provides experienced hikers with a more rigorous climb to the mountain's summit (3,121 ft.). But even the most adept mountaineers should pay attention to weather conditions before starting out on this route: The upper portion of the trail requires scrambling over exposed slabs that quickly become dangerous when wet or icy. On a sunny summer or early fall day, however, when other routes on Cardigan are choked with visitors, choosing the mountain's eastside trails is often the best way to experience Cardigan without the crowds. The loop's vertical gain is about 1,800 feet.

From the parking area at the Appalachian Mountain Club's Cardigan Lodge, pick up the Holt Trail heading west (look for the sign marker). The trail follows a wide, nearly flat woods road for almost a mile. At 1.1 miles, the trail crosses Bailey Brook and then turns slightly to run parallel to the brook. Growing steeper, the trail leaves the brook and begins a very sharp ascent. Crossing exposed rock slabs for the final 0.3 mile, the trail reaches the summit 2.2 miles from the parking area. After stopping to take in the expansive views or taking a turn climbing the fire tower, turn right (north) onto the white-blazed and cairn-marked Mowglis Trail. Follow it off the summit, dropping sharply into the saddle between the main summit and Firescrew Mountain, a shoulder of Cardigan. The Mowglis Trail then climbs to the open top of Firescrew, with more long views, 0.6 mile from Cardigan's summit. Turn right (east) and follow the Manning Trail, descending steadily with good views for about 0.2 mile. Reentering the woods, walk for 2.2 more miles before reaching the Holt Trail. Turn left and walk the short distance back to the parking lot.

User Groups: Hikers and leashed dogs. No bikes, horses, or wheelchair facilities.

Permits: Parking and access are free.

Maps: A waterproof trail map is available from the Appalachian Mountain Club (Monadnock/Cardigan, $7.95). For topographic maps, request Mount Cardigan and Newfound Lake from the USGS.

Directions: From the junction of Routes 3A and 104 in Bristol, drive north on Route 3A for 2.1 miles. At a stone church near the south end of Newfound Lake, turn left onto West Shore Road. Continue 1.9 miles and proceed straight through a crossroads. Reaching a fork in 1.2 miles, bear right onto Fowler River Road, and then turn left 3.2 miles farther onto Brook Road. Continue another 1.1 miles and turn right onto the dirt Shem Valley Road. Just 0.1 mile farther, bear right at a red schoolhouse. Drive 1.4 miles to the end of that road, where parking is available near the Appalachian Mountain Club's Cardigan Lodge. (At intersections along these roads, there are signs indicating the direction to the Cardigan Lodge.) The access road is maintained in winter.

GPS Coordinates: 43.6495 N, 71.8775 W

Contact: New Hampshire Division of Parks and Recreation, P.O. Box 1856, Concord, NH

03302, 603/271-3254, www.nhstateparks.org. Trails on Mount Cardigan are maintained by the Cardigan Highlanders, P.O. Box 104, Enfield Center, NH 03749, 603/632-5640.

🅖 MOUNT MAJOR
3 mi/1.5 hr

between West Alton and Alton Bay

Located not far from the southern end of Lake Winnipesaukee, this low-lying mountain is perhaps the most popular hike in the lakes region, especially among families with young children. It's an easy climb to Major's 1,000-foot summit and the views of Lake Winnipesaukee and the high peaks of the White Mountains in the distance are nothing short of stunning.

From the parking area along Route 11, follow a gravel-strewn jeep trail 0.1 mile until you reach a fork in the road. Here bear right for the Mount Major Trail and follow the gradually ascending slope. At 1.3 miles from the parking area, rocky slabs just off the trail offer a scenic lake overlook and a perfect spot for a picnic. Push on to reach the summit, 1.5 miles from the start of the hike. Descend the same way.

User Groups: Hikers and leashed dogs. No bikes, horses, or wheelchair facilities.

Permits: Parking and access are free.

Maps: For a topographic area map, request Squam Mountains from the USGS.

Directions: From the junction of Routes 11 and 28A in Alton Bay, follow Route 11 north to a large parking area on the left (west) side of the road. The state owns the summit area and maintains the parking lot, but the trail crosses private property.

GPS Coordinates: 43.5192 N, 71.2738 W

Contact: New Hampshire Division of Parks and Recreation, P.O. Box 1856, Concord, NH 03302, 603/271-3556, www.nhstateparks.org.

10 MOUNT KEARSARGE
2.9 mi/2 hr   👫3 ⛰9

in Winslow State Park in Wilmot

The climb to the bald, 2,937-foot summit of Mount Kearsarge, with its views of the White Mountains, Green Mountains, and southern New Hampshire, is one of the finest short hikes in New England and, while steep, a great adventure for children. Netting an elevation gain of about 1,100 feet, this loop uses the Winslow Trail to reach the summit and the Barlow Trail, a gentler route that's easy on the knees, for the descent.

From the upper end of the parking lot in Winslow State Park, pick up the red-blazed Winslow Trail. The wide, well-beaten path rises quite steeply and relentlessly and grows even more rugged the higher you go. At 0.8 mile, scramble a large boulder on the left for a good view north. A short distance farther, the trail breaks out of the trees and onto the bald summit, with views in every direction, including nearby Sunapee, Ragged, and Cardigan mountains and more distant Mount Monadnock and Ascutney. On very clear days, views extend to the White Mountains, the Green Mountains of Vermont, the Atlantic Ocean, and Boston. This is a wonderful hike during the height of the fall foliage colors (and because of this, Kearsarge's trails are usually packed during peak fall weekends). A fire tower stands at the summit, and nearby are a pair of picnic tables, along with a very large and very out-of-place-looking communications tower—the one drawback to Kearsarge's otherwise impeccable mountaintop. For the return trip, pick up the yellow-blazed Barlow Trail off the eastern edge of the summit. Follow the blazes and cairns, soon descending into scrubby pine. Follow the trail for 1.8 miles back to the parking area.

User Groups: Hikers and leashed dogs. No bikes, horses, or wheelchair facilities.

Permits: Park admission is $4 for adults; $2 for children ages 6–11; free for children ages 5 and under and New Hampshire residents age 65 and over.

Maps: A basic trail map of Winslow State Park is available at the park or from the New Hampshire Division of Parks and Recreation. For topographic area maps, request New London, Andover, Bradford, and Warner from the USGS.

Directions: Take I-89 to Exit 10 and follow the signs to Winslow State Park. From the tollbooth at the state park entrance, drive to the dirt parking lot at the end of the road.

Winslow State Park is open 9 A.M.–8 P.M. May 1–mid-November. The last 0.6 mile of the entrance road (beyond the fork at the dead end sign) is not maintained in winter.

GPS Coordinates: 43.3895 N, 71.8672 W

Contact: Winslow State Park, P.O. Box 295, Newbury, NH 03255, 603/526-6168. New Hampshire Division of Parks and Recreation, P.O. Box 1856, 172 Pembroke Rd., Concord, NH 03302, 603/271-3556, camping reservations 603/271-3628, www.nhstateparks.org.

11 MOUNT SUNAPEE
12.4 mi/7 hr   👫5 ⛰8

in Mount Sunapee State Park in Newbury

The Summit Trail up central New Hampshire's popular Mount Sunapee offers a fairly easy, four-mile round-trip route from the ski area parking lot to the 2,743-foot summit. Many hikers will be satisfied with that. But this description also covers a section of the Monadnock-Sunapee Greenway Trail from Sunapee's summit to Lucia's Lookout on Sunapee's long southern ridge. Views along the ridge, particularly overlooking Lake Solitude, make this ambitious trek well worth the time and effort. The climb to Sunapee's summit is about 1,300 feet.

From the Sunapee ski area parking lot, walk behind the North Peak Lodge about 100 feet to where two ski trails merge; look to the right for a sign for the red-blazed Summit Trail.

Ascending steadily through the woods for ap-proximately two miles, the trail emerges onto an open meadow, where to the right (south) you get a view toward Mount Monadnock. Turn left and walk to the summit lodge a short distance ahead. Some of the best views on the mountain are from the decks at the lodge, with Mount Ascutney and the Green Mountains visible to the west, and Mounts Cardigan and Moosilauke and Franconia Ridge to the north. To complete this four-mile hike, return the way you came. To lengthen it with a walk along the somewhat rugged Sunapee Ridge, head across the summit approximately 50 feet to the left (east) of the ski lift, looking for the sign and white blazes marking the Monad-nock-Sunapee Greenway Trail.

Reentering the woods, the greenway heads east and slightly south to reach the open White Ledges 0.9 mile from the summit. The trail then swings left, but walking to the right will lead you to an open ledge with an excellent view of Lake Solitude, a small tarn tucked into the mountain's shoulder (a large arrow painted on a rock tells you where to find the lookout). Continuing on the greenway, the trail passes over an open ledge 2.7 miles from the Sunapee summit before reaching Lucia's Lookout, 4.2 miles from the summit. Here, the views take in Mount Monadnock and Lovewell Mountain to the south, the Green Mountains to the west, and Mount Kearsarge and the White Mountains to the north. Hike back the way you came.

User Groups: Hikers and leashed dogs. No bikes, horses, or wheelchair facilities.

Permits: Parking and access are free.

Maps: A free map of the trails is available at the state park or from the New Hampshire Division of Parks and Recreation. A trail guide and waterproof map of the entire Monadnock-Sunapee Greenway, a trail stretching 50 miles from Mount Monadnock to Mount Sunapee, can be purchased from the Monadnock-Sunapee Greenway Trail Club ($14). For a topographic area map, request Newport from the USGS.

Directions: From Sunapee Village, head south on Route 103B until reaching a roundabout. Go halfway around the traffic circle and bear right at a sign for the state park. Continue to the end of the road and a large parking area at the base of the ski area.

GPS Coordinates: 43.3324 N, 72.0795 W

Contact: New Hampshire Division of Parks and Recreation, P.O. Box 1856, Concord, NH 03302, 603/271-3556, www.nhstateparks.org. Monadnock-Sunapee Greenway Trail Club (MSGTC), P.O. Box 164, Marlow, NH 03456, www.msgtc.org.

12 CATAMOUNT HILL

2.2 mi/1 hr

in Bear Brook State Park in Allenstown

Located in the southeast region of the state, Bear Brook, with over 10,000 acres, is the largest de-veloped state park in New Hampshire. Forty miles of trails wind through thick forest, travel-ing to an almost countless number of marshes, bogs, ponds, and hilly summits. This 2.2-mile hike ascends a few hundred feet to one of the park's highest points, 721-foot Catamount Hill, where a mostly wooded ridge offers limited views of the state park's rambling forest.

From the parking lot near the toll booth, cross Deerfield Road and follow it briefly back toward Route 28. About 100 feet past the toll booth, a trail marked One Mile Road enters the woods. Follow it for 0.2 mile, bearing left where another dirt road enters from the right. In 0.1 mile from that junction, turn right onto the Catamount Hill Trail, which is marked by a sign. The trail climbs steadily, reaching the first lookout about 0.6 mile past the dirt road, just below the summit. Continue another 0.2 mile to the summit ridge, where another view is partially obscured by low trees. Return the way you came. At the bottom of the Cata-mount Hill Trail, turn left on One Mile Road; do not take the first trail on the right, which leads to a footbridge over Bear Brook. At the second junction, bear right to return to the toll booth area.

Special Note: Bear Brook State Park is also home to an assortment of museums dedicated to outdoor pursuits. Located 0.5 mile from the toll booth are the New Hampshire Antique Snowmobile Museum, Museum of Family Camping, Old Allenstown Meeting House, and the Richard Diehl Civilian Conservation Corps (CCC) Museum. Most of the museums are housed in historic CCC buildings. Contact park for seasonal hours.

User Groups: Hikers and leashed dogs. No bikes, horses, or wheelchair facilities on this trail (access varies along other trails in the park).

Permits: During the summer recreation season, an entrance fee of $4 per adult and $2 per child (ages 6–11) is collected at the state park entrance. Children under 5 and New Hampshire residents 65 and older enter for free.

Maps: A free trail map is available at the park entrance. For topographic area maps, request Suncook and Gossville from the USGS.

Directions: From the junction of U.S. 3 and Route 28 in Allenstown, bear right on Route 28 and follow it to the entrance of Bear Brook State Park at Deerfield Road (look for the large state park sign). Turn left into a parking lot just past the entrance toll booth.

GPS Coordinates: 43.1621 N, 71.3889 W

Contact: Bear Brook State Park, 157 Deerfield Rd., Allenstown, NH 03275, 603/485-9874. New Hampshire Division of Parks and Recreation, P.O. Box 1856, 172 Pembroke Rd., Concord, NH 03302, 603/271-3556, camping reservations 603/271-3628, www.nhstateparks.org.

13 PAWTUCKAWAY STATE PARK

7 mi/3.5 hr   5 ⛰8

in Raymond

Home to a lake and sandy swimming beach, marshland, fields, forest, and upland hills, Pawtuckaway is far and away the most diverse natural area in southeastern New Hampshire. Many of its trails are ideal for hiking, mountain biking, or cross-country skiing, and you might be surprised by the extensive views from the ledges and fire tower atop South Mountain, rising less than 1,000 feet above sea level. Besides this hike, there are numerous trails to explore—try stretching this hike into a 12-mile loop by combining Tower Road with the Shaw and Fundy Trails. Fun to spot at Pawtuckaway are the numerous glacial erratics dotting the landscape; some of these giant boulders dumped by the retreating glaciers of the last Ice Age soar to over 20 feet in height.

From the parking lot near the entrance to the park, follow the paved road north for about 0.25 mile. After passing a pond on your left, a sign marker on the left indicates the beginning of the Mountain Trail. Head in a northeasterly direction along the trail, staying to the right when a junction is reached with the round Pond Trail. Approximately three miles from the hike's starting point, you will reach junction 5 (marked by a sign); turn right and ascend the trail to the summit of South Mountain. Check out the views from the ledges to the left and right of the trail just below the summit; the east-facing trails to the right will be warmer on a sunny day when the breeze is cool. Climb the fire tower for even longer views of the surrounding countryside.

User Groups: Hikers and bikes (though trails are closed to bikes during mud season, usually the month of April). No wheelchair facilities. Dogs and horses are prohibited.

Permits: During mid-June–Labor Day, an entrance fee of $4 per adult and $2 per child (ages 6–11) is collected at the state park entrance. Children under 5 and New Hampshire residents 65 and older enter for free. There is no fee the rest of the year.

Maps: A free, noncontour map of park trails is available at the park's main entrance. For a topographic area map, request Mount Pawtuckaway from the USGS.

Directions: From Route 101 in Raymond, take Exit 5 (there is a sign for Pawtuckaway). Follow Route 156 north and turn left onto Mountain Road at the sign for Pawtuckaway State Park. Follow the road two miles to the state park entrance; the parking lot is on the left.

The parking lot opens at 10 A.M. Monday–Thursday and at 9 A.M. Friday–Sunday.

GPS Coordinates: 43.0780 N, 71.1727 W

Contact: Pawtuckaway State Park, 128 Mountain Rd., Nottingham, NH 03290, 603/895-3031. New Hampshire Division of Parks and Recreation, P.O. Box 1856, 172 Pembroke Rd., Concord, NH 03302, 603/271-3556, camping reservations 603/271-3628, www.nhstateparks.org.

14 GREAT BAY NATIONAL ESTUARINE RESEARCH RESERVE

1 mi/0.75 hr   🏃🏃₁ ⛰₆

in Stratham

BEST (

Hands down the state's most ecologically diverse area, the 4,500-acre tidal estuary and 800 acres of coastal land at Great Bay National Estuarine Research Reserve provide refuge for 23 species of endangered or threatened plant and animal species. Bald eagles winter here, osprey nest, and cormorants and great blue heron are readily seen. Sandy Point Trail is a universally accessible interpretive trail and boardwalk that allows visitors to experience the vast diversity of the estuarine ecosystem.

From the Great Bay Discovery Center parking lot, a short path zigzags down the slope to the trailhead. From here, the graded, gravel trail enters a mature, upland forest of oak, hickory, elm, and beech. The trail becomes a boardwalk just before reaching the wetter ground of the red maple–sensitive fern swamp ecosystem. Here, look for jack-in-the-pulpit, spotted touch-me-not-fern, royal fern, and cinnamon fern. Continuing on, the boardwalk reaches a junction. The Woodland Trail enters the forest to the left, but this route takes the boardwalk to the right, entering the salt marsh. Almost immediately to your right, take note of the almost pure stand of feather-tufted common reed, a threatened plant species in North America (this is the last known example of the plant in the state). As the boardwalk bends to the left, Great Bay comes into view. A series of mudflats at low tide, the estuary at high tide becomes a vivid blue lake. This is a good spot for bird-watching: Blue heron, egret, osprey, kingfisher, and waterfowl all frequent this part of Great Bay. Follow the boardwalk as it forms a loop through the marsh and retrace your steps back to the Great Bay Discovery Center. Stop by the center for lots of fun, hands-on learning about the estuary.

User Groups: Hikers and wheelchairs only. No bikes, dogs, or horses.

Permits: Parking and access are free.

Maps: An interpretive trail pamphlet available at the Great Bay Discovery Center guides visitors along the boardwalk at the estuary's edge and offers information about natural history and the local environment. For topographic area maps, request Newmarket and Portsmouth from the USGS.

Directions: From the Stratham traffic circle at the junction of Routes 108 and 33, drive 1.4 miles north on Route 33 and turn left onto Depot Road at a sign for the Great Bay Discovery Center. At the end of Depot Road, turn left on Tidewater Farm Road. The Discovery Center is at the end of the road and the trail begins behind the center.

Great Bay Discovery Center is open to the public 10 A.M.–4 P.M. Wednesday–Sunday May 1–September 30 and on weekends in October. The grounds are open during daylight hours throughout the year.

GPS Coordinates: 43.0546 N, 70.8964 W

Contact: Great Bay National Estuarine Research Reserve, 89 Depot Rd., Greenland, NH 03840, 603/778-0015, www.greatbay.org/sandypoint.

© JACQUELINE TOURVILLE

Odiorne Point State Park

15 ODIORNE POINT STATE PARK

1.9 mi/1 hr

👫1 ▲7

in Rye

Just down the road from Portsmouth's bustling downtown and not far from Hampton's crowded beaches, rocky Odiorne Point is the largest tract of undeveloped land left along New Hampshire's tiny 18-mile shoreline. Nestled within a 330-acre state park overlooking both the Atlantic Ocean and Portsmouth's Little Harbor, Odiorne's most notable use was as the site of Fort Dearborn, a U.S. Military installation built during World War II. With long-abandoned bunkers looking more like grassy dunes than strategic defense points, Odiorne today offers visitors the chance to ramble along a rugged shore with unfettered ocean views. Portions of this hike are wheelchair accessible.

From the eastern end of the parking lot, the paved, handicap-accessible walkway quickly comes to a view of the ocean, taking you past a small grove of low trees known as the Sunken Forest and continuing out to the Odiorne Point promontory and picnic area. Scramble down to the rocky beach to explore the tidal pools at low tide or simply stop to take in the vast ocean views; on a clear day you can see the Isles of Shoals, a small chain of low-lying offshore islands. To the north, closer to shore, spot the hardworking Whaleback Lighthouse in Kittery, Maine. The paved walkway leads through the picnic area to form a loop leading back to the parking lot. To continue on a longer walk, follow the shoreline's well-worn path. The trail takes you first to the Seacoast Science Center—if you have kids in tow, the center's marine touch tank and many aquariums are a must-see. The path then takes you past long-abandoned bunkers, a salt marsh, and boat launch, before skirting the edge of Little Harbor and eventually leading all the way out to the jetty at Frost Point (about a mile from your starting point). Circle back from the end of the jetty and bear left at a fork just off Frost Point to return to the science center and parking lot.

User Groups: Hikers and wheelchairs (the paved portion on this route is wheelchair accessible). Separate bike paths are located elsewhere in the park. Dogs and horses are prohibited.

Permits: The park is open daily year-round. In early May–mid-October, admission is $4 for adults; $2 for children, ages 6–11; children ages 5 and under and New Hampshire residents age 65 and over enter for free. The Seacoast Science Center charges separate admissions fees.

Maps: For a map with historical and natural information about Odiorne, contact the New Hampshire Division of Parks and Recreation. For a topographic area map, request Kittery from the USGS.

Directions: From Portsmouth, follow Route 1A south for three miles to Odiorne State Park's main entrance (on the left). The parking area is just past the gatehouse to the right. GPS Coordinates: 43.0442 N, 70.7149 W

Contact: Odiorne State Park, Rte. 1A, Rye, NH 03870, 603/436-7406. New Hampshire Division of Parks and Recreation, P.O. Box 1856, Concord, NH 03302, 603/271-3556, www.nhstateparks.org. Seacoast Science Center, 570 Ocean Blvd., Rye, NH 03870, 603/436-8043, www.seacoastsciencecenter.org.

16 NORTH PACK MONADNOCK
3.2 mi/2 hr

in Greenfield

This fairly easy 3.2-mile hike ascends less than 1,000 feet in elevation to the top of North Pack Monadnock. Not to be confused with nearby Grand Monadnock, North Pack is the northern terminus of the 21-mile Wapack Trail and is located in a national wildlife refuge of almost 2,000 acres of timbered uplands. Steep in some places, the consistently ascending Wapack Trail takes you under pine trees and birches, offers nice views and places to rest

along the way, and culminates with a rewarding summit experience.

From the parking area, walk south into the woods, following the yellow triangle blazes of the Wapack Trail. For more than a mile, the trail ascends at an easy grade through forest cover, then climbs steep ledges and passes over one open ledge before reaching the summit at 1.6 miles. From the 2,276-foot summit, the views of southern New Hampshire's wooded hills and valleys are very good, especially to the west and north. Return the way you came.

Camping is allowed only at designated sites along the entire 21-mile Wapack Trail, but not along this hike. Fires are prohibited.

User Groups: Hikers, snowshoers, and dogs. No wheelchair facilities. This trail is not suitable for bikes, horses, or skis.

Permits: Parking and access are free.

Maps: A Wapack Trail map and guide is available for $11 from Friends of the Wapack. For topographic area maps, request Peterborough South, Peterborough North, Greenfield, and Greenville from the USGS.

Directions: From the intersection of Routes 101 and 202 in Peterborough, head north on Route 202. Follow for 1.1 miles and then bear right onto Sand Hill Road. Proceed 3.9 miles, including a sharp left curve (at about 2.6 miles) and a sharp right curve (at about 3 miles), until you see the trail markers on the south (right) side of the road. GPS Coordinates: 42.9001 N, 71.8707 W

Contact: Friends of the Wapack, Box 115, West Peterborough, NH 03468, www.wapack.org.

17 MOUNT PISGAH/ PISGAH LEDGES
5 mi/3 hr

in Pisgah State Park between Chesterfield and Hinsdale

Tucked away in the state's rural southwest corner, New Hampshire's largest state park includes this big hill called Mount Pisgah, where open summit ledges afford nice views of rolling countryside and Mount Monadnock to the east and Massachusetts and Vermont to the southwest. Key trail junctions are marked with signs and there's just a few hundred feet of uphill. A pleasant hike in spring or summer hike, the trail really comes to life in early autumn when the surrounding deciduous forest blazes with fall colors.

From the park entrance and parking area at Kilburn Road, follow the marked Kilburn Road Trail, bearing left at marked junctions with the Kilburn Loop Trail, and eventually turning onto the Pisgah Mountain Trail (at 1.2 miles from the trailhead). Follow the Pisgah Ridge Trail 0.2 mile to reach the hill's open ledges. Follow 0.2 mile to reach the hill's open ledges. To bag the wooded summit (which unfortunately lacks any kind of view), double back to the trail junction and ascend a short distance to the mountaintop. From the summit or ledges, head back down along the same trails, this time bearing right at junctions with the Kilburn Loop Trail.

User Groups: Hikers and leashed dogs. No wheelchair facilities. The trail is not suitable for bikes or horses. Hunting is allowed in season.

Permits: During the summer recreation season, park admission is $4 for adults; $2 for children, ages 6–11; children ages 5 and under and New Hampshire residents age 65 and over enter for free.

Maps: For a map of park trails, contact the New Hampshire Division of Parks and Recreation. For topographic area maps, request Winchester and Keene from the USGS.

Directions: From Keene, follow Route 9 west for approximately nine miles. At an intersection with Route 63, turn left (south), pass through Chesterfield, and continue three more miles to an entrance and parking area for Kilburn Road in Pisgah State Park.

GPS Coordinates: 42.8346 N, 72.4834 W

Contact: Pisgah State Park, P.O. Box 242, Winchester, NH 03470-0242, 603/239-8153.

New Hampshire Division of Parks and Recreation, P.O. Box 1856, Concord, NH 03302, 603/271-3556, www.nhstateparks.org.

18 MOUNT MONADNOCK: MARLBORO TRAIL

4.2 mi/3.5 hr

in Monadnock State Park in Marlborough

If there is a trail less traveled leading to the summit of Mount Monadnock (3,165 ft.), it's the Marlboro Trail, an uphill walk to the summit past interesting boulder formations. Leaving from a small trailhead along a dirt road almost due west of the mountain peak, this route to the summit sees only a fraction of the foot traffic experienced by popular trailheads clustered around the state park entrance to the southeast of Monadnock (see the *Mount Monadnock: White Arrow Trail* listing in this chapter). The Marlboro Trail's net elevation gain is approximately 1,800 feet.

From the parking area along Shaker Road, find the trail marker and begin walking east on the gently graded trail (look for white blazes). Enjoy the solitude on this pleasant walk through the woods. And with fewer fellow hikers to watch out for, take time to examine the mountain's diverse flora and fauna. In spring and early summer, the forest floor blooms with such delicate beauty as trilliums and pink lady slipper; mountain turtles may crawl along as you pass, and deer, wild turkeys, and even a reclusive moose may make themselves known along this stretch of the trail. As the one-mile mark approaches, the second half of the trail begins a sharp and steep ascent, leveling out somewhat (here you will notice a set of granite boulders named Rock House for their shelter-like appearance) and then pushing above the tree line to intersect with the Dublin, 0.3 mile below the summit. Together the two trails combine as a single route, bearing right to ascend Monadnock's slabs and ledges from the south. Enjoy an unparalleled scenic vista extending to all six New England states. Return along the same route to the parking area at the trailhead.

User Groups: Hikers only. No bikes, dogs, horses, or wheelchair facilities.

Permits: Parking and access are free.

Maps: A free map of trails is available from the state park or the New Hampshire Division of Parks and Recreation. A waterproof trail map is available from the Appalachian Mountain Club (Monadnock/Cardigan, $7.95). For topographic area maps, request Monadnock Mountain and Marlborough from the USGS.

Directions: From the center of Marlborough, follow Route 124 south for 4.2 miles to a left hand turn onto Shaker Farms Road. Follow for approximately 0.7 mile to the parking area on the right.

GPS Coordinates: 42.8588 N, 72.1383 W

Contact: Monadnock State Park, P.O. Box 181, Jaffrey, NH 03452, 603/532-8862, www.nhstateparks.org. New Hampshire Division of Parks and Recreation, P.O. Box 1856, Concord, NH 03302, 603/271-3556, www.nhstateparks.org.

19 MOUNT MONADNOCK: WHITE ARROW TRAIL
4.6 mi/3 hr

in Monadnock State Park in Jaffrey

At 3,165 feet high, majestic Mount Monadnock (also called Grand Monadnock) rises high above the surrounding countryside of southern New Hampshire, making it prominently visible from many other lower peaks in the region. The mountain's name comes from an Abenaki phrase likely meaning "place of an unexcelled mountain." Borrowing from the Abenaki, modern geologists use the term "monadnock" to mean an isolated peak in an otherwise eroded plain (there are actually several of these monadnocks in both New Hampshire and Vermont). With its large, rocky summit and unhindered view encompassing all six New England states, Grand Monadnock is the region's most popular peak. It's often claimed that Monadnock is hiked more than any mountain in the world except Japan's Mount Fuji—although any ranger in the state park would tell you that's impossible to prove. This hike, a vertical ascent of 1,600 feet, is one of the most commonly used Monadnock summit routes and can be a very crowded place in the spring, summer, and fall.

From the parking lot on the north side of Route 124, walk past the gate onto the old toll road and immediately bear left at the sign marker for the Old Halfway House Trail. A moderate ascent of 1.2 miles, the trail ends at a meadow known as the Halfway House site, the former grounds of a hotel built in the late 19th century for mountain tourists (and located at the midway point to the summit). Cross the meadow to the White Arrow Trail, which ascends a rock-strewn but wide path for another 1.1 miles to the summit of Mount Monadnock. The final quarter mile is above the mountain's tree line and very exposed to harsh weather. White blazes are painted on the rocks above the trees. Just below the summit, the trail makes a sharp right turn, then ascends slabs to the summit. Hike back the same way.

User Groups: Hikers only. No bikes, dogs, horses, or wheelchair facilities.

Permits: During April–November, an entrance fee of $4 per adult and $2 per child (ages 6–11) is collected at the state park entrance. Children under 5 and New Hampshire residents 65 and older enter state parks for free.

Maps: A free map of trails is available from the state park or the New Hampshire Division of Parks and Recreation. A waterproof trail map is available from the Appalachian Mountain Club (Monadnock/Cardigan, $7.95). For topographic area maps, request Monadnock Mountain and Marlborough from the USGS.

Directions: This hike begins from a parking lot on the north side of Route 124, 7.1 miles east of the junction of Routes 101 and 124 in Marlborough and 5.4 miles west of the junction of Route 124, Route 137, and U.S. 202 in Jaffrey.

GPS Coordinates: 42.8348 N, 72.1140 W

Contact: Monadnock State Park, P.O. Box 181, Jaffrey, NH 03452, 603/532-8862, www. nhstateparks.org. New Hampshire Division of Parks and Recreation, P.O. Box 1856, Concord, NH 03302, 603/271-3556, www. nhstateparks.org.

20 MOUNT MONADNOCK: WHITE DOT TRAIL

4.2 mi/3 hr 👣5 ⛰10

in Monadnock State Park in Jaffrey

BEST (

While on a trek through the Monadnock region, literary luminary Mark Twain noted, "In these October days Monadnock and the valley and its framing hills make an inspiring picture." On a sunny autumn day, a hike to the summit along the White Dot Trail is a leaf peeper's paradise, with views as inspiring now as they were in Twain's day. Passing through a mixed forest of beech, maple, birch, and evergreen and then out onto open ledges, this moderately steep climb is also the shortest, most direct route to the Monadnock summit (3,165 ft.).

From the parking lot, walk up the road to find the marked trailhead for the very well-trod White Dot Trail, just past the state park headquarters. The wide path dips slightly, crosses a brook, and then begins a gradual ascent. At 0.5 mile, the Spruce Link bears left, leading in 0.3 mile to the White Cross Trail, but stay to the right on the White Dot. At 0.7 mile, a marked spur trail turns left, leading a short distance to Falcon Spring, a burbling water source that's a big hit with kids. This hike, though, continues straight ahead on the White Dot. The trail climbs steeply for the next 0.4 mile, with some limited views, until emerging onto open ledges at 1.1 miles. It then follows more level terrain, enters a forest of

low evergreens, and ascends again to its upper junction with the White Cross Trail at 1.7 miles. The trail climbs the open, rocky terrain of the upper mountain for the final 0.3 mile to the summit. On clear days, Boston skyscrapers and even the Atlantic Ocean can be seen in the distance. Descend along the same route.

User Groups: Hikers only. No bikes, dogs, horses, or wheelchair facilities. This trail may be difficult to snowshoe, in part because of severe winter weather.

Permits: During April–November, an entrance fee of $4 per adult and $2 per child (ages 6–11) is collected at the state park entrance. Children under 5 and New Hampshire residents 65 and older enter state parks for free.

Maps: A free map of trails is available from the state park or the New Hampshire Division of Parks and Recreation. A waterproof trail map is available from the Appalachian Mountain Club (Monadnock/Cardigan, $7.95). For topographic area maps, request Mount Monadnock and Marlborough from the USGS.

Directions: From Route 101 west in Peterborough, turn left for U.S. 202 west to Jaffrey. Follow for 6.2 miles and then turn right onto Route 124 west. In 4.3 miles, follow signs leading to Monadnock State Park (on the right). Park in the large lot near the park's main entrance.

GPS Coordinates: 42.845 N, -72.088 W

Contact: Monadnock State Park, P.O. Box 181, Jaffrey, NH 03452-0181, 603/532-8862, www.nhstateparks.org. New Hampshire Division of Parks and Recreation, P.O. Box 1856, 172 Pembroke Rd., Concord, NH 03302, 603/271-3556, camping reservations 603/271-3628, www.nhstateparks.org.

21 WAPACK TRAIL: TEMPLE MOUNTAIN LEDGES

5.8 mi/3.5 hr 👣5 ⛰7

in Sharon

One of the more scenic stretches of the Wapack Ridge Trail, a 21-mile interstate footpath

view from the Temple Mountain Ledges

the Wapack follows the Sharon Ledges for 0.75 mile, with a series of views eastward toward the hills and woods of southern New Hampshire. The trail enters the woods again and, at 1.4 miles from the trailhead, passes over the wooded subsidiary summit known as Burton Peak. In another 0.5 mile, a side path leads right to the top of cliffs and an unobstructed view to the east; on a clear day, the Boston skyline can be distinguished on the horizon. A short distance farther north on the Wapack lies an open ledge with a great view west to Monadnock—one of the nicest on this hike. The trail continues north 0.7 mile to the wooded summit of Holt Peak, another significant bump on the ridge. A short distance beyond Holt, watch through the trees on the left for a glimpse of an unusually tall rock cairn, then a side path leading to a flat, broad rock ledge with several tall cairns and good views in almost every direction. These are the Temple Mountain Ledges. The Wapack continues over Temple Mountain to Route 101, but this hike heads back the same way you came.

Camping is allowed only at designated sites along the entire 21-mile Wapack Trail; there are no designated sites along this hike. Fires are illegal without landowner permission and a permit from the town forest-fire warden.

User Groups: Hikers and dogs. No wheelchair facilities. This trail is fairly difficult to ski and is not suitable for bikes or horses.

Permits: Parking and access are free.

Maps: A Wapack Trail map and guide is available for $11 from Friends of the Wapack. For topographic area maps, request Peterborough South and Greenville from the USGS.

Directions: From the intersection of Routes 101 and 123 in Peterborough (west of the Temple Mountain Ski Area), drive south four miles on Route 123 and then turn left on Temple Road. Continue another 0.7 mile to a small dirt parking area on the right. GPS: 42.8035 N, 71.9092 W

Contact: Friends of the Wapack, Box 115, West Peterborough, NH 03468, www.wapack. org. New Hampshire Division of Parks and

stretching from Mount Watatic in Ashburnham, Massachusetts to North Pack Monadnock, this hike traverses the long ridge of Temple Mountain all the way to the Temple Mountain Ledges, a 5.8-mile round-trip with, all told, more than 1,200 feet of climbing. For those seeking a slightly shorter trek along the Wapack, several nice views along the way make for worthwhile out-and-back destinations. The wild blueberry bushes found in abundance along the trail are one of this hike's special treats. Berries ripen by mid-July and usually last through early September.

From the parking area, cross Temple Road and follow the yellow triangle blazes of the Wapack Trail into the woods, soon passing a dilapidated old house. At 0.3 mile, the trail reaches an open area at the start of the Sharon Ledges, with views of Mount Monadnock. A sign marker points to an overlook 75 feet to the right with a view toward Mount Watatic (the "Wa" in Wapack and the 21-mile trail's southern terminus). Continuing northeast,

Recreation, Bureau of Trails, P.O. Box 1856, Concord, NH 03302-1856, 603/271-3254.

22 KIDDER MOUNTAIN

3 mi/2 hr 🏃3 ⛰6

in New Ipswich

This gentle, three-mile hike gains less than 400 feet in elevation, yet the views from the open meadow atop 1,800-foot Kidder Mountain take in a grand sweep of this rural corner of southern New Hampshire. To the south, the Wapack Range extends to Mount Watatic in Massachusetts; behind Watatic rises the popular Massachusetts ski mountain, Mount Wachusett. It's a great family hike, an easy way to introduce both young and old to the pleasures of hiking, and is a scenic side trip as you hike the Wapack through New Ipswich. Even Benton MacKaye, the creator of the Appalachian Trail, named Kidder Mountain as one of his favorites. MacKaye helped blaze the first Kidder Mountain Trail in 1926 while working as a school teacher in Massachusetts.

From the parking area on the north side of Route 123, follow the yellow triangle blazes of the Wapack Trail into the woods, heading north. At 0.3 mile, the trail enters a clearing and ascends a small hillside to the woods. At 0.6 mile from the road, the Wapack crosses a power line right-of-way. Walk a short distance more and turn right (east) at a sign for the Kidder Mountain Trail. The trail at first follows a jeep road under the power line corridor for 0.1 mile, then turns left, crossing under the lines and entering the woods. It gradually ascends Kidder, reaching the open summit meadow nearly a mile from the Wapack Trail junction. Feast on the blueberries that grow wild here in the summer and take in the views of surrounding hills and rolling countryside. Follow the same route back.

Camping is allowed only at designated sites along the entire 21-mile Wapack Trail; there are no designated sites along this hike. Fires are illegal without landowner permission and a permit from the town forest-fire warden.

User Groups: Hikers and dogs. No bikes, horses, or wheelchair facilities.

Permits: Parking and access are free.

Maps: A Wapack Trail map and guide is available for $11 from Friends of the Wapack. For topographic area maps, request Peterborough South and Greenville from the USGS.

Directions: The trailhead parking area is on the north side of Routes 123/124 in New Ipswich, 2.9 miles west of the junction with Route 123A and 0.7 mile east of where Routes 123 and 124 split.

GPS Coordinates: 42.7734 N, 71.8996 W

Contact: Friends of the Wapack, Box 115, West Peterborough, NH 03468, www.wapack.org.

23 BEAVER BROOK ASSOCIATION

2.5 mi/1.5 hr 🏃1 ⛰5

in Hollis

Tucked away along the edge of sleepy Hollis, a small, rural community known for its centuries-old old apple orchards and quaint village center, Beaver Brook Association is a sprawling 2,000-acre nature conservancy comprised of forest, fields, and wetlands. With over 35 miles of trails, this local jewel attracts hikers, snowshoers, cross-country skiers, and mountain bikers from as far away as Boston (a 90-minute drive from Beaver Brook). The terrain varies from ponds and marshes dotted with beaver dams and duck nests to rolling meadows, thick forest, and gentle hills. Many of the trails are ideal for beginning hikers and children; some are appropriate for people with intermediate skills. This short hike helps first-time visitors explore the area's natural diversity.

From the office and parking area, follow the wide woods road called Cow Lane less than 0.1 mile to a turn-off on the left for the Porcupine Trail. The forested path is a gentle downhill incline leading to Beaver Brook's extensive wetlands. Chipmunks, garter snakes, and tree frogs are readily spotted here, but the trail's namesake is somewhat elusive (though a sign marker about halfway down the trail helps hikers identify a porcupine habitat). At the end of the trail, turn right at the sign for the Beaver Brook Trail, a relatively flat stretch running parallel to a broad marsh. Soon reaching a boardwalk to the left, cross over the marsh and continue straight until you reach the Eastman Meadow Trail (look for the sign). Here, take a right and follow briefly before turning right again onto the wide forest road called Elkins Road. Follow the road about 0.5 mile until it ends at a trail junction. Turn right onto another woods road, cross a bridge back over Beaver Brook, and continue onto the Brown Lane barn. Walk Brown Lane a short distance and turn right onto the Tepee Trail. At first passing through a lush meadow dotted with bird nesting boxes, the Tepee Trail re-enters the forest and, in another 0.2 mile, ends at Cow Lane. Turn left to return to your car.

User Groups: Hikers and leashed dogs. No wheelchair facilities. Bikes and horses allowed on certain trails (look for sign markers).

Permits: Parking and access are free.

Maps: A trail map is available at the Beaver Brook Association office for a small fee. For a topographic area map, request Pepperell from the USGS.

Directions: From the junction of Routes 130 and 122 in Hollis, drive south on Route 122 for 0.9 mile and turn right onto Ridge Road. Follow Ridge Road to the Maple Hill Farm and the office of the Beaver Brook Association. The parking lot is just past the office to the right.

GPS Coordinates: 42.7224 N, 71.6067 W

Contact: Beaver Brook Association, 117 Ridge Rd., Hollis, NH 03049, 603/465-7787, www.beaverbrook.org, office hours are 9 A.M.–4 P.M. Monday–Friday.

Index

www.moon.com

DESTINATIONS | ACTIVITIES | BLOGS | MAPS | BOOKS

MOON.COM is ready to help plan your next trip! Filled with fresh trip ideas and strategies, author interviews, informative travel blogs, a detailed map library, and descriptions of all the Moon guidebooks, Moon.com is all you need to get out and explore the world—or even places in your own backyard. While at Moon.com, sign up for our monthly e-newsletter for updates on new releases, travel tips, and expert advice from our on-the-go Moon authors. As always, when you travel with Moon, expect an experience that is uncommon and truly unique.

MOON IS ON FACEBOOK—BECOME A FAN!
JOIN THE MOON PHOTO GROUP ON FLICKR

MOON OUTDOORS

MOON OUTDOORS
COLORADO CAMPING

MOON OUTDOORS
CALIFORNIA CAMPING

MOON OUTDOORS
OREGON FISHING

MOON OUTDOORS
CALIFORNIA HIKING

MOON OUTDOORS
BAJA RV CAMPING

MOON OUTDOORS
TAKE A HIKE NEW YORK CITY

MOON OUTDOORS
NORTHERN CALIFORNIA BIKING

MOON OUTDOORS
UTAH CAMPING

"Well written, thoroughly researched, and packed full of useful information and advice, these guides really do get you into the outdoors."

—GORP.COM

ALSO AVAILABLE AS FOGHORN OUTDOORS ACTIVITY GUIDES:

250 Great Hikes in
    California's National Parks
California Golf
California Waterfalls
California Wildlife
Camper's Companion
Easy Biking in Northern
    California
Easy Hiking in Northern
    California

Easy Hiking in Southern
    California
Georgia & Alabama Camping
Maine Hiking
Massachusetts Hiking
New England Cabins
    & Cottages
New England Camping

New Hampshire Hiking
Southern California
    Cabins & Cottages
Tom Stienstra's Bay Area
    Recreation
Vermont Hiking
Washington Boating
    & Water Sports

MOON NEW HAMPSHIRE HIKING

Avalon Travel
a member of the Perseus Books Group
1700 Fourth Street
Berkeley, CA 94710, USA
www.moon.com

Editor: Elizabeth Hollis Hansen
Series Manager: Sabrina Young
Copy Editor: Naomi Adler Dancis
Graphics and Production Coordinator:
   Domini Dragoone
Cover Designer: Domini Dragoone
Interior Designer: Darren Alessi
Map Editor: Mike Morgenfeld
Cartographers: Mike Morgenfeld, Kat Bennett
Proofreader: Nikki Ioakimedes

ISBN-13: 978-1-59880-563-5

Text © 2010 by Avalon Travel and Jacqueline
Tourville.
Maps © 2010 by Avalon Travel.
All rights reserved.

Front cover photo: view of the White Mountain
   Range with Mt. Flume and Mt. Liberty in the
   background © Benjamin Tupper/istockphoto.
   com
Title page photo: a hiker takes in the view
   from Smarts Mountain © K.D. Talbot/www.
   GhostFlowers.com

Printed in the United States of America

ABOUT THE AUTHOR

Jacqueline Tourville

Jacqueline Tourville grew up hiking in the Adirondacks region of New York State. As an adult, she discovered the diverse terrain of New England while living in Boston. Today, she's a busy freelance writer and author of the popular "Are We There Yet?" family travel column for *Parenting New Hampshire* magazine. She is the co-author of the prenatal health guide *Big, Beautiful and Pregnant,* and has contributed numerous articles about health and outdoor living for both web and print publications. Jacqueline lives in New Hampshire with her husband and two children.